BREAKING BREAD TOGETHER

BREAKING BREAD
TOGETHER

Edited by

ELAINE SOMMERS RICH

HERALD PRESS
SCOTTDALE, PENNSYLVANIA

EDITOR'S PREFACE

These meditations have been written when the children were sleeping, while dinner was roasting in the oven, during convalescence in the hospital, between final examinations and the new semester—during whatever chinks of time we could find in our days. We suspect that sometimes you will almost feel children having measles or mumps between one paragraph and another.

It has been a joy to me as editor to work with the other eleven women in preparing this book. We do not apologize for using the same themes more than once, for we never exhaust them. Who can exhaust, for example, the love of God? An effort has been made to secure permission for the use of quoted materials, and we sincerely hope there has been no offense given. You may notice that the format for various months differs slightly according to the preference of the authors. As editor I wish to acknowledge my indebtedness to *Meditations for Women* (Abingdon Press, 1947), which first suggested the making of this volume.

The twelve of us who have shared our inner lives with you in this book deeply feel the need for fellowship with one another in the Lord. We wish to break the bread of life with you in these pages, and we pray that the Lord Himself may use our words to His glory.

—*Elaine Sommers Rich*

CONTENTS

CONTENTS

THE UPWARD LOOK

Helen Good Brenneman

JANUARY 1

This One Thing I Do

". . . *But this one thing I do, forgetting those things which are behind, and reaching forth unto those things which are before, I press toward the mark for the prize of the high calling of God in Christ Jesus*" (Phil. 3:13, 14).

What time is it? Sometimes I think that question punctuates every hour of my working day. A clock must be in sight. For always there is a deadline to meet. Someone is coming, or someone is going. Time: years, months, weeks, days, seconds—where is time going?

When a Christian woman finds herself in perpetual motion, it is time for her to slow down and live. God has something to whisper in her ear. It is a word of caution:

Stop! "Be still, and know that I am God." Only in the inner quietness of the heart can the still, small voice of God be heard.

Look! Look into the Word of God. Perhaps your goals are not high enough; perhaps your purposes are not His purposes for you.

Listen! The talk with Jesus is two-way. The walk with Jesus is a two-person walk. God wants to speak to you this year, my daughter, if you will only take time to listen. He wants to speak to you in His still, small voice.

Psalm 46:10

JANUARY 2

Divine Forgetfulness

". . . forgetting those things which are behind."

A minister's wife once complained to another mistress of the parsonage because she needed to move once more.

"Oh," replied the other, "how fortunate you are! For now you can leave your mistakes behind and begin all fresh again."

But we are not all so fortunate. We cannot call the moving van each time we make a terrible blunder. Some of us would be moving all the time, and each time we would be disappointed to find that we had taken along our number one troublemaker, ourselves.

We know, of course, that God forgives us the many sins and errors of our days. But forgiving ourselves—that is another question! There are those dark times when all our blunders, our embarrassing moments, our follies, our missteps, and worst of all, our sins against God, march before our eyes in sharp focus.

I believe Satan keeps personal records of our past mistakes filed neatly away for times when he knows they will most discourage us.

2

But God does not do that. Thus saith our Lord: ". . . for I will forgive their iniquity, and I will remember their sin no more." "In the sea of God's forgetfulness," the song writer puts it.

"Forgetting those things which are behind!" We have repented; we have forsaken our sin; we have forgiveness. Now let us forgive ourselves, so that we may press toward the mark, the high calling of Jesus Christ.

Psalm 103:12

✳

JANUARY 3

Reaching Forth

". . . I press toward the mark."

It has been said that "Good resolutions, like babies crying in church, should be carried out at once." I think all will agree about the babies, but many of us have long ago given up new-year resolutions. We try to carry them out at once, but as soon as we, the same old people who failed before are subjected to the same emotional and circumstantial stimuli, we fail as utterly as we did in past years.

Spiritual goals for a new year, however, are different from new-year resolutions. For the fruit of the Spirit, love, joy, peace, long-suffering, gentleness, goodness, faith, meekness, and temperance, come not from our resolving to have them, but from our daily surrender to the Spirit of God.

A university psychologist remarked that too many of the college students who come to him for counsel have no purpose for living. They are not pressing toward a mark but

3

are aimlessly and miserably floundering about. Let us pray for them.

"Why am I here? To what purpose was I born? What shall I do with my life?"

"What doth the Lord require of thee, but to do justly, and to love mercy, and to walk humbly with thy God?"

Psalm 107:30

✳

JANUARY 4

The High Calling of Womanhood

The children were restless and the mother was tired. Motoring from Florida to Iowa, Treva and her husband found the trip a tedious one, with five small children and little number Six on the way. To break the monotony, Treva began telling stories, describing how Jesus' mother also had to take a long trip when she was expecting her child.

"Yes, Mother," pointed out her oldest tactfully, "but Mary wasn't riding on a soft-cushioned seat in a Buick."

Treva accepted the gentle rebuke, and self-pity took wings.

What an easy life women of today enjoy, compared with the women of the past! And what a privileged existence is the lot of the American woman! Think with me for a moment. Mentally disconnect your electric washer and drier (if you have one). Pick up your week's wash, and tuck it under your arm. Now follow me to a narrow stream in southern France or to a muddy river in India where you kneel beside a stone, on which you scrub clean your husband's best shirt.

4

Glad you're just daydreaming? Yet millions of women in our world today would gladly settle, not for a washing machine, but for a full stomach and food enough for their children.

If privilege and responsibility walk hand in hand, what manner living must God expect of us, Christian women in the western world?

II John 1-6

Called to Be a Wife

A Christian woman receives a two-voiced call to wifehood. There is, of course, the call of God which should determine any chosen course. But along with this call comes the beckoning voice of love, a love strong enough and convincing enough to cause her to pick up all her possessions and move out from under her parental roof.

And that is a big day. Indeed, a wedding these days is such an undertaking that nothing short of a dynamic affection would be worth all the bother! Surely if every young woman would prepare as carefully for her *marriage* as she does for her *wedding*, married life would be nearly all bliss.

Yet few women entering marriage have any idea what lies ahead of the nuptial vows. For many, the wedding is a beautiful ivy-covered entrance to a poorly furnished shanty. For once on the other side of the wedding day, a bride sometimes submits to being "just a housewife," finding it hard to see any creative joy in the little things that make up her days.

God never intended that we should have the "housewife

blues." He painted beautiful pictures of Christian home-making in His Word. He put a deepening love in our hearts, and shows us daily that happy living is made of little things, that life's joys come wrapped in tiny packages.

Someone has said, "Housework is love made visible." Jesus put it this way, "Inasmuch as ye have done it unto one of the least of these my brethren, ye have done it unto me."

Proverbs 31:10-31

JANUARY 6

Called to Be a Mother

Do not the joys of motherhood defy all description? Yet we do not always fit the psalmist's picture of the "joyful mother of children." Sometimes we feel like this:

O Lord, I've been called to children and house,
Not to office as Grace, who wears a starched blouse,
And sits at her typewriter in calmness and poise;
Her papers stay filed, and, Lord, there's no noise.

O Lord, I've been called to kitchen and sink,
Not to classroom as Sarah, who has time to think.
Her children march home at the end of the day.
"At last they are gone," I've heard her say.

O Lord, I've been called to dustpan and broom,
Not as uniformed Mary, to hospital room.
Each time I see Mary, she's pretty and pert,
While I'm in a dither in the midst of my work.

6

O Lord, I've been called to laundry by stacks,
Not as Susan, in college, to learn the facts
About many things I'd so much love knowing.
My mind's on my housework, while Susie's is growing.

O Lord, please forgive me; I'd never change places
With the Susans, the Marys, the Sarahs, the Graces,
For although I must hurry for all I am worth,
I love being mother above all things on earth.

An elderly saint once wrote me in a letter, "The great-est missionaries . . . the greatest asset the church has . . . the greatest full-time mission workers . . . are our God-fearing mothers. God bless every one of them. May their posterity rise up and call them blessed."

Psalm 113:9

JANUARY 7
Called to Be a Daughter of the King

I look back with pleasure upon my years as private sec-retary.

"Please get me such and such a file." "Kindly mail these letters special delivery." "Would you telephone so-and-so and give him this message?" "Answer this letter yet this evening."

And so on and on, I endeavored to be a "handmaid" to a leader in the church, relieving him of lesser responsibil-ities so that greater jobs could be accomplished.

But what a challenging task it is to be a handmaid to the Lord Himself! I see Him sitting at His desk in the

7

heavens, dictating His holy will to His daughters upon the earth.

"Take that young child and train him for me," I hear Him say. "Send my servant (your husband) forth, well-fed and confident in your love." "Witness to that lonely girl at the factory." "Encourage that busy young mother by giving her a helping hand."

To all His handmaidens He says, "You are daughters of the King. Carry out my business upon the earth which only you can accomplish. Conduct yourselves as princesses in my kingdom."

A high calling, to be personal secretary to Jehovah-God? Yes, it is our privilege to "take dictation" each morning, as we begin our day with Him. Throughout the day, too, we are tuned to His will, transcribing His purposes into our everyday lives.

Like Philip's daughters, we must prophesy. Like the elect lady to whom John writes, we must love. Like Ruth of old, we must live virtuously. Like Mary, we must ponder His will in our hearts. Like Mary Magdalene, we must wash His feet with tears of repentance and devotion.

We must be about our Father's business.

Luke 1:38

JANUARY 8

Laying Aside Those Weights

"Wherefore seeing we also are compassed about with so great a cloud of witnesses, let us lay aside every weight, and the sin which doth so easily beset us, and let us run

8

with patience the race that is set before us, looking unto Jesus . . . " (Hebrews 12:1, 2a).

Travel light. Thus we were exhorted as our student group prepared to tour Europe. But what could be left behind, I puzzled, eliminating one possession after the other. It was not easy to travel light.

Yet, when we arrived on the Continent, how we wished we had obeyed the injunction more literally! How hard it was to run for a train, heavy suitcases dragging the ground on either side!

Travel light, the apostle wrote in his letter to the Hebrews. Lay aside those dead weights, for you cannot run a race with a trunk in one hand and a footlocker in the other. And the race you are to run has a prize at the end!

Travel light. Anything which impedes your progress as a Christian is a hindrance and must be left behind. Sin—the sin which easily besets *you,* must be dropped, or it will weight you down. Good things used wrongly or selfishly are weights and must be eliminated. Poor habits, formed early in life, are burdensome obstacles.

You know what your list of weights is; I know my special variety. But Christ is ready to help us lay those weights aside, for He was tempted in all points like all of us, yet without sin.

Travel light!

JANUARY 9

The Weight of Pride

". . . not to think of himself more highly than he ought to think."

What spiritual conquests we could make if we were actually to lay aside the weight of pride, to be our own true, best selves!

A tiny boy once asked his mother, "Mommy, why do you have your company hair on?"

His mother, who had been busy with the care of a new baby, suddenly realized that she had been growing careless about her appearance. Yet how many of us wear company faces, church faces, town faces, or talk on the telephone in company voices? Like seasoned actresses, we find ourselves playing roles, wearing masks. We become "all things to all men," not for the purpose of winning others to Christ, but in order to make a good impression on our friends.

Pride is a wolf that appears in sheep's clothing on a thousand occasions. It keeps us from receiving spiritual therapy available through confessing our "faults one to another." It makes us ungracious receivers, for we cannot accept favors without easing our pride by repaying them. It makes us apologize for our housekeeping when someone drops in unexpectedly, and robs us of the blessings of hospitality when every window is not shined. It keeps us poor keeping up with the ever-present Joneses.

Few people can honestly say, "In my humble opinion . . . ." For most of us are troubled by pride in some form. We might as well frankly admit that "It's not my brother nor my sister, but it's me, O Lord, standing in the need of prayer." Only then can we experience spiritual growth.

Romans 12:3

The Weight of Ill Will

"Mommy, you doesn't love Betty."

"Why, of course I like her," denied the mother, guilt nevertheless written plainly on her face. For she knew full well that what she had said about Betty was as far from a compliment as Betty was from what she ought to be.

"No, you doesn't. I know you doesn't."

Probably the most revealing and disconcerting invention since the Lord made children (who can often discern and report what they were not meant to see) is the tape recorder. Consider the hostess who hid this treacherous machine behind the sofa and went out to the kitchen, leaving the unaware guests to record their opinions on many subjects, including her! How much of what we say today will sound "true, kind, and necessary" when played back on God's eternal tape recorder?

On a little slip of paper enclosed in some merchandise I once read, "This little 'Thank You' note is in appreciation of your order. If you are pleased with our service, kindly tell your neighbors. If you are not pleased, kindly tell us. . . ." Good, sound, Scriptural advice!

Ill will—disgust, impatience, condescension, "better-than-thouism," faultfinding, quarreling, malicious talk, grudge-holding, gossiping, nagging—what a family of misery! How hard to run up and down the stairs with such a weight on our backs! And how unnecessary, when Jesus Christ stands at the foot of the stairs ready and willing to unload us of our burden!

Ephesians 4:31, 32

11

The Weight of Worry

"I know I shouldn't worry," she said, "but Bill is so irresponsible about his health. Suppose he should get t.b. or have a nervous breakdown, the way he's working. And Phyllis—I wonder if that fellow she's going with is as nice as she thinks he is. And, oh, dear, I worry every day about the grandchildren."

Does this sound familiar? The speaker is a Christian, but with each anxiety she impairs her health and makes her family uncomfortable.

> "One wept all night beside a sick man's bed;
> At dawn the sick was well, the mourner dead."

Have you ever thought about the abundant supply of worry material available to the experienced worrywart?

Members of your family could get run over, fall off a cliff, slip on an icy pavement, be robbed by a bandit, be bitten by a dog with rabies, contract poliomyelitis, or be hit by a falling meteorite. Even the chandelier, hanging innocently from the ceiling, could suddenly descend upon their heads. Our homes and property are also possible sources of worry. One's house could burn down, a jet plane could crash through the roof, termites could enter the basement, roaches the kitchen, or burglars the attic. And how about our own health? A mole could turn into a malignant tumor, a scratch into blood poison, indigestion into heart disease.

What shall we do with this weight of worry, this bundle of anxiety which keeps us from being truly productive?

"Casting all your care upon him; for he careth for you." It is as simple as that.

Matthew 11:28-30

The Weight of Possessions

The little party of travelers turned eagerly into the entrance of the refugee camp, a place they could call home, at least for a while. Strapped to their backs were all their earthly possessions, everything they owned in this world. Hundreds of miles behind them, miles they had covered on foot, were their homes and all the things they held dear. Now their possessions were so few, so dirty, and so tattered.

But could they have plodded the weary miles with their houses, their farm buildings, their libraries, their pots and pans on their backs?

A young couple lived happily in another part of the world, a brightly lighted, gay, and comfortable plot of ground in America. All Mary's life she had dreamed of the home she would create, and George provided the funds. They lived and laughed together, sharing their laughter and their party desserts with their friends. But in their quiet moments, the moments they thought on God, Mary and George felt condemned. Finally, they determined to spend part of a year in Christian service.

But somehow home was not the same when they returned. The living room chairs were too comfortable, the desserts too sweet. For George and Mary had seen across the spiritual tracks. God had laid His finger upon them.

To all of us Jesus says, "Your 'things' are not your own. Possess them as though you possess them not. Use them in my service."

And to some of us He may say, "Sell all that you have . . . come . . . follow me."

Luke 12:15

The Weight of Fear

"I hope you don't mind that I dropped in, Jill," Jane said as she grabbed a tea towel. "I guess it's the blue end of my cycle, or something. But you know how things have been with us financially, Jill. Since little Johnny was sick we just aren't making it, and I know people are talking about us. I heard something in a roundabout way just the other day about—about us not being good managers."

Jill saw the tears her sister tried to hide. "You really are letting things get you down now, Sis," she rebuked gently, "when you begin being afraid of what people think. Don't you know that people whose opinions are worth anything will think the best about you? And, well, people who want to think otherwise will do it no matter how well you manage. Why not just try to please God?"

How wise Jill was in her advice! For of all the fears that do so easily beset womankind, "what people think" probably rates highest on the list. A perfect formula for misery is to "Take a small measure of overheard gossip, add a generous dose of imagination, and brood over it constantly for several days, weeks, months, or years." Women who make this their practice over a period of years usually are no longer able to distinguish truth from their fertile imaginations.

Whether our fears are of personal failure, of what people think, or some particular obsession of our own, God is the answer.

"I sought the Lord, and he heard me, and delivered me from all my fears."

I John 4:18

14

The Weight of "Busyitis"

"I'm late, I'm late, I'm late,
For a very important date.
No time to say hello, good-by,
I'm late, I'm late, I'm late."*

The children sat Indian fashion around the radio, listening intently to their old favorite, *Alice in Wonderland*. Pearl, ironing in the next room, chuckled at the flustered rabbit. Then she sobered.

"That was me today," she thought to herself. " 'Busyitis,' that's what I have. Can't I be busy without getting busyitis? How ridiculous I must look, not only to my family but to my friends and neighbors! No time for devotions, no time to play with the children, no time, really, for the most important things of life—God and people."

How often we as homemakers are like the ostrich, our heads buried deep in our housekeeping sand. We are so busy that we do not come up for air. And what a poor view of the world the ostrich gets!

"Busyitis" causes the homemaker to neglect the deeper needs of her children. It makes her forget that husbands need more than good food and clean shirts (important as they are). It gives the impression to friends that she is too busy to be bothered. It gets her out of step in her walk with God.

The cure? God's touch. The quiet time, when we, like Mary, choose that good part, which shall not be taken away from us, no matter how busy we are.

Luke 10:41, 42

* Used by permission of Walt Disney Productions.

15

The Weight of Self

"Poor philosopher," I mused, as I listened to one speak on "Are people basically selfish?" Even Christ had a selfish nature, he said, for those who do good to others do it "to satisfy their own inner needs."

Is it not true, though, that the heart is "deceitful above all things"? How often Old Lady Self walks sweetly in, disguised in satiny garments of unselfishness, humility, benevolence, and "do-good-ism." How often our deepest motives are to gain attention, to hear our neighbor say, "My, what a fine Christian woman she is!"

Self is an actor who plays many roles with ease. Sometimes she walks onto the stage in the form of self-pity. The audience is supposed to pull out their handkerchiefs and weep with the unfortunate self. Sometimes self struts onto the stage as a real *somebody*. At this point the audience must respond with the expected compliments, respect, and awe. If all else fails, self portrays herself as untalented, inefficient, homely, and of little value, waiting anxiously for the audience's assurance that the opposite is really true.

Fortunately, our Lord has told us what we should do with this troublesome self which, like Stevenson's Little Shadow, goes everywhere with us. As Christ allowed Himself to be crucified, so we are to die with Him, that He might live gloriously through us. Die to self. Live to Christ.

Poor, worldly philosopher. How little he knows of the Christian's Calvary! How little he knows of Easter!

Galatians 2:20

16

The Sin Which So Easily Besets Us

What woman does not shudder at the thought of an unsuspected diagnosis of cancer? For cancer, too late discovered, is deadly. Yet, how few of us are willing to take the simple precaution of a once-or-twice-a-year checkup with our physician.

But far more frightening is the deadly disease of sin. Sin, like cancer, thrives on neglect, spreading rapidly if undetected in its early stages. You can call sin by more respectable names: faults, mistakes, human error, human nature, but it continues its destructive work within us. Arsenic, neatly displayed in an ornamental salt shaker, remains arsenic. A hydrogen bomb, wrapped in gay Christmas paper, if this were possible, could still destroy a city.

Physically, you cannot run the race of life with cancer eating away at your body. Spiritually, you cannot run the Great Race with sin undetected by God's bright, X-ray light. And once a year is not often enough for a spiritual checkup. Only the Spirit and the Word can make an early diagnosis; once a day is not too often.

There is, however, one significant difference between sin and cancer. There are no incurable stages of sin, if the sinner comes repentant to receive therapy from the Great Physician. For He who said, "They that be whole need not a physician, but they that are sick," has also said, "Whosoever will may come."

I John 1:5—2:2

Patient Running

Run with patience? On the surface this is indeed a paradox. We are to run a race, yet we are to be patient about it! Probably the Revised Standard Version will resolve our perplexity, for it translates it thus: "Let us run with *perseverance* the race that is set before us."

The alarm goes off—early. Out of bed we hop and into our day's work we dash, as though there were no other days in the week. But in our hurry, we forget that it is more important to *be* than to *do*. And, as any efficiency expert might have predicted, we are ready to fold up by 2:30 P.M. The trouble? Impatient running, the kind that can not possibly persevere.

Dorothy wants to be an ideal mother, and she wants her children to be model children. She forgets that physical, intellectual, and spiritual growth are slow. It seems quicker to nag than to work patiently for character development. Dorothy's goals are fine, but her running is impatient.

Each of us has a race to run, an individual course chosen for us by God, the Father. But the running, to be perseverant, must be patient. Better to be a plodding tortoise than a weary, never-arriving hare.

Isaiah 40:31

JANUARY 18

Looking unto Jesus

It was on one of those rare island experiences in a woman's life, as described by Anne Lindbergh in *Gift from the Sea,* that I found time to meditate upon the thoughts she so poetically presents in her book. Only, while Mrs. Lindbergh's island lay in the Atlantic, my little island of solitude was a bed on fifth floor, maternity ward, Mercy Hospital.

And while I could not run breathlessly alongside her to collect treasures from the sea, I could close my eyes and consider the life values which each lovely sea shell brought to her mind.

One of the treasures which she took home with her from the seashore was the moon shell, reminding her that every woman needs to be alone, some part of every day, some part of every year. For as she so vividly shows, a woman must continually be giving herself away, and one cannot unceasingly give, unless one's own inner springs are replenished and the soul fed.

To Mrs. Lindbergh's emphasis on the need for the "inner look," I feel that Christian women need to add the "upward look." It is not enough to be alone with oneself. We must be alone with our Creator, and our times of quietude and meditation must be enlightened by whisperings of His Spirit and through reading His Holy Word.

As one author has put it, we must use our "window to the sky."

Psalm 23

✳

JANUARY 19

Ask and Receive

"Ask, and it shall be given you; seek, and ye shall find."
Overheard in the nursery:

19

Charles: "Lois, my teddy bear is sick. What shall I do?"

Lois: "The Lord will make him well."

Charles: "Shall I call Him up? What's His number?"

Lois: "809 Heaven."

Charles: "Hello, is this the Lord? Well, we have a sick teddy bear down here. Would you please come down and take care of him? Okay, good-by."

"Be careful for nothing; but in every thing by prayer and supplication with thanksgiving let your requests be made known unto God."

Overheard at a cribside:

"Dear Lord, I thank you for the nice rain we had today, and I thank you that it won't rain tomorrow, so that we can go and play."

What great principles of prayer are not best understood by a little child? Out of the mouths of babes and of sucklings issue forth prayers that are simple (without vain repetitions); forgiving (what child holds a grudge); honest, forthright, specific, and filled with faith.

Take a lesson from your child, or your niece, or your grandchild. Humble yourself as a little child, and ask Christ, in plain English, for those spiritual blessings for which you so much long. Add your heart's cry of thanksgiving and praise and believe that you shall receive.

Matthew 21:22

JANUARY 20

I Just Want to Be with You

"But don't you want to play in your nice playroom?" It had seemed like a good idea. Arranged in storybook order were the miniature refrigerator and stove (constructed from orange crates), the breakfast set (gift from grandparents), little chairs, and toy telephone.

The catch to it all was that this fine playhouse was upstairs, and Mother was down.

"No," insisted the three-year-old, "I just want to be with you."

"I just want to be with you, dear God," I say, as I rise in the morning, beginning the endless tasks that await me. "But how can I be with you in the midst of all this work?" And then I think of Brother Lawrence and his classic statement, "The time of business does not with me differ from the time of prayer, and in the noise and clatter of my kitchen, while several persons are at the same time calling for different things, I possess God in as great tranquility as if I were upon my knees at the blessed sacrament."

I smile as I mentally place a high chair with a demanding baby in Brother Lawrence's monastic kitchen, and as I insert three preschoolers playing chase.

But the thought remains the same. God's ear catches those petitions of our hearts, above the screams of small children and the noise of the vacuum cleaner. In the silence of a worship service, in the confusion of everyday living, God is near, ready to hear and to help.

Psalm 139:1-14

JANUARY 21

Window to the Sky

It was a panel discussion in the true sense of the word. Not a stiff symposium, where everyone reads a formal paper. Just a handful of women talking over their problems around a microphone.

"We all know that we should take more time to read," the chairman said. "But how can we find the time?"

She turned to Mabel, a mother of eight children who has in recent years read the Bible through a number of times.

"When do you do your reading, Mabel?"

We all listened for a magic formula, for few of us had done as well as Mabel.

Mabel described the close family life at home and told about the family devotional hour after dishes are washed each evening. "For my own Bible reading, I spend fifteen minutes each morning after the children are all off to school and fifteen minutes each afternoon after the last baby is in bed."

It was that simple. But those regular fifteen-minute periods add up. And for Mabel it was a "window to the sky," the time when she allowed a stream of inspiration to penetrate the roof of her busy life.

No one can regulate another woman's household or advise her when she can find that blessed quiet time. No one can tell another how long that quiet hour should be. But the important thing is that we *choose* that good part, that we see its importance, and that we discipline ourselves to take it.

Acts 16:13, 14

JANUARY 22

Spiritual Nutrition

"Do you suppose the Lord minds when I just grab a spiritual sandwich?" I asked my husband one day. It was canning season, the time of year when lunches turn out to be sandwiches and suppers end up being soup.

My minister-husband frowned over the implications of my question.

"Surely the Lord understands," I added, trying to reassure myself, and him.

"You mean," he smiled, "that you have your devotions for the Lord's sake, instead of your own?"

I got the point.

It is true that we have our times of spiritual feasting, days when we let our Martha activities go to the winds while we sit, in special conferences or Sunday services, at Christ's feet. On the other hand, there are days when every moment is accounted for from the time we crawl from our beds until far past our regular bedtime. Can we, like spiritual camels, carry over the Bread of Life from one day to the next? Do we not need Him more on our busier days?

All day I have poured from a dry, empty cup.
I come to Thy fountain, Lord; now fill me up.
My heart is a vacuum; my cistern is dry.
I thirst; for the Water of Life now I cry.

No wonder the children have grumbled and sighed,
Molehills turned mountains, thorns multiplied;
Small wonder my soul is suffering from drought;
My schedule was full; the Lord stood without.

O Lord, grant me wisdom to take time for Thee.
Let the beauty of Jesus be seen in me.

Amen.

Mark 6:31

23

A Message or a Nixie

I am indebted to Sam, a Christian mail carrier, for the following thoughts on the Christian as a human message from the Lord.

In post-office jargon, a "nixie" is a letter which cannot be delivered or for which delivery is abnormally delayed. A letter becomes a nixie for any of the following reasons: "There is no such post office, street, or street number in the state named. The letter is unclaimed, refused, or illegibly or insufficiently addressed. The addressee has moved, leaving no address, or is deceased. The house is vacant or there is no mailbox. The letter is unexplainably delayed en route (for instance, a year from the United States to Arabia) or missent (as far, perhaps, as England).

In the post office a nixie becomes a nixie through no fault of its own. It is a victim of circumstances or of the mail handlers.

But it is different with human letters. In II Corinthians 3:2 and 3, we are told,

"You yourselves are our letter of recommendation, written on your hearts, to be known and read by all men; and you show that you are a letter from Christ delivered by us, written not with ink but with the Spirit of the living God, not on tablets of stone but on tablets of human hearts" (RSV).

Therefore, Christian friends, *you* are either a human letter, a message from God to be delivered in some form of Christian service, or a human nixie, a message from God, lost in the world or delayed in its hazards and snares.

II Corinthians 3:2, 3

24

Look Up for Commission

In the year that King Uzziah died, Isaiah saw the Lord in a vision. Isaiah was not looking for a commission. But his vision of the holy God showed him up as a sinner, a man of unclean lips. Now, at his request the Lord quickly took care of his sin, purging him of his iniquity. Then Isaiah was in a position to hear God's call to Christian service.

"Whom shall I send, and who will go for us?"

A prompt reply. "Here am I; send me."

What happened after you saw God in His glory, took a look at yourself, and cried to God for mercy? What did you answer when God said, "Whom shall I send, and who will go for us?"

You might have said, "Here am I, Lord; send the preacher, the missionary, and the deacon." You may have said, "Thank you for saving me, Lord, and for forgiving my sins. I'll see you later in heaven."

The "here-am-I-send-me" homemaker, or secretary, or teacher may not have been called to the mission field. But she has a sense of calling in her vocation. She knows that living her Christianity before her neighbors and friends will open doors that are locked to her minister or a missionary. She knows that the Great Commission was directed straight at her.

Look up for cleansing, look up for salvation, look up for all your spiritual needs to be supplied. But expect with it a commission—a call to Christian service. Look outward. And be glad!

Isaiah 6:1-8

25

3

Look Up for Guidance

It was a strange way to begin a honeymoon. Married in Amsterdam, we chose to begin our lives together in a quiet hotel high on the banks of the North Sea, close to the Dutch-Belgian border. No sooner had we arrived than we felt an urge to try walking across to Belgium, asking directions of strangers whom we met along the way. But the instructions were fuzzy.

Soon we were lost. And worse still, the tide (which was out when we began our adventure) suddenly came in. Evening set in. It began to rain. And there was nothing to do but jump across the many little rivulets which now surrounded us.

Would we ever get back to civilization? Each time we jumped a stream of water, the lights of our hotel seemed farther away. And so barren was the shore that we had only the distant hotel light to guide us.

Many hops, skips, and jumps later we did cross our watery obstacle course, wending our way, hand in hand, toward *The Light* that stood for warmth, hospitality, hot coffee, and cheer.

An unusual beginning for a honeymoon, yes! Yet was it not symbolic of many an experience which we have had since, times when unexpected tides came in, when we walked hand in hand through No Man's Land with only the Light of Jesus Christ to beckon us on?

"I said to the man who stood at the gate of the years, 'Give me a light that I may find my way.' But he replied, 'Go out into the darkness and put your hand in the hand of God. This will be better than light and safer than a known way.'"

Psalm 32:8 and John 16:13

Look Up for Peace of Mind

"Now come on, Son," I insisted. "Hurry up and put away your toys. It's time to go to bed."

He looked at me with pleading eyes. He might have asked, "Why hurry me? I have all the rest of my life to tear around as you do."

Instead, he simply said, "Don't wait on me so fast."

It is no wonder, in our bustling, nail-biting America, that there should be a large market for books on peace of mind. Even though our friends in other lands have made us self-conscious about our fast living, no one yet has come up with a satisfactory course, "How to quit hurrying in three easy lessons." Even Christian workers find themselves sacrificing the ministry of prayer and the study of the Word for feverish activity and multiple committee meetings.

Yet the kind of peace which Jesus gives does not scratch items off a busy schedule, keep the baby from getting colic, unhook the telephone or doorbell, or insure us from unexpected guests at suppertime.

Jesus' peace is not a pair of pink glasses through which we see the world as a placid bed of sweet williams nodding gently in the breeze.

Jesus' peace is not the kind which sells on the popular market. It is "not as the world giveth," for He said, "In the world ye shall have tribulation."

Jesus' peace is just a fruit of the indwelling Spirit of God. His peace leaves us in our helter-skelter world, but lifts our spirits above it. His peace does not come in three easy lessons. It just comes. When we abide in Him.

John 14:25-27

Look Up for Security

A speaker said recently that his idea of security has changed with the years. In 1920 he thought of security as the accumulation of stocks and bonds. In 1930 security seemed embodied in the Social Security Act, in old-age. compensation. But, he pointed out, from 1940 on to the present time, security is no longer an individual matter. Security these days is usually thought of in terms of military safety and protection.

Jesus knew, many years ago, that the day would come when men's hearts would fail them for fear. A realistic survey of our hydrogen age, with its civil defense, air-raid shelters, and war propaganda, plus an honest look into the Scriptures about future times, affords little security for the sinner.

As the spiritual puts it, "Oh, sinner, what will you do, when the stars begin to fall?"

But for the Christian there is a satisfying answer that defies circumstances. Jesus described coming events thus:

"Nation shall rise against nation, and kingdom against kingdom: and great earthquakes shall be in divers places, and famines, and pestilences; and fearful sights and great signs shall there be from heaven. . . . And ye shall be hated of all men for my name's sake."

But Jesus hastens to assure us ". . . there shall not an hair of your head perish. In your patience possess ye your souls. . . . And when these things begin to come to pass, then *look up*, and lift up your heads; for your redemption draweth nigh."

Luke 21:25-28

Look Up for Victory

It was VE-Day in the Allied world, and in America the throngs stormed the cities to celebrate the coming of peace. Yet, in the suburbs of the nation's capital, we observed a strange contradiction of peace and victory. In the heavy traffic one car bumped into another; the drivers became involved in a heated argument, and their wives joined in the violent dispute that followed. On their way to celebrate a supposed national victory, these citizens were defeated in their personal lives.

John writes, "My little children, these things write I unto you, that ye sin not." The writer of Hebrews says, "Let not sin therefore reign in your mortal body." Jesus says, "I am come that they might have life, and that they might have it more abundantly." And the whole New Testament trembles with spiritual power, power through the Holy Spirit, power for victorious Christian living.

It is comforting to discover that others have the same temptations and life struggles as we do. But how much more consoling to find that the One to whom we look for victory knows from experience just what we need!

"For we have not a high priest who is unable to sympathize with our weaknesses, but one who in every respect has been tempted as we are, yet without sinning. Let us then with confidence draw near to the throne of grace, that we may receive mercy and find grace to help in time of need" (Hebrews 4:15, 16, RSV).

Psalm 40:12, then 40:1-3

Look Up

I have a neighbor who does not seem to need God. She never sends her children to Sunday school. Nor does she attend church herself. Yet, she is intelligent and strives to be a good mother.

I try to think of how to convince her. Why Sunday school? Why church? Why God? I find myself trying to put into words sacred intangibles, things I have taken for granted all my life.

How will her children distinguish right from wrong? How can she insure their future happiness? How can she explain shaky world events? What purpose will they find in living? How will they satisfy that deep longing for things eternal? How will they face crises, make life's momentous decisions?

But there I stop. Are not all these things simply by-products of a relationship with Jesus Christ?

What those children are missing most is life's greatest adventure—a personal encounter with the Lord of all life.

I must make her hungry, not for the spiritual toothpicks, salt shakers, napkins, or centerpiece, but for the Bread of Life Himself. And to do this I must look up to the Lover of my soul. For the joy of His abiding presence means more than all other blessings.

"Look unto Jesus," my life must shout to my neighbor.

Revelation 3:20

✷

The Author and Finisher of Our Faith

"Looking unto Jesus the author and finisher of our faith; who for the joy that was set before him endured the cross, despising the shame, and is set down at the right hand of . . . God."

In the beginning, God. In the end, God. We ought, every one of us, to have the opportunity of explaining eternity to a child. "Who made God? How could He always be? How could He never end?" Explain it, did I say? Explain what our own minds cannot comprehend?

It is as difficult for us to understand eternity as it is to comprehend infinity. Our temporal lives are framed by our birth to the left, our death to the right, the earth beneath, and the sky above. But you cannot put Jesus Christ into that kind of frame.

"In the beginning was the Word, and the Word was with God, and the Word was God. . . . All things were made by him; and without him was not any thing made that was made."

"I am Alpha and Omega, the beginning and the end."

Neither the earth beneath His feet nor the sky above could frame our Saviour. For He was there when God said, "Let there be a firmament in the midst of the waters, and let it divide the waters from the waters." And God has said, "The heaven is my throne, and the earth is my footstool."

Yet, in between the beginning and the endless future, Jesus allowed Himself to be temporarily framed by time. He ran the race of life ahead of us. Now He sits, cheering us on, and waiting to reward us at the finish line.

II Timothy 4:7, 8

The Upward Look

I will lift up mine eyes unto the hills,
From whence cometh my help.
My help cometh from the Lord,
Which made heaven and earth.

He will not suffer thy foot to be moved:
He that keepeth thee will not slumber.
Behold, he that keepeth Israel
Shall neither slumber nor sleep.

The Lord is thy keeper:
The Lord is thy shade upon thy right hand.
The sun shall not smite thee by day,
Nor the moon by night.

The Lord shall preserve thee from all evil:
He shall preserve thy soul.
The Lord shall preserve thy going out and thy coming in
From this time forth, and even for evermore.

Psalm 121

FEBRUARY

THE GREATNESS OF GOD

Barbara Claassen Smucker

FEBRUARY 1

God's Glory

With each day there is dusk—the hairbreadth of time between daylight and night. A distilled hush marks the time. In the west the "heavens declare the glory of God" with the prayer of sunset. Like a flame that has died to a glowing ember, it offers beauty and praise instead of light and heat.

It is the time, too, for evening dinner, for the washing of dirty hands, for the clanging of the supper bell, for the hurried end to the busy day.

But there should be a pause first for that holy time of sunset, for the relinquishment of the day's bustle and an intake of God's peace. Walk to a quiet spot near a window or out of doors and with the heavens declare the glory of God. Even the busiest day should end with the serenity of the heavens.

"The heavens declare the glory of God" (Psalm 19:1).

Joy from God

Jean Francois Millet was a famous French painter whose life was closely bound to the soil, the seasons, and the humble, peasant people. In his painting "The Angelus" a farmer and his wife pause beside a waiting spade and a burdened wheelbarrow. The sun is setting, and they bow their heads for evening prayer.

It is easy to imagine that soon the farmer will reach for his spade and the woman will stoop for the worn handles of the wheelbarrow. Their backs will bend with the burden of their work and their feet will trudge heavily in wooden shoes over the dusty fields. But the eyes of these two peasants will glow with the embers of the sunset, for they have shared with the heavens in declaring the glory of God. They will return to their meager home with peace and quiet joy.

". . . and the firmament sheweth his handywork" (Psalm 19:1).

God's Promise

It is easy to feel sometimes that life is static . . . that the long, hot days of summer will *never* end . . . that a young mother will be confined *always* with the constant care of her babies . . . that the bleak, bare earth of winter will be a *permanent* landscape.

The boy who is a high-school freshman and hasn't matured thinks feverishly, "I will *never* grow."

There are faces that go with static lives. They grow old with downward wrinkles and drooping eyes. With a frame around them they could be portraits of gloom and despair.

Such self-imposed pessimism is unnecessary, for God promises change.

"Weeping may endure for a night, but joy cometh in the morning" (Psalm 30:5).

A sundial has these words around its face, "It is always morning somewhere in the world."

Job believed this. In the face of insurmountable suffering he cried,

> "If a man die, shall he live again?
> All the days of my appointed time will I wait,
> Till my change come" (Job 14:14).

FEBRUARY 4

Praising God

God's world has moments of beauty so fleeting that often I completely miss them. I think, "Tomorrow when I have more time, I'll walk to the woods and see the changing leaves of fall."

Tomorrow the blustering north wind rides through the sky and every leaf is swished and scattered over the land.

Or, I scrape a hole through a frosty winter window one morning and gasp. Out of doors the frozen, glistening limbs of the shrubs and trees present a fairyland of white-spun lace. Even the ugly rusted pipe that sprawls on the ash heap has become a glowing wand of grace and artistry.

"This afternoon, when I have more time," I say, "I'll

put on the children's snowsuits, boots, and mittens and take them out into this miracle of beauty wrought by God." The afternoon sun burns bright and warm and the limbs and shrubs drip mud-brown drops. The moment of exquisite beauty has passed.

It is possible to say, I shall pray at 2:00 after the dishes are washed, and the children tucked off for a nap, and refuse to respond to a moment of inspiration that might arrive at 1:14.

If God's presence is made known at odd and unexpected moments, I must take time for that moment of spiritual refreshment and praise His name!

> "Praise ye the Lord.
> Praise ye the Lord from the heavens:
> Praise him in the heights" (Psalm 148:1).

FEBRUARY 5
The Builder of Man

I listened amused one morning as our four-year-old Becky defended her father against the boasts of another four-year-old friend.

"My father is bigger than your father," she battled defiantly. "And he's stronger than your father, too."

"Well," said her friend, smiling confidently that now she would score a point in her favor, "my father can build a chair and a table and a doll bed and—and—"

Truthful facts couldn't be denied. Becky paused. She forgot comparisons and said with finality, "Your father can't build a man."

"Yours can't either," answered her friend and they both laughed.

How insignificant man becomes—even fathers—in the face of something only God can do—the building of a man. The greatness of this job is unsurpassed.

"Thou art worthy, O Lord, to receive glory and honour and power: for thou hast created all things, and for thy pleasure they are and were created" (Revelation 4:11).

FEBRUARY 6

Creating for God

A round ball of soft modeling clay, a package of flower seeds, a paint box, an untouched piano, a sewing machine and a piece of bright calico, a typewriter, a pad of blank, white paper and a freshly sharpened pencil, a saw and a pile of wood. The list could be multiplied into pages. Jumbled together, the items are just words. Separately, they are potential statues, flower gardens, paintings, musical compositions, a child's gay dress, a book, a poem, a cabinet.

The linking chain to join one with another and to bring order from the jumble is a creative man, woman, or child. Children of God the Creator take His potentials and build for Him, and the act of building becomes an experience of worship.

But if creating is separated from God, it can become a witch's brew. Its wily mixtures simmer and twist over the earth in every direction. Evil creates evil. A bomb's potential is murder. Poisonous gas is made to choke a victim. Gossip is manufactured to harm a neighbor.

To be a worthy creator in the sight of God my prayer should be:

"Create in me a clean heart, O God;
And renew a right spirit within me" (Psalm 51:10).

FEBRUARY 7

God the Creator

"O Lord, how manifold are thy works!
In wisdom hast thou made them all;
The earth is full of thy riches" (Psalm 104:24).

A row of books in the bookshelf can be surprisingly uniform. If they are encyclopedias, they stand side by side, like soldiers, with the same dress, same position, same size. I can become obsessed with their uniformity—dusting them, keeping them neat, lining them in the proper alphabetical order.

Then, I open the covers of those "uniform" books. Such mad and glorious variety! One of them pictures a blown-up housefly. "The Mighty Insect." In another the "Renaissance in Italy" is discussed with a beautiful interior of St. Peter's in Rome. A tall observation tower overlooks a forest in the next book and is found under the topic "Conservation."

Sometimes my neighbors, my husband's school associates, even my children are lined up before my eyes in the same outward neat uniformity as a set of books. I expect them to be like me—same color, same background, same interests, same customs. I am thrown temporarily off base when I discover variety and interests as widespread as the encyclopedia.

Instead of frustration and scorn, I should bow down in wonder and awe, praising the greatness of God the Creator.

"Thou art worthy, O Lord, to receive glory and honour and power: for thou hast created all things, and for thy pleasure they are and were created" (Revelation 4:11).

✳

FEBRUARY 8

God's Gift of Age

Why do women cry out against the inevitabilities of life? God, our Creator, is a great God. The seasons of His world flow by with meaning and rhythm. The seasons of life are equally creative and rhythmic.

Childhood is the seed. Youth is the rosebud. Middle age is the rose in full bloom. In old age, the fragrant petals are collected for sweet and lasting perfume. Each age has something beautiful in it and each is dependent on the others.

Our small daughter, when selecting pictures for her room from a portfolio of famous paintings, chose two old men by van Gogh. "I like old people," she explained.

"She misses them," I realized. In suburbia where we live there are no old people. It is a society without maturity— a garden of neat, fresh vegetables without herbs and spices.

Why hide gray hairs and conceal the dates of birthdays? Age is inevitable and it can become enviable. E. Stanley Jones says, "Never retire—change your work. The human personality is made for creation; and when it ceases to create, it creaks, and cracks, and crashes. You may not create as strenuously as before; but create. Otherwise you will grow tired resting. Create, create, create!"*

Proverbs 16:31

* E. Stanley Jones, *Abundant Living* (Abingdon-Cokesbury, 1942), page 293.

39

The Quietness of God

I buy my groceries at the *super*market. I purchase sheets and pillowcases at the *gigantic* January white sales. I buy my son the *fastest* bicycle on earth. I jump on the national band wagon proclaiming *bigness*. This band wagon must keep pace with all that is modern. It must roar with the speed of a jet-propelled plane. It must soar with the ear-shattering quake of a hydrogen explosion. It must reach a pinnacle of the *biggest*, the most *successful*, the *greatest* band wagon in the *world*. And then what? Man can make nothing greater than the greatest in the *world*.

And how does God's greatness compare with this band wagon measuring stick?

"Be still, and know that I am God" (Psalm 46:10).

> Drop Thy still dews of quietness,
> Till all our strivings cease;
> Take from our souls the strain and stress,
> And let our ordered lives confess
> The beauty of Thy peace.
>
> *—John Greenleaf Whittier.*

Strength from God

"Praise ye the Lord. O give thanks unto the Lord; for he is good: for his mercy endureth for ever" (Psalm 106:1).

A young German friend wrote to me after the second

World War. Her life had been completely altered. She had once been the beloved daughter of wealthy parents. She had been carefree, gay, pretty, and untroubled about her future. Now her parents were dead. The wealth was gone. She was sober, prematurely aged by starvation and terror, and insecure about her future.

Stripped of all human support and all earthly possessions, she had in desperation turned to God. At the lowest ebb of her life she was receiving God's free gifts of grace and mercy.

"I am now finding strength and joy in the music of Beethoven," she wrote, "the poems of great German poets, and most of all in God and prayer. I have made a vow never again to forget the real essentials of life."

Sometimes in the strife-free, smooth-running moments of life, only the edges are left for God and prayer.

Continuous prayer and commitment can be preparation for joys and sorrows to come as well as daily strength and sustenance.

"Seek the Lord and his strength, seek his face continually" (I Chronicles 16:11).

FEBRUARY 11

Grapevine Lives

There are times when our thought lives twist about like a grapevine hovering over our own little patch of world. And if there are grapes, they grow green and sour.

Mrs. Greene is a filthy housekeeper, I think. My house is spotless. Mrs. Lowe's children are borderline delinquents. Mine misbehave, "but they are nothing like hers."

41

There is a rumor that the Johnsons' marriage is tottering. Who could I find to tell me the intimate details? The minister called on Mrs. Smith twice in one month. He hasn't even brushed by my door in over three months. And just think, Mrs. Grey brought only one slightly burned apple pie to the church potluck dinner. What did she think her family of eight was going to eat? My two perfectly baked apple pies?

It is a tangle, all right, and like a ball of yarn chased by a cat, it gets more tangled the longer it unravels.

What does God do when He steps into such a life? Is it possible to twist and hide and cringe and gossip in the littleness of our sheltered world when we stand before the glory and greatness of God?

"For he that will love life,
  And see good days,
  Let him refrain his tongue from evil,
  And his lips that they speak no guile:
  Let him eschew evil, and do good;
  Let him seek peace, and ensue it.
  For the eyes of the Lord are over the righteous,
  And his ears are open unto their prayers:
  But the face of the Lord is against them that do evil"

(I Peter 3:10-12).

*

42

God in All

God is not exclusive. He is not a Jew or a Gentile. He is not black or yellow or white. He is not the friend of one nation and the enemy of another.

Through His Son Jesus Christ, God revealed His all-inclusiveness.

Christ gave counsel to Nicodemus, a man of wealth and high authority among the Jews. He also spoke to the woman taken in the very act of adultery. "Go and sin no more," He told her.

When the multitudes assembled on the hills to hear Jesus, He spoke to the men and women, and also to the children.

"Suffer little children to come unto me," He said, "and forbid them not: for of such is the kingdom of God" (Luke 18:16).

Christ captured the unlearned Peter. He seized the mind, heart, and soul of scholarly Paul.

The ministry of Jesus was not stuffed into national and racial pockets. It was open to all—to the Jews ("God's people") and to the Gentiles ("foreign people").

"For he is our peace," Paul said in Ephesians 2:14, "who hath made both one, and hath broken down the middle wall of partition between us."

At Pentecost even the barrier of language did not separate the people. They could understand one another in Christ. "The multitude came together, and were confounded, because that every man heard them speak in his own language" (Acts 2:6).

God is indeed all and in all!

"There are diversities of operations, but it is the same God which worketh all in all" (I Corinthians 12:6).

God Is Great and Good

> "God is great and God is good,
> And we thank Him for our food.
> By His hand we all are fed.
> Give us, Lord, our daily bread."

This is a simple prayer which many children say before their meals.

"How is God great? How is God good?" with upturned, trusting face a child asks.

Muriel Lester once gave this advice: "Whenever you are with a child and see something beautiful, associate that beauty with God."

The soft snow of winter is beautiful. It is made by God.

The fragile blossoms of an apple tree in spring are beautiful. God made them.

The hushed beauty of a sudden rainbow is a promise made by God.

The holy beauty of a manger scene at Christmas time celebrates the birthday of God's Son.

Patiently the child matures and, as a Danish folk song ends, is "Slowly growing from seeds to flowers."

"And let the beauty of the Lord our God be upon us . . ." (Psalm 90:17).

Genuine Nonconformity

The Christian in his faith is often tugged in two different directions. The missionary teachings of the Bible send men

and women out into the world with deeds of compassion
and words of truth.

Another side of Christian life calls its followers to be
separate and nonconformed to conventional standards of
culture. Some Christians are called to emphasize the outgoing field of the missionary. Others are led to build up
defenses against evil and sin.

Both ideas are taught in the Bible. Both are vital. In the
latter, however, it is important that nonconformity partakes
of a true Christian character. It is possible to be peculiar
and odd merely for the sake of being different. Also it is
possible to live under the illusion that minor external differences have created a major tension with the world. It is
akin to the blind guides which strained at a gnat and
swallowed a camel. Matthew 23:24.

Genuine nonconformity focuses on some of the great
challenges to the Christian way of life, such as war, racial
prejudice, class, and nationalism.

Romans 12:2

FEBRUARY 15

Conformity or God

Josephine Wetzler, conductor of School Time Programs
on Prairie Farmer Station, WLS, says, "Today we are putting children into a production line of conformity. When
the species conforms to its environment, growth stops."

I shudder. The media of education and influence are
highly skillful and technical today.

"In radio," Miss Wetzler continues, "we have to capture
the child's interest in the first five seconds. We have to
have a hook—get our foot in the door."

In this production line of conformity, the cultural stamp comes down with its uniform likes, dislikes, demands to the state, dress, hair style, and even a stamp-patterned, pleasant, undemanding God.

To reveal the greatness of God to the growing child and to prepare him for true discipleship—which means defying production line conformity—religious education must get its "foot in the door" early with good equipment, sound teaching methods, and attractive materials. All of which, however, can be meaningless showpieces without fully surrendered Christian disciples as teachers and mothers and fathers.

"Do not be conformed to this world but be transformed by the renewal of your mind, that you may prove what is the will of God, what is good and acceptable and perfect" (Romans 12:2, RSV).

FEBRUARY 16

"The Voice of God in the Soul of Men"

Conscience is a nuisance word. It pops up at undesirable moments when life is running smoothly, when all seems well with the world—my world. I have a comfortable rapport with my neighbors. We mow our respective lawns. We chop down the dandelions before they pepper the air with their feathery seeds. We tie our dogs so they don't gallop over others' gardens. Everyone is friendly in a nodding, smiling sort of way. My little world is pleasant and secure.

One day a swimming pool is built in the neighborhood. I learn that only people of one race and color are to be admitted. My conscience prods me unmercifully.

46

"In Christ there is no East or West, in Him no South or North; but one great fellowship of love throughout the whole wide earth." I cannot sing hymns in a church without believing them if I have chosen Christ as the Lord of my conscience.

The greatness of God through Christ places prejudice and discrimination at the little end of the telescope of perspective. I am compelled to risk ending my smooth-running environment to speak and work against a public project which limits participation to those with white skin.

"How much more shall the blood of Christ, who through the eternal Spirit offered himself without blemish to God, purify your conscience from dead works to serve the living God" (Hebrews 9:14, RSV).

∗

FEBRUARY 17

God Loves the Least

A city is a small town under a magnifying glass. Its buildings are towering; its population spills out of a million doors; its superhighways cut great swaths through its center. Its poverty and slums spread through its core like decay in a tooth.

Our car stopped one cold afternoon at a red light on Madison Street in Chicago. This is a long street filled entirely with lonely men who drift aimlessly in and out of saloons, cheap stores, and dirty hotels. There are hundreds of these men. They seem to share a mass misery.

Near our car a massive man with shaggy hair pushed himself along the sidewalk on a board with rollers. He had no legs. He held a hat in his hands and wheeled about in front of the other men, begging. One passer-by kicked the hat from his hands and walked away. The legless man retrieved it. Another man spit into the hat. The beggar seemed to pay no heed. He held his hat aloft until at last a coin dropped into its emptiness. At once he shoved his board and wheels into the open door of a crowded saloon.

God loves this wretched man, I thought! And as though to match my thoughts, the neon lights of a cross blinked on before a store-front mission next door. Someone behind those lights was courageously fulfilling the words of Jesus when He said, "Verily I say unto you, Inasmuch as ye have done it unto one of the least of these my brethren, ye have done it unto me" (Matthew 25:40).

FEBRUARY 18

Mustard-Seed Jobs for the Kingdom

It is often the task of women to accept the little mustard-seed jobs of life. There are, of course, the exceptions like the "big" jobs of women doctors, lawyers, and an occasional ambassador. These must be graciously granted without rancor. They must be evaluated individually and without the blustering pride called "women's equality."

But the tasks of many women involve such "little" things as printing Tim's name on towels and sheets for summer camp; checking that Tom finishes his paper route; devising a scheme to make Susan's piano practicing a picnic instead of a pill; planning the week's menus to reduce Dad, add pounds to Becky, eliminate eggs for allergic Peter, stuff teen-age Jim, and squeeze all of it into a pre-inflationary budget; and on the Sabbath to shed the week's busyness and guide the household into an atmosphere of peace and spiritual refreshment.

48

"Nothing I ever do is really big or important," many women cry at the end of such a week. "My jobs are all the little ones."

Big becomes synonymous with important—little with unimportant. There is a legend that at the time of the crucifixion the dogwood tree was big and strong. It was chosen as the timber for the cross. The tree was horrified. It grieved at the misuse of its bigness.

Jesus sensed the tree's suffering and declared that never again would it grow large enough for a cross. It would be small and slender. Its blossoms would be in the form of a cross, and in the center would be the nailprints and the crown of thorns. In its purity and beauty it would come forth year after year, little and unimportant looking beside the towering pine and the majestic oak, to remind each passer-by of Christ and His death for all mankind on the cross.

"The kingdom of God . . . is like a grain of mustard seed, which, when it is sown in the earth, is less than all the seeds that be in the earth: but when it is sown, it groweth up, and becometh greater than all herbs . . ." (Mark 4:30-32).

FEBRUARY 19

God Loves Every Man

I once had as a friend a noble, elderly man of wealth and culture. He surrounded himself with choice furniture, rugs, and paintings. It was not ostentation. He had an eye for the artistic and beautiful. The thick-carpeted floor, the sparkling cut glass chandeliers, the ornate chairs with lions' heads carved into the armrests made his home an art treasure.

49

He could detect at once the real against the artificial, the honest against the false. His friends followed the same pattern. They were from many walks of life. But each one was as finely chiseled as the chandelier, as genuine as the oriental rugs. The man's position and wealth gave him the privilege of being selective. He was the art collector, not the artist; the buyer of pottery, not the molder of its clay; a judge of man, not a builder of men. And, for all his greatness and honesty, he was exclusive. He never fully accepted Christianity.

Christ opened His arms to everyone—the weak, the timid, the frail, the confused, the diseased, the sinner, the woman adorned in trinkets and the man clad in jewels, a terrified creature possessed of demons and a brilliant scholar of the synagogue. In each He saw a child of God.

God through Christ seeks *every* man and gives to *each* His love.

"For God so loved the *world,* that he gave his only begotten Son, that *whosoever* believeth in him should not perish, but have everlasting life" (John 3:16).

The blessings of cultural and hereditary advantages must flow as a river of compassion to the unlovely and the lost. They must never become a dam to keep the clear water from spilling over and adding refreshment to the murky streams and the parched river beds below.

John 3:16

FEBRUARY 20

A Bond with God

I often say to my children, especially when we have company, "Share your toys, your books, your basketball, and your dolls with your guests."

When they are very small, they hold back. They even tug and offer vocal protests. It is hard to learn to share a treasured possession.

A stingy, grasping creature like old Scrooge of Dickens' "Christmas Carol" is repulsive. He surely had no blessings as a miser. Yet it took the jarrings of a full-fledged ghost to make him believe that it is truly "more blessed to give than to receive."

A Chicago minister, many years ago, left a secure pastorate to share a dream of a "house by the side of the road and be a friend of man." He and his family had few possessions and little money and yet he had faith and a dream and a desire to share them both.

Today on a high hill at the portals of a forest preserve near the city, this minister and those who shared his dream have hewn a Community Center Foundation. There is a chapel, a retreat lodge, a craft shop, and a summer camp grounds for disturbed, unhappy boys and girls. Sick souls from the city come daily to seek counsel from the minister and rehabilitation from the shared beauty of the forest and the house by the side of the road.

In giving we link ourselves with God, the Giver of every good and perfect gift.

"Every good gift and every perfect gift is from above, and cometh down from the Father of lights . . ." (James 1:17).

FEBRUARY 21

God Is All

God in Christ is all and in all. I wonder. Is it possible for me to stretch my mind and soul to the possibilities of this great fact? It means that a Christian recognizes the fundamental unity of mankind, and knows that in Christ all divisions according to race, religious rites, culture, and social position are done away.

Is my world filled with divisions? I ask myself. Do I measure everyone by the way I dress, by the food I eat, by the church service I have always attended, by the color of my skin?

And if my world is little and squeezed in like a shriveled lemon, can I push the roof of heaven very high?

A man who belonged to the church I attended once protested against a morning radio service which my church sponsored because, he said, "It goes outside my town."

It isn't necessary to travel around the world to sample differences at first hand. They can be found in the smallest hamlet—across the railroad tracks—in the home of a Negro family—in the county seat jail—in a home of wealth and culture.

But when Christ enters these doors with me, I know there will be a unity inside despite the many outward differences.

"Where there is neither Greek nor Jew, circumcision nor uncircumcision, Barbarian, Scythian, bond nor free: but Christ is all, and in all" (Colossians 3:11).

✳

FEBRUARY 22

Needing God

When a man turns his back on friends and family and heads toward the independent hermit's hut, he usually discovers the impossibility of being sufficient unto himself.

The need for food, medical care, shelter, and legal protection brings people knocking at his door. Modern man has interlocked himself with material dependencies.

Without the grocery store I could not survive. And behind the grocery store are scores of helpers: the clerks, the food manufacturers, the tin can makers, the glass factory workers, the miners, the farmers, and many more. I need the grocery store to nourish my body.

But another part of me seeks nourishment, too. It is my soul.

Here again I am dependent—on God, the Bible, my minister, my friends, unknown neighbors. This time the dependency is interlocked with need and love. It cannot be given or received without love. It must be based on the words of Jesus when He stated His rule of life, "This is my commandment, That ye love one another, as I have loved you" (John 15:12).

FEBRUARY 23

A Gift from God

A gift is usually thought of as a package knotted and tied with expectation. For some, Christmas is a collection of such packages. So are birthdays. There are occasional unwrapped gifts, like money from the will of one who has died and wishes his loved ones to have his earthly possessions.

Sometimes, it almost seems that the giving and receiving of packaged gifts is a drive that has made higher wages a twentieth-century obsession. With extra money tangible things can be bought—gifts for ourselves—gifts for our home —gifts for our children.

When Jesus departed from this earth, He too left gifts for His friends. But they were different. He left His teachings. He left His love. He left His disciples of whom He had become a part.

And, He left His peace. It was not the kind of peace sought between nations, or the temporary peace that quiets a family quarrel, or the peace of escape in the bomb shelter. Christ left His peace deep within people—a peace of heart and mind—a peace as certain as the earth's seasons, as indestructible as God, and as permanent as eternity.

For all time Christ gave this gift of peace. It can never be purchased or folded or tied or placed in a package.

"Peace I leave with you, my peace I give unto you: not as the world giveth, give I unto you" (John 14:27).

FEBRUARY 24

God of the Wind

A spiritual encounter with the living God never runs along one pattern. It is like the wind of the Spirit blowing where it wills.

Anna planned to be a missionary. Everything in her young life led to this fulfillment. Then, her mother died. She was shocked. How could God be good and let this happen? She lost her faith and her desire to be a missionary.

Anna married. During the first twelve years of marriage she never prayed, or attended church. One day a church was built near her home. Its members accepted her doubts and struggles. Slowly her faith returned. Her husband joined her. Today she is again a church member—praying, studying the Bible, and striving toward true discipleship.

Katie, Anna's neighbor, has not known the rough and turbulent winds of the Spirit. All her life she has been in the center of Christian living and witness. To her it seems unbelievable that Christians could ever doubt or deviate from their Christian faith.

Not far from Katie lives Sarah. Her parents were atheists with humanistic idealism and sensitivity to human need. She has never gone to church or accepted Christ. Yet friends praise her goodness and kindness. In serious moments, however, life to her has many unanswered questions. She seeks for God in a cautious way.

God's greatness permits freedom. Yet He pursues each person like a powerful, shifting, unpredictable wind.

"The wind blows where it wills, and you hear the sound of it, but you do not know whence it comes or whither it goes; so it is with every one who is born of the Spirit" (John 3:8, RSV).

*

FEBRUARY 25

God of Gods

The doorbell rings. I open the door and standing before me are two common-looking people with Bibles and pamphlets under their arms. In firm, but quiet-spoken tones they ask to come in. A few minutes' conversation reveals they are Jehovah's Witnesses. To me their beliefs are strange, their spirit fanatical, but their courage great.

Mankind wants a living God. Do these witnesses appear as a judgment on vague, conformist, lukewarm Christianity?

In our mailbox at Christmas is a small invitation asking us to come to a neighbor's home to celebrate Hanukkah.

In our window a lighted star hangs, reminding us of Bethlehem. A manger scene decks our mantel, portraying the birth of the Messiah. Yet our Jewish neighbors at this season have their eyes on the military exploits of the Maccabees celebrated in Hanukkah.

War, persecution, and cruelty make it hard for the Jew to believe that the living God came down to earth at Bethlehem. Judaism persists and still looks for the Messiah.

God's greatness must be found in those who worship Him through Christ, or other gods appear and other religions are taught that are "but broken lights of Thee. And Thou, O Lord, are more than they" (Alfred Tennyson).

"For the Lord your God is God of gods, and Lord of lords, a great God" (Deuteronomy 10:17).

FEBRUARY 26

God the Father

One day I walked into the nursery of a Chicago settlement house. Settlement houses arise in the areas of slum and decay of the city. They do a brave job lifting the loads of poor and desolate people and easing the pains of unwanted children.

This nursery was gay and bright in its exterior. Low, colorfully painted tables held crayons, wooden beads, puzzles, and boxes of clay. A half circle of eager-faced boys and girls sat about a storyteller. They were motionless with interest.

The reader turned a page and held up a picture for all to see.

"This is Daddy," she said, "who has come home from work to play with his children."

"Do the children have a daddy?" a small square boy elbowed his way toward the book. His fat leg hooked the chair of a pale child in a faded blue dress. She fell to the floor and began screaming and kicking.

A social worker drew me aside.

"This sort of thing happens every time 'daddy' is mentioned," she said. "The storyteller forgot. You see, most of these youngsters come from broken homes. They never see their fathers. A daddy is something they need and want terribly."

Human fathers are denied these children of the slums, but concerned adults can become their Christian brothers and sisters. Through them these unwanted youngsters may someday understand Christ's family reference to the heavenly Father—a God of love with personal concerns, that reach out to all mankind.

"A father of the fatherless . . . is God in his holy habitation" (Psalm 68:5).

FEBRUARY 27

God Our Refuge

Fear is a menacing creature that clutches at the heart and pinches the mind. Its eyes are hollow and withdrawn. Its tongue twitches with distortions. Fear does not know God.

One distraught mother worried herself into physical pain. She feared each day that some evil would come to a member of her family when he or she left the safe vigilance of home.

A man, so fearful of an impending operation, walked from the hospital, stating he would rather die than face the surgeon's knife.

With not too much imagination today, it is possible to get "international jitters." Mounting stockpiles of hydrogen bombs in opposing national camps do not induce a serene kind of security. Reports that intercontinental atomic missiles could destroy most of this planet are saturated with fear.

Sleeping pills, dope, alcohol are used by some to escape fear; but they are always a temporary escape.

A lasting release from fear, and a lasting insurance for a real security are found in these words of St. Theresa:

> "Let naught trouble thee:
> Let naught frighten thee:
> All things pass.
> God alone changeth not.
> Patience can do all things.
> Whosoever has God, has everything.
> God alone sufficeth."

"The eternal God is thy refuge, and underneath are the everlasting arms" (Deuteronomy 33:27).

FEBRUARY 28

God's Order

Elise Boulding, a Quaker writer and mother of five, has an apt phrase for the housewife's Today. She calls it the "trap of dailiness" and says "the great enemy of the kingdom is Today."

Many Todays are ushered in with the clang of an alarm clock. It is a miniature fire alarm that sets off a rushed and hurried series of breakfast, scramble for buses, trains, car pools, and a disarrayed house that screams from one end to the other to be picked up and pulled into order again.

The housewife buries herself in a long cup of coffee and then braces herself for the tugs and pulls of Today. The neighbor's children unexpectedly arrive for the morning. The drapery committee from the church calls to say they will come at two o'clock instead of three.

"Don't go to any trouble," the chairman's sugary voice quivers, "just a cup of coffee and some of your fresh, homemade cinnamon rolls will do for refreshments."

The baby cries for breakfast and a bath. Two white shirts must be ironed for the big sons' party tonight. What will the dinner menu be? Evening arrives and a splitting headache with need for an aspirin.

Would Today be different if it started fifteen minutes ahead of the rush with prayer? God is present with His strength, His love, His steadiness, His direction. In prayer God's presence is sought. The busy program of Today's housewife might unfold itself in life's pattern as the time for this type of labor. A new reverence might be developed for the neighbor's children and the committee chairman. Order might be restored and with it peace and joy.

"It is God that girdeth me with strength,
And maketh my way perfect" (Psalm 18:32).

59

Abandoned Joys

An Englishwoman once came to Kansas on a lecture trip. Each morning early, before the sun began to bake the earth, she set off for the country with long, full strides. She trod happily across treeless, flat fields and down long, straight roads.

Car after car stopped her with the request,

"Please can't we give you a ride? Where do you want to go?"

"No, thank you," she answered, "I want to walk. I want to pray with the rhythm of my steps. I want to breathe the freshness of the air. I want to hear your birds sing. I want to look at the sky."

"She must be crazy," someone said from the car and drove away.

In the complexities of motorized America, the simple joy of being able to walk, given freely to most men by God, is abandoned. Motorboats, motorcars, motor lawn mowers carry our unused legs swiftly from place to place.

"Let's enjoy the good fresh air of the country," we suggest as we pile six people in the car, roll up the windows, and turn on the heater.

Is man in this pursuit of a more mechanized civilization a better man? Now and then it might be well to remember that man created cars and boats and airplanes and motorcycles. God created legs and eyes and ears. No man-made substitutes have ever equaled them. These taken-for-granted gifts of God are indescribably precious and structurally miraculous.

"So God created man in his own image, in the image of God created he him; male and female created he them" (Genesis 1:27).

EVERYTHING BEAUTIFUL IN ITS TIME

Helen Wade Alderfer

MARCH 1

A *Time to Live*

Hugh Means wrote of "the gift of living together, lost so often in the attachment to worthless personal possessions." His words strike an aching chord in my heart, for I think of houses filled with fine furniture that mean the often-repeated command to small hands—"don't touch"—as though the costly furniture were of more worth than the child. I think of long lines of young women, many of them mothers of small children, punching a factory time clock for an added income to meet a too high standard of living; while all the small but infinitely important deeds of a a mother-at-home die a-borning. With pain I recall all the unimportant trivial things that have kept me from the abundant life.

St. Francis of Assisi was one who knew the joy of appreciation without the need for possession, who gained the sweetest joy in a life of poverty and love.

The gift of living! How we long for it! And all the while Jesus, who ever puts people above things, waits to tell us how to achieve it. It is all in perfecting His command, "Follow me."

61

"If we live in the Spirit, let us also walk in the Spirit"
(Galatians 5:25).

✳

MARCH 2

A Time to Pray

Majestic, lovely St. Bartholomew's church in New York
City is fronted by a sign welcoming all to enter for prayer
and meditation; and for over 200 years people from the
busy pounding streets have entered to pray in solemn quiet.

At Greenfield Village stands Henry Ford's proudest
effort, a little white chapel only 75 feet from its doorstep
to the tip of its simple spire. Visitors overwhelmed and
wearied by the many old craft shops and restored historical
houses, and the many relics from the past have stopped at
the little church and in its simple beauty come to prayer.

How quick the heart is to remember and to say, "But,
Lord, if only I were there in St. Bartholomew's or in the
chapel at Greenfield Village; but you see where I am here
in my own house, not exactly the setting most of the time
for prayer."

To the heart that listens, His answer comes clearly, "The
church [that is] in thy house . . . ." And to the eyes that
see, everywhere there are quiet rooms, corners of rooms,
window sills that look out on waiting fields and woods.
And, lo, the place is anywhere, the hour is any time.

"I will therefore that men pray every where, lifting up
holy hands . . ." (I Timothy 2:8a).

✳

A *Time for Thanks*

Think what it would mean to celebrate Thanksgiving, not once a year, but once a month or once a week or, better yet, once a day; hearts overflowing with thanks for every good gift, hands carrying some of the bounty to those in need of its sharing—all of this a literal application of "giving thanks always for all things."

What if every day we named the things for which we give thanks, beginning with the big usually thanked-for-things and coming down, down to the tiniest ones, the ones children remember, like "the stars in Mother's eyes," "the lickings of the cake pan," "the little icicles on the roof"— all this in grand accord with Jesus' request that we be like little children.

Then we would find that some little spring that has been slowly drying up would be sparkling and alive again, that every day would be like a fountain upspringing in the heart.

Nine there were who went on (let me not be one); one returned to give thanks (let it be me). For I would not grieve Him again, cause Him to ask, "Where are the nine?"

> So much I have;
> Lord, give me one thing more—
> A thankful heart.

"And to stand every morning to thank and praise the Lord, and likewise at even" (I Chronicles 23:30).

A *Time to Love*

A study team fanned out over a certain city to check on the 400 children considered well-adjusted by their public school teachers. Armed with clip-board, paper, and pencil, what would they find? The world waited eagerly; surely they would find that such children came from families with a certain number of children, a certain income, a certain kind of parents.

Startlingly, the team found that some were from poor homes, others from wealthy homes; some were only children, others from families of 8 or 10 or 12; some had calm, well-adjusted parents, others had flighty impossible ones or had no living parents or lived in broken homes. But always these 400 children had one certain thing. They had someone who loved and needed them.

This is exactly what Jesus taught along the dusty Galilean road when He put His arms out in love and said, "Suffer the little children to come unto me." This is what He would have parents ever learning, "Let them come to you and then give yourselves to them, not some poor substitute of a toy or piece of clothing. Give them the gift of time, down-on-the-floor game time, out-in-the-woods-and-fields hiking time."

"Life is more than food and raiment," Jesus said in an effort to help us see that each child is more than a body to be fed and clothed and housed, more than a mind to be educated. Each one is a precious eternal soul to love and guide.

Time for that love I pledge today.

"To every thing there is a season, and a time to every

purpose under the heaven . . . . A time to love . . ."
(Ecclesiastes 3:1, 8a).

✳

A Time to Be Praised

Sometimes we found her in the woods with her four.
("Oh, we brought nothing back. We just looked and
looked.") Sometimes she was storytelling in the orchard
to hers and others. Always there was good food in her
cheerful kitchen; from it I carry a memory of crusty bread
new-baked and spring-cold milk, of blue willowware on a
red-checked cloth. I see her and those she loved at peace
with life and filled with the joy of living. When I read,
"Her price is far above rubies," I think of Anna.

There are for all homemakers, endless meals and washing of dishes; and always floors to be scrubbed, clothes to
be washed and ironed and mended. But with it there are
little faces to kiss, little hands to hold, little feet to lead in
straight, true paths. And those who do it all for love of
God know how high and sweet is the calling of a homemaker.

> Say not that hers was a house kept well;
> Not there her honor lay.
> Nor tell that she visited the sick
> And any found in need;
> Though it was ever so.
> Strength and honor were hers,
> And all her ways were ways of kindness;
> Only think not of that.
> Safely did her husband
> Put his trust into her keeping,

And her children called her blessed.
Remember but one thing:
This woman feared the Lord
And so she shall be praised.

". . . a woman that feareth the Lord, she shall be praised"
(Proverbs 31:30b).

$$*$$

MARCH 6

A Time for Sorrow

Who never ate his bread in sorrow,
    Who never spent the darksome hours
Weeping and watching for the morrow,
    He knows ye not, ye Heavenly Powers.

—Goethe.

There is a cry that goes out when sorrow comes, "Can
the heart that grieves find strength to recover?"

What tears Mary and Martha must have wept at the
death of their loved brother! And with it was the pain of
supposition—"If only Jesus had been here!" Then He came;
weeping and loss and suppositions were over. Whatever
Mary and Martha may have thought about Jesus before
Lazarus' resurrection, they now knew for a certainty that
Christ was the Son of God, no mere man or friend, but
Saviour. He held the keys to the gate marked "life."

Here is light for our wondering "why?" and our often
questionings when the fabric of family life is tested by
physical suffering or death, when the lovely sun of day
turns to blackest night.

The heart *can* bear it when hope is torn away and the

fondest dreams of life are destroyed; for the Spirit of God gives strength for life. He seals no bit of life away; He unlocks it.

"From whence cometh my help?
My help cometh from the Lord, which made heaven and earth" (Psalm 121:1, 2).
"I will fear no evil: for thou art with me" (Psalm 23:4).

MARCH 7

A Time for Joy

Having a certain amount of money or possessions, being a certain age, or attaining a certain position in life—none of these mean a monopoly on joy. How wise the one who wrote, "Joy is not in things; it is in us."
My heart sings:

Because something that has been held a frozen captive in the earth is ready to spring to life, and hope rings like a chime.

Because there are little houses on little streets where love shines out and draws the traveler into warmth.

Because there are friends, "pilgrims and strangers," who make life's highway not only a present path of dear shared joys but one that lifts the eyes to the sweep of the stars above.

Because there are signs of compassion in people who say with Llewellyn, "There is no room for unkindness. All men are born the same and equal."

Because there is the knowing that man does not live by bread alone but by the Word, more precious with each reading, with each remembrance.

Because there walks with us One who came to make our joy full.

"And my soul shall be joyful in the Lord:
It shall rejoice in his salvation" (Psalm 35:9).

*

MARCH 8

A *Time to Sing*

Once a year the Bach family, of which Johann Sebastian was a member, held a family reunion which was a great festival of music, looked forward to and practiced for all year. The uncles and aunts and cousins came from far and wide to sing and play and listen to music; on that special day of the year the Bach family scaled a mountaintop to stand in close fellowship with God.

Perhaps Johann Sebastian Bach would not have become the musical genius he was if one family had not lived their music as an expression of their love for God. His music would be lost to the world and its inspiration would be lost to the musicians who followed him as well as to the world of music lovers who have listened to his work.

Remembering the Bach family, who built on love of God and of music, I will remember that the notes of thanks and adoration sung at the wash line, above the dishes in the sink, or around the table, are in themselves a link in the chain of praise across the centuries. I will rejoice that God who notes a sparrow's fall misses no least note of joy.

"I will sing unto the Lord as long as I live:
I will sing praise to my God while I have my being" (Psalm 104:33).

A *Time to Speak*

One lovely spring morning in a little church in the Philippines five women were baptized into the Christian faith. These five were neighbors of a woman who had lived so well the life of love that her pastor could say of the five, "They were brought by this woman."

Paul wore himself out going from place to place in witness for Christ. Church history includes a mighty army of those who served in their time and place. We, the twentieth-century witnesses, must take our places and speak the words that only living witnesses can speak.

The Samaritan woman at the well became a sermon on missions. "Lift up your eyes," Jesus said to the disciples. And when they looked up, they saw the countryside of Samaria stretching before them vast and waiting.

God of all harvests, give us clear eyes to see, a sure voice to speak.

> Oh, let it not be said, my friend,
> That we talked of many things
> of many people
> of a few ideas
> But not at all of God.
> For then you will return to your work
> And I will turn again to mine—
> Both of us sad and hungry.

"But thanks be to God, who in Christ always leads us in triumph, and through us spreads the fragrance of the knowledge of him everywhere" (II Corinthians 2:14, RSV).

A *Time to Write*

At furlough time a missionary nurse told a group of women, "I cannot tell you what letters have meant. They have been a bond that has helped to keep me strong in times of loneliness and weak faith." Her words painted a picture of the village in a far country where she lived, of evening time and with it thoughts of loved ones separated by thousands of miles; and then of the letter and the lonely evening shadows being pushed back. Sometimes nothing should stand in the way of writing a letter.

The Bible speaks of the cup of cold water given in Christ's name; a letter of appreciation fits in with His plan, too. Amy Lowell said that for every letter that she wrote she chipped a piece from off her heart. Such extravagance makes for the kind of letters that gladden the heart.

Somewhere there are those who wait for the words we write. We must ask God what they should be, say with Browning's David, "Speak through me now." They should go on their way with a winging prayer that they will be weighted with joy for the ones who receive them.

Once the Author of all good writing promoted these words:

"You yourselves are our letter of recommendation, written on your hearts, to be known and read by all men; and you show that you are a letter from Christ delivered by us, written not with ink but with the Spirit of the living God, not on tablets of stone but on tablets of human hearts" (II Corinthians 3:2, 3, RSV).

A Time for Silence

Perhaps you find that a busy life schedule leaves no time for days away from home. The cottage by the sea or the cabin in the mountains cannot be your retreat. And even as you accept that, you know that the spirit must have a place to recreate for days of crisis or ordinary sameness. Some place, a small woods or a garden spot, a stone or a fallen log, one small quiet place there must be; for the spirit demands a silent hour.

Today I took lunch in a paper bag and walked to the little woods that joins the garden. There I ate in quietness, noting each small awakening of spring and feeling anew the sweet stirrings of faith that God gives with every springtime.

A gray squirrel stood far off querying my presence; sparrows scolded me or him and fluffed their winter coats in the breeze. Such thoughts as I had not had all winter of God's goodness delighted me. A sadness for the winter's busyness and loss came clear.

"Be still, and know that I am God" (Psalm 46:10).

MARCH 12

A Time to Build

> A house is built of logs and stone,
>   Of tiles and posts and piers;
> A home is built of loving deeds
>   That stand a thousand years.
> —*Victor Hugo.*

71

Building a house—poring over blueprints, planning, dreaming, changing, and at last beams against the sky, shape and form, and stone and brick in place. A house! Hard, tangible reality that the hands can touch!

Building a home is so much more subtle. How measure accurately the intangibles that go into it, the feel of home that children never forget no matter how far in place and time they travel from it, the feel that friends and strangers touch when they cross the doorstep?

Who knows how many kind words and tender thoughts, whispered prayers and joyful songs it takes to form an aura of sweetness? Who can measure how much of gentleness, mercy, and forbearance it takes to create a godly home?

Home needs no measuring cup or stick, for home is all good things in great abundance, moment by moment casting in of the best until no smallest child in it, no veriest king of a guest can ever doubt but that here has been a-building a very temple to the living God.

Who will this day build a home?

"Except the Lord build the house, they labour in vain that build it: except the Lord keep the city, the watchman waketh but in vain" (Psalm 127:1).

MARCH 13

A Time to Choose

We talked one evening of what we would do if Jesus came to our home, as He did to the home in Bethany long ago, how we would maybe see Him coming up the path just as evening fell and we would hurry to open the door wide for Him.

"And you would put the flowery dishes on the white tablecloth, Mother."

"And He could use my room."

"I wonder what He would say to us?" blue eyes shone in anticipation of the blessed words.

That little talk at evening started a thought. Would Jesus feel at home with us? What would the furnishings of our home tell Him? Would He know that He was the honored Guest or would He feel that He was one of the lesser ones?

"Today," I said in my soul, "I must put my house in order."

> Still He stands at doors—
> "Is there room?"
> And we choose
> As did the keeper of the inn,
> As did the keeper of the stable:
>   Poverty or riches?
>   Light or darkness?
>   War or peace?
>   Sorrow or joy?
> Each to himself,
> Keepers of our own hearts' doors
> We choose alone.

"Choose you this day whom ye will serve; . . . as for me and my house, we will serve the Lord" (Joshua 24:15).

6

A Time to Read

The Book Sir Walter Scott asked for when he was dying was the Bible. It is also a book to live by. To our shame it is called "the least read best-seller among the race of white men."

Secular reading has its place, too, but not just any book. In a world where there is much of the cheap and tawdry, there are still books that "upward lead."

Keep a book of poetry with the cookbooks, ready like a fresh breeze to blow away the little vexations of the day. Have a devotional book at your finger tips when you sit down, another book to take you to far places and open the heart in sympathy and understanding to those in other lands.

Some books belong on your bookshelf to be read many times. Someone said, "You would never boast of having heard Beethoven's ninth once; just so a good book should be read often." Some books are meant to be loaned; take one to your neighbor, even as you share prized recipes or flower slips. You will give her the gold that nothing can take away, not the weight of years nor eyesight that dims.

Take a few minutes today, your insurance of the delight and perspective that you need to be the kind of wife your husband deserves, the kind of mother your children will love. Be sure of this—good reading is not a luxury to be snatched or something for which you must apologize. God adds His blessing to it.

"Study to shew thyself approved unto God, a workman that needeth not to be ashamed, rightly dividing the word of truth" (II Timothy 2:15).

A *Time to Work*

Jesus' eyes sweep the world we see from the kitchen window. "Look, the fields! The Jericho road runs past your door. Go ye, also, into the vineyard."

For several weeks a newspaper serialized a book which was in essence the story of Jesus' life on earth. A reader wrote to the editor of the paper, "I am so excited wondering how the story will come out that I can hardly wait for the paper to come." This was no native of a remote jungle village, but someone who lives on a street with people who know the story she has never heard.

The thought of the thousands to be taught, the countless doubters to be strengthened, the world of straying ones to be guided, the vast "vineyard of the Lord" is almost too great for one poor laborer to think upon.

But God never passes out work by the thousands—just to each his small allotment. To each He gives a little workable parcel which is altogether possible if the hands are willing to put down the earthy tasks for a heavenly one.

I am ever learning, dear Lord, but today help me to learn indelibly that spring house cleaning must wait if I have failed to work your vineyard, the one outside my kitchen window. Amen.

"I must work the works of him that sent me, while it is day" (John 9:4a).

A *Time for Faith*

Once when Mr. Wesley was in a very important conference, the discussion centered on the subject of faith. No one seemed able to give a satisfactory definition. Finally they called in a woman whom they knew to be a person of good sense and strong Christian character. They asked her what faith was and she answered, "It is taking God at His word." "That will do," said Mr. Wesley. "That is enough for us all."

And so it is. We set out bulbs, knowing that winter will not go on indefinitely, for God has promised the changing of the seasons. Plows turn the earth and make it ready for sowing in that glad expectation. The eye notes the lengthening days and the heart does not doubt either the time of planting or the time of harvesting.

It will be spring again; the sap of life will rise. A winter of fear and pain it may have been, of war and disillusionment, but faith remembers that the prince of darkness has always waged a losing fight. God who promised "seedtime and harvest" meant for us to take Him at His word.

Even so this day as the divine cycle turns, the heart prepares for spring. Rejoice in it!

"Now the just shall live by faith . . ." (Hebrews 10:38a).

"Now faith is the assurance of things hoped for, the conviction of things not seen" (Hebrews 11:1, RSV).

*

MARCH 17

A Time to Dream

It is good to dream dreams, not idle schoolboy dreams of riches and fame, but warm, forward-looking dreams of women who plan with God.

It is good to dream of the day when all men will be at

peace and children everywhere can live in love and safety. Women have prayed that dream in their hearts since wars began.

It is good to dream of that glorious day when people everywhere will have the Word of God in their mother tongue, when no spot of God's beautiful world will remain barren of His saving knowledge.

It is good to stop and remember that Jesus walked dusty roads and sat beside cool streams where His thoughts and dreams were often of the kingdom of God that He had come to build.

Out of this busy day it must not be said that there was no time for a high dream of a world in which God can work perfectly in hearts, beginning always in single hearts—yours —mine.

". . . grow in grace, and in the knowledge of our Lord and Saviour Jesus Christ" (II Peter 3:18).

MARCH 18

A Time to Do

Someone chided the kindly neighbor who carried dinner each day to a family in which there was much illness: "Why do you spend so much time helping others? Your own family will suffer."

"This I can do," she answered. "There are many things I am not able to do, but this is one I can do."

She is one who would have stopped to help the man who fell among thieves. She is one who would have taken her Samuel to the temple, saying, "This I can do." Always it can be seen that when the heart willingly says these words, a dozen deeds of love spring to the eye.

77

Perhaps this good neighbor woman one day had dreams of doing mighty works for God in a foreign land, before vast crowds of people. Or was it a dream of written words or songs that would bring sounding honor to Him?

And then it seemed as though she let go the dreams and did the common things, the often unseen things. Who can dare to guess how she has rejoiced the Father's heart, what high honor she has brought to the kingdom!

"As we have therefore opportunity, let us do good unto all . . ." (Galatians 6:10a).

✳

MARCH 19

A Time for Hospitality

The Shunammite woman said to her husband, "Let us make a small roof chamber . . . and put there for him [Elisha, holy man of God] a bed, a table, a chair, and a lamp, so that whenever he comes to us, he can go in there." And for this she was greatly blessed, even to the restoring of life to her son.

An American woman said to her husband, "The storeroom—we shouldn't really have one: the things it holds could well be used by someone in need. Let us make it into a guest room, always ready for pilgrims and strangers who are in need of a resting place on their way." And for this she was greatly blessed, even to the restoring of her peace with God.

And as warming to the heart is the story of the good friend, without the smallest space that could be reserved as a guest room, who dedicated a table board to the Lord. She kept it always in the table so that no notice was necessary, but anyone could stop and find a place ready and waiting. She was greatly blessed by bread broken in love, good conversation, and often and often angels entertained unawares.

"Be kindly affectioned one to another with brotherly love; . . . given to hospitality" (Romans 12:10a, 13b).

MARCH 20

A Time for Simplicity

We live in a world of things, many things—in the stores, often in our homes. Sometimes we are aware of the parade of them. Sometimes they subtly become a part of our thinking and living. The newest becomes a *must*; the luxuries become necessities. Life is measured by quantity, not quality.

The happy Greek philosopher, Diogenes, said, "How many things there are in the world that Diogenes does not need." His words are in bold contrast to the advertisements that would make us believe that no one can be happy without this or that article.

Even our very life program is endangered as a multiplicity of demands are made upon it to the extent that complexity and lack of co-ordination are the usual.

Remembering how simply our Master and Example lived, how often He taught that man's salvation and even his delight are not composed of a multitude of things, we must rethink our life structure.

Somewhere at the core of life we must put the sure knowledge that simplicity stands on its own high peak of worth, that nothing can make up for excess.

"Now thanks be unto God, which always causeth us to triumph in Christ, and maketh manifest the savour of his knowledge by us in every place" (II Corinthians 2:14).

MARCH 21

A Time for Spring

The winter days are lengthening; on sunny slopes wild plum and japonica bloom, underfoot the more shy—wake-robins, spring beauties, and dogtooth violets appear. These bring to memory an old inscription engraved on the tombstone of an early American naturalist, "Lord, 'tis a pleasant thing to stand in gardens planted by Thy hands."

It is a time to think of the growth in our spiritual lives. Life, for an adult, is more than measuring at the doorjamb to see how many inches the year has added. Life is a growing of the inner person; and we hunger for that growth as we long for hardly anything else.

As the flowers on the earth are proof positive of another springtime, we look for signs of growth in our spiritual lives. We take tests such as those in I Corinthians 13. Have the admonishments to bear all things, to endure all things, and to love, above all to love, become more of a pattern, less of a burden?

And there is no peace until the inner tender shoots of growth appear.

"For, lo, the winter is past . . . the flowers appear on the earth; the time of the singing of birds is come . . ." (Song of Solomon 2:11a, 12a).

A *Time to Keep*

The vase shone like a jewel in the dingy room; sunlight on the ruby glass caught warmth and light like a prism. "It was my mother's," the tired woman said and for the telling her eyes caught some of its light.

Several years after a concentration camp experience one of the prisoners told of the difficult days, difficult because there was not enough food, no privacy, little medical attention, indefiniteness of stay. Nerves frayed. People became churlish and dishonest and unlovely. But a lover of music led a camp chorus. "It was like a miracle that there was one who could lead us in the great hymns of the church. I think it saved many of us from going to pieces." I thought when she recounted those days that she held up an experience that shone like the ruby glass in the mountain cottage.

Praise be to God for memory. For even on such a day as this when the early spring sky is cold and gray and when troubles are pressing in; there wait memories for the drawing forth—ruby red, and singing in a gray day.

"They shall abundantly utter the memory of thy great goodness, and shall sing of thy righteousness" (Psalm 145:7).

A *Time to Give*

The day the widow put in her mite she set an example to shine down every century since. We do not know, but

I have always imagined her to be a young widow, sorrowing still in lonely loss for a dearly loved husband, frightened yet at being an only parent to her children.

Out of her need she gave, holding back no least bit. Her gift rebukes my niggardly ways, my holding back selfishly not only of material gifts but of time from those who ask it, love from those who need it.

The unnamed widow of the Bible teaches that life is putting in everything you have, giving in lovely abandonment, not from the surplus but from the need.

Once another widow put in generously every Sunday. Noticing it a wealthy man offered to put in her share with his. "Oh, no," she cried, "would you rob me of the joy of giving?"

Lord, make us people of the giving heart, the open hand. Let no hardness of withdrawal keep one gift we have from those who wait in need. Let it not once be said that we turned away from one in want. In Christ's name. Amen.

"You will be enriched in every way for great generosity, which through us will produce thanksgiving to God" (II Corinthians 9:11, RSV).

MARCH 24

A Time to Share

Thank God for the Bible, no longer chained to the pulpit as in the sixteenth century, no longer scarce as in the seventeenth, no longer expensive as in the eighteenth and sometimes in the nineteenth, but available in the twentieth as never before. And this for a small price and in an increasing diversity of languages. Not all the changes of the centuries have robbed it of its power. For myself I rejoice in this, but when last did I know a driving need to share the Good News?

Our children bring us the wonders they find, wild flowers, pretty stones, or small creatures. Finding them, they could not possibly keep them to themselves; for there is in them a great need to share with someone the good things they find.

Christ could have said that He came that we might have life and stopped there, but He didn't. He added, "and that . . . [ye] might have it more abundantly." It is out of that abundance that the sharing is done. How abundant Christ's life was! How He shared it! Never did He hold one hand behind Him and give with the other. Never did He speak to one person or to a crowd with a mere part of Himself. Never did He say when the demands of life pressed in, "Today I am too tired; today I had planned for myself; today I am just too weary to face people."

O Christ of the abundant life, help me pattern my life after yours. Help me to be done with this small, pinched, selfish life and to find in its place the free, life-breathing, abundant life you meant for us all to have. Clarify my walk in life that its purpose may be first to share the life you came to give. Amen.

"Let the beauty of the Lord our God be upon us: and establish thou the work of our hands . . ." (Psalm 90:17a).

MARCH 25

A Time to Shine

Sometimes when the glow of shared fellowship was warm around her, it seemed that she must break forth in brightness. But she sat on with pursed lips and a frozen stare, feeling perhaps that lightheartedness was not seemly in a Christian. Sadder than her face was its effect on others; some of the gloom did brush off.

The one who wrote a book with the title, *The Lost Radiance of the Christian Religion,* must have known such a person. The sad title is one that could with profit be on the bookshelf, if only for the occasional stab to wakefulness that it might give. It would be good for the days when we forget that theologies and religious standards were not meant to depress but to help us catch the radiance of Christ's life.

Artists have pictured Jesus in many ways but always from the imagination. He has never been pictured in any other way, and so there is only one way to judge what He did look like—by His reflection in the lives of His disciples.

Foggy or clear the reflection? Jesus was a radiant person; would anyone know it looking at me?

"By this shall all men know that ye are my disciples" (John 13:35).

MARCH 26

A Time to Forget

No one lives who does not have in the warp and woof of his being countless things forgotten. Sometimes there are unforgotten things there, too; lines of faces often reveal the sharp memories that burn and do not bless.

As fine as the memory that serves well is the memory that can reject those things that are better forgotten.

Paul wrote, "Forgetting those things which are behind,

and reaching forth unto those things which are before, I press toward the mark for the prize of the high calling of God in Christ Jesus." And with what certain purposeful steps he pressed forward, unhindered by the dragging weight of bitter memories.

Here is dawning another new day, fresh-minted from the Father's hand. Enter it with all the best-be-forgotten things left behind and before you all the lovely opportunities for rich thoughts, kind deeds and words that come to those who walk hand in hand with God.

"Remember ye not the former things" (Isaiah 43:18).

MARCH 27

A Time to Remember

"For God so loved the world that he gave his only forgotten Son," three-year-old Faith said in an effort to repeat the verse she was learning in Sunday school.

"It's 'begotten,' dear," I corrected, repeating the verse for her.

She said it dutifully and then ran to play.

But the verse was not ended for me. As I went through the motions of the day that had been planned full long before it began, "forgotten" kept coming back like a small haunting ghost. "Forgotten" while I tried frantically to keep to the housekeeping schedule I had set? "Forgotten" while I rode a treadwheel of modern busyness?

Was my small child surprised to see me come to her, hands empty, only me in the middle of the morning? In the shade of the sandbox we sat together. I told her of some of the wonderful things Jesus had done when He

85

lived on earth. I answered small, deep questions and found in that hour a sweet peace. For us He was not forgotten; remembrance sweetened all the day.

"Seek the Lord and his strength, seek his face continually. Remember his marvellous works that he hath done" (I Chronicles 16:11, 12a).

∗

MARCH 28

A Time to Be Old

Many dear saints have proved "Grow old along with me! The best is yet to be" is true. Their homes are homes of peace and comfort where rich memories come from the skein of life and where the words fitly spoken are so often the needful words for those who are too eager, who cannot wait for time to make ready the way.

One of them who lived nearly as the Master meant all of us to live said in time of sorrow, "It is well; it has always been well with me and my Father." That is traveling to heaven first-class. D. L. Moody said that "What time I am afraid, I will trust in thee" is second-class. "I will trust, and not be afraid" is first-class.

I think of my grandmother's small cloth sack of Bible references. At every day's beginning she took one out, a measure of strength for that day. I think of someone else's grandmother who began writing poetry when she was eighty and said that from then on everything seemed to make a poem. How fitting that, in the Bible, old age and honor are so often linked together!

Thanks be to God for the saints who travel the last miles of the pilgrim way with cheer and grace.

"As the clear light is upon the holy candlestick; so is the beauty of the face in ripe age" (Ecclesiasticus 26:17).

✳

MARCH 29

A Time to Be Young

How wonderful to be young with strong back and keen mind to attack the gigantic problems that need solving, the long bridges that need building. How hard, too, to be young, pulses pounding with vitality while the hands prove awkward for the task, while in the background are the frowns of those who have forgotten Paul's words to Timothy, "Let no man despise thy youth."

No, youth does not always arrive at its destination. Stephen is stoned in Jerusalem; Borden of Yale dies on the way to the mission field; even sometimes heart and hands and feet grow old and weary before the work is done.

But youth is always on the way—optimistic, inspired, leaning forward as they run, overreaching, tender and usable, so that despised or not they are the means by which God builds churches in far and lonely places or in the middle of great cities.

If it is a friendly hand youth are needing today let them not want for its clasp. If it is an encouraging word they need to hear let their ears not need to strain for it. And always let the prayers flow in a wide moving tide for them so that they will feel their strong current holding them up. Then even the very old can say, "We are labourers together with God."

"I can do all things through Christ which strengtheneth me" (Philippians 4:13).

A *Time to Meditate*

Who can read the stark statement, "Meditation is a lost art," without a sense of rebellion? Is there too much noise? Is it the speed? Is it the complexity of life? Who has ever computed the demands that exact their part of each day?

How disconcerting to have to face the fact that we have added truth to that modern statement. (We, who have on our tongue tips such choice truths as "Be still and know," "In quietness and in confidence shall be your strength," "He leadeth me beside the still waters.") What bravery it takes to face about and resolve that beginning here in one resolute heart (and has God ever worked in anything but single hearts?) meditation will not be a lost art.

Thomas a Kempis wrote, "If thou wilt withdraw thyself from speaking vainly and from gadding idly, as also from hearkening after novelties and rumors, thou shalt find leisure enough and suitable for meditation on good things." In a world where many things cannot be changed, perhaps this is the one thing that can be corrected. Even surrounded by noise and speed and complexity of life, if this one thing can be altered, what golden moments, yea verily hours, will then be free for thoughts of God and good!

"Thou wilt keep him in perfect peace, whose mind is stayed on thee" (Isaiah 26:3).

A *Time to Be*

Jesus Christ does not measure a person's worth by any man-made standard of evaluation. If you read Matthew, Mark, Luke, and John with only one goal in mind, to see what importance Christ put on a human being, you will find that He considered no one unimportant. Every person was of exactly the same worth: Jew or Gentile, rich or poor, well or sick, not-quite-honest-in-business like Matthew the tax collector, too-much-a-lover-of-money like the disciple who carried the money bag. They all balanced out the same for Christ who looks at souls, not at the outside covering of souls.

A gift of inestimable worth this—to be a child in the great family of God's children, equally loved, equally needed!

Color lines break up, prejudices fall, both snobbery and inferiority melt away—all alike refined in Jesus' evaluation of a soul.

With dignity and humility will I carry this rich gift today, pondering its worth, letting its truth make joyous the day.

"For God so loved the world, that he gave his only begotten Son, that whosoever believeth in him should not perish, but have everlasting life" (John 3:16).

7

IN PRAISE OF LITTLE THINGS

Ethel Yake Metzler

APRIL 1

In Praise of April Weather

April with her temperamental moodiness gathers all the seasons into one poetic medley. And April keeps me constantly conscious of the weather. I rejoice when the crocuses defy her biting wind—grumble when the boots I put in storage for the summer must be ferreted out for wood-tramping feet. I leave the doors flung open to the faintest breeze that hints that May may see spring firmly established.

It's as Robert Frost said in "Two Tramps in Mud Time":[*]

The sun was warm but the wind was chill.

You know how it is with an April day

When the sun is out and the wind is still,

You're one month on in the middle of May.

But if you so much as dare to speak,

A cloud comes over the sunlit arch,

A wind comes off a frozen peak,

And you're two months back in the middle of March.

(The date of Easter varies, of course, from year to year. We suggest that you use April meditations 20 to 30 during the following Holy Week, shifting the others accordingly.)

[*] From *Complete Poems of Robert Frost.* Copyright 1930, 1949, by Henry Holt Co., Inc. Used by permission.

Sometimes I wish I could manipulate God's April weather laws and get with Midas-touch the golden jubilant weather I know must be somewhere in the near future. Then I remember God's words to Noah: "While the earth remains, seedtime and harvest, cold and heat, summer and winter, day and night, shall not cease." And I praise God for April—month that in itself holds almost all the promise.

Come, April—bring your winds and undulating weather— your tastes of spring and energizing hints of summer—your lethal reminiscences of winter. Come, crocuses, hyacinths, azaleas, and blooming cherries. North may have more of winter—but only to make spring the better. I've faith in God's fair weather!

Genesis 8:22; Psalms 104; 147:15-18

APRIL 2

In Praise of the Sun

I hung the curtains at the sun-drenched windows of our bedroom and watched their yellow, rose, blue, and violet flowers burst into full bloom. The children shouted in delight. I too was pleased, for furnishings chosen for one home often do not enhance another. But these did. The sun danced through their cheerful design from early until late afternoon.

I love the sun—its light and warmth—the way it gilds the hair of children; the way it pours warmth through floor-to-ceiling windows, and makes the afternoon warm and lazy, deceivingly suggesting that daylight lasts forever. And I love its evening light slanting through greening trees and casting their endlessly moving shadows into a pattern on our wall.

Saint Francis loved the sun. He called it Brother Sun, and though he couldn't know in 1200 A.D. how utterly dependent earth is on its constancy of heat, he sensed, as did the psalmist of old, that when we consider the sun, we cannot but stand in awe of its creator and feel insignificant by comparison. Yet He who spoke the sun into existence is our maker, sustainer. The sun is our servant and joy.

God planned carefully for the sun to give us light and warmth. Were it moved farther from us by a comparatively small distance, we would freeze. Were it closer, we would be scorched. It is placed just right in relation to the earth to maintain life.

I praise God for this blazing radiant energy, sustainer of life, brother to us, God's human creation.

Psalm 74:16; Genesis 1:14-19

APRIL 3

In Praise of Color

The jeweled freshness of the greens in our yard made me catch my breath and offer a prayer of praise for color one April morning. A light night rain had washed away the last traces of snow, and the tender early grass sparkled.

A downy woodpecker's saucy head moved malletlike, drilling the bark of an old, gnarled apple tree. Its red patch flashed in the sun and set off its spattered coat of black and white.

Crocuses edging the garden were pushing blue and

violet, yellow, red, and white. And against the azure sky, the turned loam lay mellow black.

I praise God for color. Heightened colors before a storm. The soft, startling brilliance of the rainbow. The fruit hues: apricot, plum, lime, lemon, cherry, grape, currant, pineapple, and avocado. And precious stones flashing rose, blue, and gold, found long ago in a clear rippling stream and secreted in my treasure box.

I love the way a boiling bath intensifies the green of asparagus, limas, and string beans before I plunge them into cold water and then into the freezer. I love the seafoam white of icing, the ruby glaze of strawberries frozen into ice cream.

Ezekiel and John on Patmos, awed by the glory of the Lord, described it with colors—sapphire, bronze, fire, and the rainbow. The radiance of the new Jerusalem was like a most rare jewel, "a jasper, clear as crystal"; and the city itself was as a cluster of crown jewels.

For us here, food and the good earth with its vegetation and bird and animal life varied and delightfully colored. And there—the regal grandeur of gems.

Ezekiel 1:26-28; Revelation 21:10, 11, 18-21

APRIL 4

In Praise of Tastes

Spring evenings I like to come in from stirring in the yard and garden to a steaming pot of mint tea, brewed to taste and flavored with sugar and a drop or two of lemon or lime. Add a slice of raisin toast with apple butter or strawberry jam, and I can imagine no better combination of flavors.

All sorts of flavors delight my taste buds, and I like to think that I can distinguish many degrees of sweet, sour, salty, and bitter, and their combinations. Shad with its delicate fish and rich satisfying flavor; avocado, bland and delightfully different; sweet sour pork combining succulent tomatoes and tart pineapples with egg-dipped pork, fried in hot peanut oil; blue cheese, indescribably teasing; or dried apricots sweet and delectable.

I have never tasted caribou, walrus, or grasshoppers, but I have sampled partridgeberries, yoghurt, and opossum; learned to like asparagus, raw tomatoes, and sardines, and longed for blackberries!

Our Jewish ancestors who had acquired a relish for the leeks and garlic of Egypt, but became satiated with quail and manna in the desert, found the honey of Palestine a pleasant change. We, too, need the variety of flavor God's world of foods offers. "Behold," God said, "I have given you every plant yielding seed which is upon the face of all the earth, and every tree with seed in its fruit; you shall have them for food."

I thank God that His foods satisfy my yen for flavor changes as He satisfies my soul. Our Lord is good. As David said, "O taste and see that the Lord is good!"

Genesis 1:28, 29; Psalms 19:7-10; 34:4-10

APRIL 5

In Praise of Fragrances

Each time I pluck rhubarb from its row under the apple tree, I am tempted to loosen a piece of fungus growth from a fruit tree stump nearby and take it into the house to dry and burn, just for its distinct penetrating odor.

94

I like the individual essence God has given to many of the plants, animals, and substances He has created. I enjoy the acrid pungent odors of a chemistry lab, the scent of printer's ink and volatile cleaners, the antiseptic chasteness of alcohol, Lysol, bleach. And from a distance even the choking fumes of ammonia.

The aroma of baking bread, the ethereal breath of lilacs, the clinging scents of toilet soaps brighten a day. On my dresser stands a little earthen jug filled with a potpourri of rose petals. Each morning I catch a whiff of its delicate perfume and thank God for fragrances.

The Apostle Paul thought of Christ as a fragrant offering and sacrifice to God. The love that emanated from His life in words and deeds was delightful to His Father. Paul desired that the Ephesians exude that same sweetness in their daily lives. So, when I enjoy God's gifts of delightful aromas, I like to thank Him by loving service. I like to think my thanks ascend in Christ's name as the aromatic incense arose at the time of sacrifice in the temple. Then God's people of old bowed to confess their sins, receive forgiveness, and give thanks. And the incense carried heavenward their heartfelt prayers.

Exodus 30:1-10, 22-38; Ephesians 5:2; Psalm 141:2;
II Corinthians 2:14, 15

APRIL 6

In Praise of Sound

I detected the warble of a wren the other morning when the back door was left open. And in its wake, the joyous melody of the lark. The children joined me on the porch and we stood quietly listening.

We spotted the wren and laughed to see his throat expand and contract with his sparkling song. We noted the difference between the two bird calls, and compared them with the robin's noisy competition. While we waited we heard a half-dozen other different calls we couldn't identify —and but hope someday to add this dimension to our listening pleasure.

Accustomed to the symphony of nature's pleasant sounds I sometimes scarcely note them. Tree toads cheeping, rain pat pit-a-patting, wind moaning, dry and papery leaves skittering over the ground, thunder rolling, the puppy grinding away on a bone— these may pass unnoticed if I am preoccupied with mundane things.

But these wonderful sounds of nature that tell us God's world is alive, awake, responding to His goodness are special heralds calling me to praise and prayer. For I know how it is to miss the faint echo of the wood winds or the haunting melody of the strings, to try to catch words meant for my ears but lost because of their deafness, to strain to hear a minister's words, to mistake the announced song number, to see a cardinal singing in a tall larch—but hear him only faintly.

Now that I can hear, each joyous sound bids me thank the Lord for ears that hear, and to add a song of praise to creation's symphony.

Psalm 150

APRIL 7

Morning Canticle

To Him who made the soft weak sounds
The cedar waxwing sings,

Who painted daffodils a butter yellow
And dyed red the cardinal's wings;

To Him who guards the awesome night
Until the morning's sun,
And calls my soul to praise and prayer
Before the day's begun;

To Him who floods my mind and heart
With songs of joy and love
And gives me voice to pour them forth
And lift in prayer above;

To Him be praise,
To Him be praise throughout my days.
Amen.

Psalms 3:5, 6; 4:7, 8; 139:17, 18

APRIL 8

In Praise of Leaven for the Loaf

"When can we punch it?" the children question after we've stirred up a batch of roll dough. And because the time always seems to go so slow, we take a breather outside in the late morning sun of the April day and almost forget about our dough until we open the door to go in for lunch. "Oh, the rolls! They're ready," the children shout and punch the cloth-covered bowl experimentally.

Then we knead and pat our smooth elastic ball and set it aside for another hour or so in the warmth of the sun. And

I always think of the story Jesus told about the kingdom of heaven.

That day Jesus told three stories about sowers. And though the people listened and listened, they seemed not to understand. Then in one short concluding sentence He described His kingdom, the kingdom of heaven: "[It] may be compared to yeast which a woman took and worked into a bushel of flour until it all had risen."

So I have found it—the kingdom of heaven—a subtle power which when mixed with the flour of my life leavens the whole. A portion of Scripture, a poem, hymn, or a plan of action for "doing unto the least of these" or for nurturing my children—mulled over in my mind is the yeast at work. Quickly it becomes action, enlivening my routine duties, sparking my will to worship, making me truly a participant of two worlds—heaven and earth.

I thank God for a story about the kingdom of heaven on earth that I, the mixer of dough, can understand.

Matthew 13:18-33

APRIL 9

In Praise of the Gentle Touch

I bathed the feet of my littlest one as she lay exhausted and crying in my lap. Tiredness had mounted almost to hysteria when she was accidentally awakened after falling asleep at the end of a long trip. Gently I rubbed the warm cloth over her tense muscles and rejoiced to see them relax. I warmed the cloth again and she motioned for me to return it to her feet. Her crying ceased.

In another moment she slid from my lap and took my

98

hand, leading me to her bed, and I knew her needs were satisfied.

Then I remembered friendly hands easing the hair around my damp neck and ears and tracing a delicate pattern across my aching shoulders when as a child fatigue teased and tortured me and I wriggled and wiggled trying to find a comfortable position on a church bench proportioned for adults. That understanding touch, sharing my distress, soothed my aching muscles and made the long hour bearable.

Isolated and loathed because of the religious and cultural restrictions imposed upon him, a leper came to Jesus wanting His help. Desperately he cried, "If you want to, you can cure me."

Jesus—knowing that above all the leper desired the touch of a loving hand, the fellowship of understanding, the consent of the able to minister to the ill—stretched out His hand. And touched him. "I do want to!" Jesus said. "Be cured!"

Devout followers have since uttered Christ's words, "I do want to," and stretched forth their hands to give the gentle touch. I too would join the throng—not only when my little ones ask care—but whenever I see a need that my hands can reach.

Mark 1:40-42

APRIL 10

In Praise of the Tug on My Skirt

My three-year-old ran anxiously toward me when he spied me through the crowd. I remember his look of relief

99

when I smiled reassuringly. But then I felt the clutch of his hands upon my skirt as he literally wrapped himself in its folds, and a stab of annoyance jabbed at my adult preoccupation. Stooping down, I quietly chided him, "Better not do that. You could tear my dress."

But he only held on more tightly. It wasn't rebuff that he'd come for. Suddenly I thought of Christ caught in the mass of restless expectant people when He wanted to retire to the Sea of Galilee. They milled around Him trying to edge close enough to touch Him, to receive power and healing.

My hand slid down to cradle my son's head as it pressed against me. He had come to find strength and healing, too—to find himself. Here security could envelope him, cushioning the pressures of the unfamiliar. Here he could feel a cessation of his fear. Here a sudden strength could replace his anxiety, if I accepted his weakness and did not rebuff him. I caressed his head and gradually his clutch relaxed and he pulled my hand down to hold his own.

I praise God for little hands tugging my skirt. They are a call to worship, an opportunity to remember Jesus who did not recoil from grasping hands; who gladly healed the ill who crowded around Him; and who blessed the woman who touched the hem of His garment to receive healing with gracious words, "Go in peace."

May I give as generously and understandingly to those who clutch my skirt that in my presence they may find strength and security as I do in Thine. Amen.

Mark 5:24-34

APRIL 11

In Praise of a Little More Loving

The Scotch plaid pencil box, row of books, typewriter, papers, and little aluminum tray with its teapot entice my children to my desk. When I go to answer the phone, baste a roast, or find a book, up they climb into my chair. The pencils go helter-skelter; the keys on the typewriter go click-click and then get bottled up. And when I return, a little voice says, "Mommy, hold me. I wanna see. I typing." And once in a long, long time, I hear, "Mommy type." And that's when things really are a mess!

I'm tempted to hurry the little one away so I can get back to work. But past experience warns me of that procedure and I lift little Mary to my lap. We sip tea together, choose some pencils and crayons (kept especially for this purpose), paper and paper clips and get Mary started at her office job.

Jesus lifted the little children who came in curiosity to see Him onto His lap and loved them. How happy they must have felt that day to be part of the excitement, accepted, and enjoyed.

I praise God for this beautiful example of Jesus who knew how quickly little children perceive the motives of adults and are always eager for a little more loving.

One day when it seemed little Mary had had more than her share of loving, and yet was not satisfied, I made up a song at bedtime to sing in the dark before the children drop off to sleep. "I'll hug my Mary tight and love her more each day, and then she'll get a little better every way."

Then her brother said, "And love me more each day, too. It makes me better."

Mark 10:13-16

In Praise of Growth

"Sing my one-year-old song," Mr. Five requested on his birthday. That sounded strange, but then I remembered what he meant. He wanted his "Bear-Went-over-the-Mountain" tune with the growing-up words. How would it sound with the new addition he was so proud of—his fifth year? So we sang:

> Michael used to be one year old,
> And then he was two years old,
> And soon he was three,
> And then he was four,
> But now Michael's five years old.

Gladly, eagerly children grow. They stretch toward each new experience as tulips stretch toward the morning sun. They accept the importance of sleep, vitamin-rich vegetables, fresh air and sunshine, for they want to grow. Mr. Five put it this way, "I won't stay little forever, will I? Not until you're a grandma—will I?"

No. I guess not! He'll grow in years and health and understanding. And may I help him grow in perceptions, depth of soul, and love for God—the way Jesus grew. And the way God wants me to grow.

How arrested is my growth at times! I scrupulously obey the laws of good physical health—but forget the laws governing spiritual growth. I postpone my daily devotions; I rationalize disobedience to the truth I know; I turn from God's scrutinizing gaze.

But when I bathe in the sunlight of God's goodness and mercy, when I do what I know to be His will, and when I listen to Him speak as I read the Bible, I grow. I thank God that I may grow toward the measure of the

stature of the fullness of Christ. And pray that He will
grant me the will and energy to grow eagerly, as a child
rejoices to grow.

Philippians 3:8-15; Colossians 1:9-14

✳

APRIL 13

In Praise of Ten Words

When the bones in my neck creak with each turning of
my head and my knees crunch on steps I cannot avoid, I
long for the maidens of the "virtuous woman" the author of
Proverbs lauds.

Give me but one maiden, I groan inwardly, to put away
the food and do the dishes. Or a maid to wash the hand
laundry. Or to mend and sew. Or to care for the children
and straighten up after their play.

Almost bitterly I remember how the good wife also
works, making cloth, sewing garments, planting vineyards,
providing food for her household. She even considers a
field and buys it. She looks well to the ways of her household and does not eat the bread of idleness.

For me there is only one commendation in this description of the good wife by King Lemuel's mother, and it is
hidden at the end. But since for it I qualify it stands out
boldly: "A woman who fears the Lord is to be praised."

Sick though my body, inadequate though my looking to
the ways of my household, sporadic though my providing
food for my family, insufficient though my vineyards or the
cash to buy new fields, incapable though my hands to
weave cloth or tailor garments for the merchants, I do fear
the Lord.

I fear Him with all my heart and soul and mind. I claim Him King and Master, Lord, Saviour, Friend, and Omnipresent Comforter. He is my Bread and Meat and Wine! Strength, Beauty, Mercy, Love, and Father. I cast on Him my anxieties and repeat David's psalm of praise:

> As a father pities his children,
> So the Lord pities those who fear him.
> For he knows our frame;
> He remembers that we are dust.

I thank God for ten wonderful words: "A woman who fears the Lord is to be praised."

Psalm 103:11-18

✳

APRIL 14

In Praise of Rain After a Drought

I know how it is to feel the springs go dry. To awaken at morning afraid to tackle the day—my body tired, my mind a dusty wilderness. I know how it is to want to pray, yet be unwilling to confess how parched and dusty are my mind and soul.

During such droughts I hear the echo of Mark van Doren's "Why Sing at All."* But I don't want to believe singing could refresh my dried and shriveled soul. Any song I started would choke in my throat, I protest. But the echo persists:

> . . . the tongue's attempt
> May startle the chambered silence, and awake
> Some spring whence joy, thin, flowing,
> Trickles a while; then rivers; and then a lake;

* From *A Winter Diary* and Other Poems by Mark Van Doren, Macmillan, N.Y., 1935.

104

And as the echo fades, the words and music from a Bach motet form a refrain in my mind: "The Spirit also helpeth our infirmities . . . with groanings which cannot be uttered." The rain is starting—with a song!

A song had roused my hope. But really it was Hope that roused my song. God's ever-present Comforter had brought to my mind the promise of His help and with that promise—rain. Suddenly I'm singing "As Torrents in Summer":

> So hearts that are fainting
> Grow full to o'erflowing
> And they that behold it
> Marvel and know not
> That God has been raining—
> Far off has been raining
> At their fountains.

Isaiah 55:10; Romans 8:26-28; Philippians 2:12, 13

APRIL 15

In Praise of a Degree of Poverty

When I was a teener dreaming dreams of *Better Homes and Gardens* houses, I used to wonder why my mother saved bread wrappers and the wax paper from cereal boxes. Really I knew—or thought I knew. But how she could keep acknowledging it every day, week after week, was beyond me. I hated being poor. Every carefully folded wax paper I identified with our poverty.

Now that I find myself dusting off cereal crumbs and tucking away the lining paper, I laugh at the trouble I put myself to hating my mother's conservation. The truth has finally dawned that she was being thrifty not only because my father's income was meager, but also because she enjoyed conserving her resources.

Her wax paper came in handy many a time. A guest would comment on her peonies, coleuses, or tea. She would go to the house for her shears, damp cloth, and wax paper. When the bouquet was cut and carefully wrapped, it was ready for a half-day trip without wilting.

She was doing as she had made up her mind to do— sharing what she had cheerfully, for God loves a cheerful giver. Besides, she enlarged her ability to share by utilizing the materials that lay within her reach. She capitalized on her poverty.

I praise God for a degree of poverty that has increased my awareness of the possibilities of thrift. I like to make my own cooky mix instead of buying it, because it's fun to use my resources creatively. Some have found joy in voluntary poverty. A group of missionary-minded women decided to try shopping with care and cooking creatively to save extra dollars for a special project.

Paul suggested to the Corinthians that they should not sow sparingly, for their reaping would be in direct proportion, but remembering that God is able to provide for every need, should give freely, joyously, as they were able —even though they were poor.

II Corinthians 9:6-12

In Praise of Windows

Before mid-twentieth-century designers cut picture windows into their ranch-style homes, my parents built a house with large, low windows that let us look out on our friendly street, the mountains, and our back yard. Perhaps that is why my eye always measures the size, location, and lowness of windows and why I remember the views from all nine homes of six years of marriage.

Windows invite me abroad—to sail with the wind rousing the trees, to fly south with the birds, to converse with the people walking by, or to meander with the children to school.

Or I may see a Turner landscape, an Audubon portrait, a Daumier study of humanity, or the delightful motion of a Degas. Sometimes I squint my eyes, let the colors intensify, the outlines emerge, and compose my own painting. Seldom do I succeed in transferring it to canvas, but having visualized my composition, I'm satisfied to turn back to washing dishes, wiping up spilled cereal, making beds, and dusting.

I thank God for windows. As a telescopic lens they bring the distant near; as a generous philanthropist they offer me the world. As a silent monitor they help me measure my thoughts and judge my actions.

They make me think of God who is above and beyond, yet at work in the world and living within me. They make me thank Him for the wonderful world of nature, for the thousands of little worlds within our universe that I could explore. And for the people whose lives I may touch unseen by prayer as they pass my window.

Psalm 29

In Praise of Silence

Occasionally I waken with the dawn. The trucks grumble uphill into the morning workday world. And all is silent. I dare scarcely breathe for fear of shattering the bliss of this unexpected gift of early dawn—silence. Silence to think and pray and tune in to the voice of God.

Although I am often cheated of silence by the roar of jets overhead and trains nearby, 200-horsepower motors at my door, a timer and mixer in my kitchen, and the family radio, I do know the soul-refreshing therapy of stillness because I listen for the overtones of God's world rather than its rattle-de-bum.

At nap times, in the empty moments when the children leave for school or go out to play, or when the house settles into its foundation for the night, I listen for the whispers of silence.

I hear God speak, explaining the children's pleas and pleases, their shouts and cries. I hear Him asking about my actions and attitudes, my words and thoughts. And suddenly I find myself telling Him about my inadequacies, my temper, incompetence, insufficient knowledge, lack of understanding, trouble with details, and preoccupation with distractions. I thank Him for the love, forbearance, patience, concern, understanding, wit, and humor He lent me. And I ask Him to give me stillness of soul in my world of noise.

I thank God that in quietness and confidence I may regain strength.

Isaiah 30:15; Philippians 4:4-9

APRIL 18

In Praise of Song at Eventide

One evening my desire to sing and play overcame my reticence and I sat at the piano in our apartment. Ours was the only piano in that apartment house; so my playing was soft and my singing too. But I had hardly begun to read the Bible after playing when my neighbor who worked during the day stopped by to ask why I had never played before when she was home. I explained. But she insisted that I play each evening, for the walls seemed to subdue my mistakes and the hymns were a delight to her TV-distracted soul.

They cannot help being—hymns such as "Jesus, Thou Joy of Loving Hearts," "O Love of God, How Strong and True," for they come from full souls, Bernard of Clairvaux and Horatius Bonar. Bernard, who with eleven other monks built an abbey in a valley whose name meant wormwood, was a man of such spiritual leadership that the valley's name was changed to Clairvaux, light. In a sermon he said, "Jesus is honey to the lips, in the ear melody, in the heart joy. Medicine also is that name. Is any sad? Let Jesus come into his heart, and thence leap to his tongue."

So at eventide, I sing:

> Jesus, Thou Joy of loving hearts!
> Thou Fount of life! Thou Light of men!
> From the best bliss that earth imparts,
> We turn unfilled to Thee again.

And praise God that I can utter my prayer in song.

Colossians 3:16, 17; Isaiah 35:10; Revelation 15:3;
Psalm 100

109

In Praise of a Garden

In our eighth-grade songbook was a pleasant arrangement of these words:

The man who wants a garden fair—
Or large or very big,
With flowers growing here and there,
Must bend his back and dig.

Whether I've inherited the desire from Eve, or not, I want a garden. For almost as far back as I can remember I've dug the earth, given into its care minute snapdragon seeds, and delighted to see the fragile stems and leaves unfold as water and sun welcomed them to our world.

That first garden must have been exquisite, for God had planted it Himself, and in the cool of the evening sought its shade and the company of the man and woman who tended it. Here was variety beyond our imagination, trees and plants, flowers, and fruits—luxuriant, delicate, succulent, sweet, fragrant, magnificent.

And when I work the ground, plant and transplant, water, weed, fertilize, and feed the plants in my small garden, I think perhaps God may deign to walk in it too. And I have seen Him there when the first mint pushes up and the crocuses magically appear in the snow. I have heard Him, too, when the wind delights the maple and the early robins sing cheer-up in the morning dew.

I praise God for the pleasure of observing and participating in creation year after year after year, as I plant a garden.

Genesis 2:8-10, 15, 16; Psalm 147:7-9; 104:10-24

✳

(For a Holy Week Sunday)

Palms and Hosannas

Jesus set His face toward Jerusalem that first day of Jewish Passover and with His disciples joined the crowd walking the rocky dusty miles. Today He would fulfill the words spoken by Zechariah the prophet centuries before. He would let Jerusalem's crowds hail Him King.

Near Bethphage, He sent ahead two disciples to fetch a donkey and its colt. When the disciples returned, they spread their coats on the animal and assisted Jesus to mount. Sudden resolution seized the crowd. They laid their garments before Him in the dust, tore branches from the palm and myrtle trees, and shouted:

"Hosanna! Blessed be the King that cometh in the name of the Lord. Peace in heaven and glory on high. Hosanna in the highest."

Only the Pharisees in the crowd held back: "Master, rebuke thy disciples. The mob has gone wild. It is blasphemy!"

Jesus answered, "If these shall hold their peace, the stones will cry out."

Jesus and the royal procession marched toward Jerusalem. The great city with its high yellow ocher walls, deceivingly bright in the spring sun, broke into sharp relief as Jesus ascended Jerusalem's hill. Here was His city. Here could have been His royal throne. But Jerusalem had had only stones for God's prophets. And it had a cross for Him. Jerusalem would not accept Him. Jerusalem would go on worshiping a God of its own making. Jesus wept.

Outside the city gates a crowd from the city met them.

111

As a mighty river they overflowed Jerusalem's narrow dirty streets and moved toward the temple.

Festival travelers choking the city shouted, "Who is this?"

And the multitude chanted: "This is the prophet Jesus from Nazareth of Galilee."

"Who is this?" This is Jesus, the promised one, fulfilling the words of Zechariah: "Behold thy king comes to you meek and sitting upon an ass and the foal of an ass."

"Who is this?" This is Jesus, Son of God, whom today you acclaim King—but crucify tomorrow.

John 12:1-19

✳

APRIL 21
(For a Holy Week Monday)

A Coil of Rope

As King that cometh in the name of the Lord, Christ entered the temple gates the morning following His kingly reception. Within earshot of the high priest's penitential prayers, agents were dealing dishonestly to make an extra dollar changing Roman money to temple coinage and selling sacrifices for more than they were worth.

With authority Jesus moved toward the tables and benches of the filching concession merchants who crowded the Court of the Gentiles. "Have ye not read?" He said. "My house shall be called a house of prayer; but ye make it a den of robbers." He drove the dove sellers and money-changers out of the temple and overturned their seats and tables. The Pharisees ran to prattle the news to the high priest.

The blind and the lame crowded around and Jesus healed them. The women drew closer and their children shouted the song they had heard the day before, "Hosanna to the Son of David!" Their spontaneous praise rejoiced Christ's heart. God's house was indeed meant to be a sanctuary for praise and prayer.

But the high priest, by this time alerted to the devastation taking place in the outer court, came running. At the sound of the children's voices he shook his head and pretended to rend his clothes, crying in horror at such sacrilege.

Jesus looked on him with eyes that read his soul and said, "Yea, did you never read, Out of the mouth of babes and sucklings thou hast perfected praise?"

O Lord, no wonder Thou didst say, "Except ye . . . become as little children, ye shall not enter into the kingdom of heaven."

Matthew 21:12-16; 18:1-5

APRIL 22
(For a Holy Week Tuesday)

Questions and Answers

"By what authority do you do these things and teach?" the Pharisees demanded when Jesus began to address the crowd Tuesday morning. Their plans were well laid. Today they would question Jesus closely and catch Him for a capital offense—blasphemy. On the testimony of two witnesses that was equal to death.

"Consider a question I shall ask, and I'll answer yours,"

113

Jesus responded. "The baptism of John, was it from heaven or men?"

They dared not comment. They could not hazard their reputation with the people who had approved of John by saying his baptism was of men. And to accord it as divine—that would destroy their case against this man. Caught, trapped before the day had hardly begun, they remained silent.

"What think ye?" Jesus continued, not letting them gather together their forces. "A man had two sons whom he asked to go work in his vineyard. The first refused, then afterward changed his mind and went. The second consented, but then went and did as he pleased. Which then did the will of his father?"

Readily they answered that simple question.

And readily Jesus retorted: "The publicans and the harlots go into the kingdom of God before you. For John came unto you in the way of righteousness, and ye believed him not: but the publicans and the harlots believed him: and ye, when ye had seen it, repented not afterward that ye might believe him."

And when the day ended, several parables, questions, attacks, and counterattacks later, Jesus threw one last question to these men who prided themselves in knowing the Jewish Scriptures—and not one of them could answer Him. And from that day forth no man dared ask Him any more questions.

Matthew 21:15-46

(For a Holy Week Wednesday)

Predictions and Rest

As the sun's slanting rays burnt the temple's gold to bronze, Jesus and His disciples moved toward the outer gates. Perhaps the thought that this was the last time He would descend this holy hill was in Christ's mind and made Him seem strangely quiet and far away from His disciples. To bring Him back to themselves, to stimulate His flow of words, they pointed out the beauty of the temple glittering in the sun.

But Jesus was seeing beyond to the devastation her rulers were dooming her to. "As for these things, the days will come when not one stone will be left upon another."

So quick and decisive was this answer that the disciples ceased speaking and they moved in silence through the familiar streets and out the stony road to the Mount of Olives. There they rested. But the disciples could wait no longer to inquire, "When shall these things be? and what shall be the sign of thy coming, and of the end of the world?"

They wanted to know—and He answered, but His words were not quieting. Jesus spoke of war, desolation, famine, earthquakes, death, torture, flight in the dark of night, persecution, and tribulation which should come upon them.

As to His final appearance, not even He knew the day or the hour. "Watch and pray," Jesus said. Be ready, for it will be an hour when ye think not. Watch as a householder who knows that thieves have connived to break into his house. Watch as though you were waiting for a bridegroom. Watch as though you were taking care of a treasure for your lord who is soon to return.

"And while you watch, show mercy, love, and kindness to the hungry, thirsty, naked, the stranger, and prisoner. Good done to these is good done to me."

Matthew 24:1—26:1

✳

APRIL 24
(For a Holy Week Thursday)

I Am He

Jesus knew this was His last day with His disciples before His death. For this death He had been born. For this death He had lived. Tomorrow He would die.

"With desire I have desired to eat this passover with you before I suffer," He told His followers as they gathered in an upper room to eat the meal Peter and John had prepared. Not one of the group offered to wash His feet dusty from the day's traveling. They were engrossed in an argument as to who was the greatest among them.

He slipped from the table, laid aside His garments, took a towel, and stooping washed the feet of each. Nor did He leave to chance their catching the meaning of His actions: "Know ye what I have done . . .? Ye call me Teacher and Lord: and ye say well; for so I am. If I then, the Lord and the Teacher, have washed your feet, ye also ought to wash one another's feet. . . . A servant is not greater than his lord; neither one that is sent greater than he that sent him. . . . Love one another even as I have loved you."

Jesus also lifted bread from the plate, blessed it, and divided it among the disciples, saying, "This is my body which is given for you: this do in remembrance of me."

He passed the cup from one to the other after He had

given thanks, saying, "This cup is the new covenant in my blood, even that which is poured out for you."

The disciples did not understand as He foretold their fear and desertion in His hour of capture and debasement. But when the force of His words finally flooded them with sorrow, Jesus could speak the words of comfort He longed to share with them. These truths about His Father and the Holy Spirit calmed and strengthened His soul also as each moment brought the cross nearer. "Let not your heart be troubled . . . . I go to prepare a place for you. . . . I am in the Father, and the Father in me . . . . Ask anything in my name, that will I do. . . . And I will pray the Father, and he shall give you another Comforter, that he may be with you for ever, even the Spirit of truth."

Peace flooded His soul, and He commended peace to them. He asked them to abide in His love, to expect persecution, and to welcome the Spirit.

They sang a hymn together and walked toward Olivet and Gethsemane. There sorrow overcame Him, and the effort of prayer and submission to the will of His Father drew blood as sweat to His brow. His disciples slept.

Roman soldiers, Jewish rulers, and a crowd of hired accusers clattered into the garden. Jesus turned to His disciples oblivious, asleep. "Sleep on now. The hour is come. Behold, the Son of man is betrayed into the hands of sinners."

"Whom seek ye?" Jesus asked the approaching soldiers.

"Jesus of Nazareth," they answered.

"I am he," Jesus replied. And they took Him.

John 17

117

(For a Holy Week Friday)

Song of the Marys for Mary on Good Friday

Oh, Mary, see Him now,
Hold your hand upon your brow
And wish 'twere His.

Oh, Mary, shade your eye,
Look upon His face and cry
To know His pain.

No eye may naked be
Marking His hands, His feet, and tree
Whereon He bows.

Oh, Mary, wipe your tear;
Quiet, He speaks, oh, listen, hear;
His words are yours.

For this—your loss, your woes—
He offers solace, comfort, and bestows
On you a son.

Oh, Mary, turn away—
He dies. He did not come to stay—
He told us this.

You have a son again—
Love to share your inmost pain—
For death young life.

Oh, Mary, go to mourn.
We'll wait the new week's silent morn
To honor Him.

Oh, God—of heav'n above,
This day, and all our deepest love—
Make that morn bright!

—E. Y. M.

Luke 23:26-49

APRIL 26

(For a Holy Week Saturday)

Deeds and Devotion

It was Friday evening—and almost sundown when the Sabbath began. John took Jesus' mother to his home, but the other Marys and the unnamed number of women who had ministered to Jesus in Galilee, Jerusalem, and in Bethany stayed at the cross to watch.

Jesus was theirs more than they were their own. They could not leave Him alone upon a hill of bleached bones with only those who long before had hardened to the gory brutality of crucifixions.

They waited.

Silently through the gloom stole Nicodemus and Joseph of Arimathaea, their servants carrying the myrrh and aloes, burial linen, and tools to loose Jesus' hands and feet from the bite of wooden pegs. In sight of all, they did their humble service—these men of secret faith. And when their small party started in quiet procession from the hill of death, the women followed. They could not leave Him—

119

He who had so often shared their sorrows and received their care. They would see where He was to be laid.

They went with Him as far as they could. They saw the new-hewn tomb, its solid closing monolith. They saw Nicodemus and Joseph of Arimathaea anoint His body with myrrh and aloes.

Tonight and tomorrow they would rest as the Jewish Sabbath law instructed. But on the morning of the next day, they would return and with spices of their own preparing do homage to His body—the body of the Son of God. Though intrigue and hypocrisy convicted Him, though a cross killed Him, and a tomb removed Him from sight, they were certain He was God.

Perhaps no man had ever seen God—but they—they were women. And to their humble souls and sensitive minds His face and words, His hands and deeds had been the Father's. Had He not Himself said, "He that beholdeth me beholdeth him that sent me"?

Matthew 27:55-61; Luke 23:49-56; John 12:45

APRIL 27

(For an Easter Sunday)

Earthquakes and Angels

Trembling Mary Magdala awoke on the first day of the week. Dew hung on the garden's grass and the air moved expectantly as she passed between the rows of herbs and flowers. Morning would soon break, for light was gently nudging the horizon. She quickly wended her way over the rough paths toward the tomb.

Abruptly she halted. The stone—who would roll it away?

The guards—would they refuse her entrance? Suddenly the dawn was cold. She shifted the weight from hand to hand—her spices—she had prepared them herself for Jesus her Lord. Resolutely she moved toward the tomb.

It was open—and empty!

Her Lord? Who had taken Him? As Mary deliberated, the other women joined her in the eerie predawn light. They, too, stooped down to look inside the tomb but were blinded by angelic light. Keeping guard were two dazzling messengers. Their brilliance filled the tomb and filtered out the passage.

"Why seek ye the living among the dead?" they asked. "Ye seek Jesus who was crucified. Behold, he is not here. He is alive, as he said. He goeth before you into Galilee. Go tell his disciples and Peter."

Jaded into action the other women moved away in the swiftness with which they had come. But Mary Magdala remained. Her Lord? Where was He? She had come to honor Jesus—to enrich His body as He had her soul. The spices in her hands were heavy and fragrant. Spices for her Lord. Where was He? Had someone stolen His body? Tears blinded her eyes. Mutely she cried.

"Why do you cry?" a gentle voice asked.

She turned to share her grief. "Gardener, if you have taken Him away—oh, lead me to Him."

Then into one lovely word the Gardener of souls gathered the meaning of the empty tomb, the divine messengers with their blinding beauty, the trembling thundering earthquake. "Mary."

Morning broke. Heaven touched earth. Mary's sorrowful soul sprang to life, and she flung herself at His wonderful feet and called Him "Lord."

John 20:1-16; Luke 24:1-11

121

9

(For a Day After Easter)

Easter Chorus from Faust

Christ is arisen.
>Joy to thee, mortal!
Out of His prison,
>Forth from its portal!
Christ is not sleeping,
>Seek Him no longer;
Strong was His keeping,
>Jesus was stronger.

Christ is arisen.
>Seek Him not here;
Lonely His prison,
>Empty His bier;
Vain His entombing,
>Spices and lawn,
Vain the perfuming,
>Jesus is gone.

Christ is arisen.
>Joy to thee, mortal!
Empty His prison,
>Broken its portal!
Rising, He giveth
>His shroud to the sod;
Risen, He liveth,
>And liveth to God.

—*Johann Wolfgang von Goethe.*

John 20:19-23; Luke 24:13-36

(After Holy Week)

One Yet to Be Convinced

No hearsay for Thomas. No idle tales. No spiritualist visions of distraught men could convince him. Women's stories of angels and earthquakes, and a gardener disguised as Christ were not for him. Imaginations run wild—that's what they were. Thomas knew death when he saw it. And Christ had died.

Unconvinced though he remained, Thomas joined the disciples night after night for their evening reveries and worship. Sometimes he wished he could believe, and almost envious of their exuberant accounts of His appearings, he hoped.

And then it happened—just as they had described His previous visit. While they were speaking, Jesus Himself was with them, greeting them. "Peace be with you."

Jesus knew Thomas for what he was—a man quick to believe when shown, but slow to act on the word of another. "Reach hither thy finger, and behold my hands; and reach hither thy hand, and thrust it into my side: and be not faithless, but believing."

Thomas touched; he felt the wound in Christ's side, the scars on His hands. How good to know for certain that He who had died was alive! And though Christ's words were almost chiding, Thomas could not care, for now he too had membership in the kingdom of God.

John concludes his account of this divine stooping to human need with these words: "Thomas, because thou hast seen me, thou hast believed: blessed are they that have not seen, and yet have believed."

"These are written, that ye might believe that Jesus is

the Christ, the Son of God; and that believing ye might
have life through his name."

John 20:24-31

APRIL 30
Prayer After Holy Week

Lord, at Thy end I found in Thee a ray
So powerful its focus on my soul no hand could stay.
And though I could not pinpoint this to time
Or be so adamant or careless as to say
This was my end, I felt its blazing penetration
Burn sin to clay.

I know as time and place and stimuli and notion
Combine and proffer me the world's unending ocean
Of well-wrought, beautiful, and gracious things,
I shall most surely feel again a terrifying tension
Bowing the counter poles of self and deity—
My soul's prostration.

Then shall my yearning and despair for precious things
Unleash my soul in prayer until aside it flings
All worldly thirst. And I shall quietly embrace
The poignant, ceaseless longing Thy gentle Spirit brings
To quaff Thy crucifixion cup, and losing self
Find Thee and wings.

—E. Y. M.

Philippians 3:7-14

FAITH OF OUR MOTHERS

Winifred Schlosser Waltner

MAY 1

The Pledge She Kept

When my mother died, we found among her things a gilt-edged Bible which had been given her by my father when they were friends in college. On the back flyleaf of that Bible, dated over fifty years ago, was the following inscription in her fine neat hand:

"This Sabbath day, to the depths of my soul, I say *Amen* to all God's will. I am not worthy the least of His notice. Verily, I am 'less than the least of all saints.' I covet, I burn, I long to know Christ more fully and the *fellowship of His sufferings* and the power of His resurrection. I *must have* His presence and power, His melting, tender heart of love or I will frustrate the grace of God. I will undo His work in spite of myself. Oh, I ask for nothing else but to be at work with Him—in public and private—in church and in the factory—at home and abroad! I do this day register my longing desire after God. 'Blessed are they which do hunger and thirst after righteousness: for they shall be filled' (Matthew 5:6). 'Bring ye all the tithes into the storehouse, . . . and prove me now herewith, saith the

Lord of hosts, if I will not open you the windows of heaven' (Malachi 3:10)."

Time brought a change to the color of the ink. It saw a change in Mother's handwriting and in her body. But it saw every yearning of her heart in these words come true.

Malachi 3:10

MAY 2

College Girl Mother

I once knew a college girl who was like a mother to all the girls in the dormitory. When I came back to visit my alma mater, she took me around through the new and old buildings and showed me my former room. A junior then, she had already won the love and confidence of her whole dormitory. She looked up the new girls and made friends. She knew the problem girls and had their confidence. Even girls that were older came to her for advice. There was something so sure and solid about her Christian experience that she was able to communicate it and radiate confidence and faith. As we went down the halls, doors opened and friendly voices begged her, "Come on in." We went into many rooms and I met many of her friends whom she had brought to know the Lord. One year after graduation, when she was married and happily looking forward to motherhood, a fatal disease overtook her and she was swept away.

As I read the letter telling the shocking news, the memory of all the girls to whom she had played the role of a mother in her college days immeasurably softened the hurt and sense of loss in her going.

Lord, may it be said of me, whenever life overtakes me, as it must have been said to her, "Well done, thou good and faithful servant: thou hast been faithful over a few things, I will make thee ruler over many things: enter thou into the joy of thy lord" (Matthew 25:21).

MAY 3

A Brother-Mother

If you have no mother, a brother may do. At least one had as good as Mother's words for his sister.

The time had come for his sister to go a thousand miles away from home to school. The two had never been separated far before, although they had been away from home and parents at boarding school and had faced the odds of life together there. The imminent parting loomed difficult. They walked in silence the three miles to the station, and at the inevitable end the boy framed his thoughts somewhat awkwardly in words.

"You're going away from home now, and there won't be any props to lean on. But remember the one big Prop that we will always have. Don't ever forget Him."

She knew he meant Jesus Christ. She knew he was a little worried that she might leave the faith or at least feel fearfully alone so far from home and acquaintances. It was a younger brother's tenderest attempt to play the part of a parent at parting, and she sensed that much more thought had gone into his words than came out in those few sentences. They never left her. Nor did the Faithful Prop.

"For he hath said, I will never leave thee, nor forsake thee" (Hebrews 13:5).

Make Me a Little Cake First

When the prophet, who was fed by the ravens, came to the widow asking for a bit of food, and was told that there was not enough meal and oil left except for a little cake for herself and her son, the prophet still persisted, "Make me thereof a little cake first."

The mother of a college student was overjoyed to receive a letter from her absent one noting the same persistent plea and its winning way in the matter of time. Time is a scarce commodity in a student's life. There is always the temptation to use the Lord's day for studies. Many students take for granted that this day must be used to catch up on the week's overload of assignments. But this student had been taught the right use of the Lord's day and could not feel right about putting it to the same drudgery as a week day, though it did seem a squandering of hours to spend it in glorious freedom and rest.

"But I kept thinking, 'God meant it for that,'" the letter read. "And an odd little phrase from an old story in the Bible kept coming to me, 'Make me thereof a little cake first,' and so I've taken my Sundays for worship and rest and freedom, and it's wonderful how, just like the widow's oil and meal, my time for the rest of the week has stretched farther than it ever did before. I get all my work done in six days because I know I can't count on the seventh, and now I look forward to taking those hours off on Sundays feeling good and not guilty."

"Make me thereof a little cake first . . . . And she went and did according to the saying of Elijah . . . . The jar of meal wasted not, neither did the cruse of oil fail" (I Kings 17:13-16, ASV).

MAY 5

Nooks Around the House

"There are nooks around the house that I cannot see without thinking of Mother," said a recently bereaved one.

"I never see that rocker without remembering her sitting there, or that chair at the table without remembering it was her place, or this little room without thinking of her in every part of it."

In the same way there are spots around the house that are precious to me because of times when God has become real to me there. I never scrub a certain corner of the kitchen floor without thinking of a time when I was doing that very thing and God's presence overwhelmed me.

It was late Saturday night and I should have been through with my work long before. As I washed out the little corner and saw all the dirt, I thought how incredible it was that God's Son should have come down to live in our inglorious world from His world of light. How could He stand it? I looked at my own dirty apron and rubber gloves. How could He endure us, much less love us? But then the thought came: "He does love us. He loved us enough to die for us."

And right there at that last corner of the kitchen floor at the tired end of the day I sat down and wept for gratitude at such divine love and knew that my adoring worship was accepted.

"Behold, I am with thee, and will keep thee in all places whither thou goest" (Genesis 28:15).

Pricked to Prayer

"Bishop Lajos Ordass, Hungary, imprisoned, May 1950.

"'More than bread, we need prayer. Give us your gifts of prayer that the cross may not become heavier, but if heavier, then that we may have the strength to bear it. . . . You do the praying; we'll do the suffering.' . . . The eyes of all were upon the undaunted figure of Bishop Ordass as he disappeared into prison. Standing innocent before his accusers, he said, 'I receive the judgment with humble mind and faith, as I know in any event the blessed will of God will be done.'"

Why did Mother pray so much? She knew its importance. The above words, found on a slip of paper in Mother's Bible, were notes from a sermon she had heard, and were typical of the barbs with which she let God prick her will to prayer.

My God, strengthen Thou the faith of those who suffer for Thy sake. Let it not fail. Let them be a light to those who persecute them. Grant them an abundant entrance into Thy house of light. Let the day soon come when all will know Thee and Thy kingdom will be in every heart. In Jesus' name. Amen.

"An angel of the Lord stood by . . . [Peter], and a light shined in the cell . . . . And . . . he came to the house of . . . Mark; where many were gathered together and were praying" (Acts 12:7-12, ASV).

MAY 7

Beam of Influence

A woman, who was retiring after forty years in the service of her Lord, was asked to tell of her call of God to that ministry. She concluded her talk with these words:

"I had no idea of all that was involved when, at the age of fourteen, I gave my heart to God. But one thing was eternally settled. I was going with God. No halfway measures. I had decided to follow Jesus.

"But now I tremble as I look back and realize how important it was that I put my hand in Jesus'. What if I hadn't! Think of the forty-odd years of influence on the wrong side. And think of the children. They probably would not have been saved, not living for God now and preaching the Gospel and starting in turn a beam of influence that goes out from them to so many others.

"Oh, thank God for His grace which reached down and saved me."

"The path of the just is as the shining light, that shineth more and more unto the perfect day" (Proverbs 4:18).

"Her children arise up, and call her blessed" (Proverbs 31:28).

MAY 8

Foster Mother

One of the most unselfish persons I know is a Chinese girl who was brought up as the adopted daughter of a single lady missionary. She is now the foster mother of three little Chinese girls who came to her in much the same way as she came to her foster mother.

During famine time in China a Christian Chinese evangelist walked home along a lonely, deserted road. He heard a tiny cry and looking about, he saw that it came from a bundle of rags at the roadside. This was a tiny new life, a brand-new victim of the famine. The mother and father undoubtedly had starved. He picked the baby up and took it home to his wife, who fed and cared for it willingly for a few days. But they found it difficult to provide food for their own six children; so when the missionary called they offered the baby to her.

Skipping over a long story of indecision and prayer and legal red tape, we may say that a radiant Christian life blossomed out of that adoption, and that after education in American colleges, this adopted Chinese girl chose to return to her own land to witness for Christ in the far northwest. One by one she picked up three waifs like herself to care for. Somewhere there, now beyond the reach of letters, but not beyond the reach of the Father's loving hand, a foster mother has been living out Christ's love under difficult circumstances.

"There was a certain Jew . . . . And he brought up . . . Esther, his uncle's daughter: for she had neither father nor mother, and the maiden was fair and beautiful; and when her father and mother were dead, Mordecai took her for his own daughter" (Esther 2:5-7, ASV).

MAY 9

Creative Mothers

"I love the creative parts of homemaking like baking cakes and sewing dresses," said a mother, "but it is the routine cleaning, dishwashing, ironing, and such that irk me."

Everyone loves to be creative, from the little child making a building of blocks, or an older boy fashioning a fort of snow, to an old woman crocheting beautiful afghan blocks of wool or piecing a quilt. Many a mother has said to herself, "If only I were not so busy, I would like to take up something creative like painting or music." But the most enduring creation to which a woman can turn her hand is the building of a character, the molding of the life of a little child, or, if one is not a mother, the life of anyone to whom one so much as speaks. This is done, a day at a time, no, a moment at a time, by all the little words and motions which go into contact with another. A cake is gone in a day, a coverlet in a few years, but the creation of a personality, in which God allows woman a major part, outlasts even this life. It is then doubly true of mothers that "Every idle word that . . . [they] shall speak, they shall give account thereof in the day of judgment" (Matthew 12:36). Those words are the chief instruments with which, often unawares, a mother is doing her most creative piece of work.

"See that ye despise not one of these little ones" (Matthew 18:10, ASV).

MAY 10

Her Marked Bible

Looking through her mother's Bible, a little girl noticed that there were many little marks, under certain words. Philippians had red lines under the words "joy" and "rejoice," and I John had them under "love." Here and there whole verses or long passages were underlined. Those she could understand, but why did her mother have so many single words underlined?

She asked and her mother said, "Oh, you can tell what is important by what is repeated often."

So the girl set about to look in her own Bible for something repeated often. It was the first Bible of her very own, and she had got only as far as Exodus in reading it. But, pencil in hand, she proceeded to underline the most obvious repetition in the book. It was, "God said . . . God said."

Finally her pages looked very well marked, but she felt that these words lacked the spark of interest that her mother's findings had. She told her disappointment, and it took her mother to point out to her again that she had, indeed, found one of the most important facts in the book. It was full of what the Lord God of hosts, the Creator of the ends of the earth, had said, through one mere man, Moses, to all the people of the world, even to little girls like her.

"And God said unto Moses, I AM THAT I AM: and he said, Thus shalt thou say unto the children of Israel, I AM hath sent me unto you" (Exodus 3:14).

MAY 11

What Are You Doing in Your Heart?

A five-year-old girl was playing with her toys in the living room within sight of her mother washing dishes in the kitchen. No words passed between them, but each was aware of the other. The happy sounds of the little girl's chatter to her dolls assured the mother that she was close by and was all right. And the familiar sounds of dishwashing assured the little girl that her mother was close by and all would be well.

Presently a distressing thought troubled the mother. She stopped for a moment and looked out of the window while a cloud crossed her face. At the sudden silence in the kitchen the child stopped playing too and a corresponding cloud crossed her face.

"What are you doing in your heart?" she called out. That was enough to bring back the humor to her mother's eyes.

"I should have been praying, but I guess I was just thinking."

Lord, I want to be a perfect crystal shining so flawlessly, transparently, and clear, that all who look into my face can see my heart and, seeing, may be sure that Christ is living there.

"As . . . [a man] thinketh in his heart, so is he" (Proverbs 23:7).

MAY 12

Mother's Built-ins

Built-in cupboards in the kitchen, built-in closets, shelves, and storage space all over the new house—that was a mother's dream.

"Then I wouldn't get so tired with my housework, and so impatient with the children. I believe I'd actually be a better Christian if I had a better house," she assured herself.

135

That same year a missionary family came to visit her church and stayed with her for a few days. "They were wonderful people," she recalled, "such marvelous parents as well as missionaries, so patient with their children and so understanding with mine."

She had an unforgettable conversation with this missionary mother. It went something like this.

"Do you mean you have to cook on an open fire, like a bonfire?"

"Yes, exactly. Except that it is in the middle of a sandbox in the center of the kitchen. That is the way all the women in the jungles of Mindanao cook. A little tripod stands in the center to hold the cooking utensil up, and the smoke goes through a hole in the thatched roof. We may be able to have more convenience someday, but that is the way we have been doing it these three years."

"But you never wrote about any of these things. You never complained."

"No, we did not feel like complaining. It is not very convenient, but we did not go there for convenience."

Nothing very significant took place in the conversation after that, but the questioning mother took note in her heart.

"She's got built-ins, all right. She's got built-in love and built-in patience, and all the other true wealth built right into her. It is not apart from her, like cupboards, but a part *of* her, like what it takes to be a Christian."

"Christ in you, the hope of glory" (Colossians 1:27).

Mother's Mending Pile

On Mother's mending pile, close to the sewing machine, there is a little dress which must be let down, because sister has grown too tall for it. There is also a skirt which must be taken up at the hem, because another little sister has almost grown into it. There are two coats with sleeves to be let down, and a pair of big brother's slacks to be shortened for little brother. Everything useful in the family has to be tailored to fit the one who needs it.

At family prayers there is a thought about God which must be expanded for big sister and brother because they have shown by their questions that they have outgrown their simpler childish view. There is also a verse from the Bible that is too deep for little brother and must be adapted to fit the grasp of a younger mind.

The mending pile is never done, though Mother works away at it, and neither is the thinking pile, though it is worked at just as faithfully, because the growing keeps right on. And we would have it so.

Help me, my God, faithfully to transmit Thy truths to my children and to any others who may look to me for that help. Help me not to let the pile grow too long unattended, lest I never be able to catch up with it. In Jesus' name. Amen.

"When thy son asketh thee in time to come, saying, What mean the testimonies, and the statutes, and the judgments, which the Lord our God hath commanded you? Then thou shalt say . . . for our good always" (Deuteronomy 6:20-24).

137

Mother's Little Conscience

Mother has a little conscience that rides in the car with her every day. The conscience is six years old and goes by the name of Johnny. There are so many errands to run and duties to do that sometimes Mother's mind is not on her driving and she exceeds the speed limit. But there is always Johnny. Ever since he learned to read the numerals on the dial, he has been her monitor.

"Aren't you going too fast?" he asks. "Or doesn't it matter if we don't obey the speed limit?" With a question put that way, who would not be more observant?

And at home Johnny asks, "Aren't sweets before meals bad for grownups? You told me I couldn't have a cooky because it was before dinner." So Mother merely rearranged the cookies on the plate for dinner instead of sampling one.

How unaware of our own sins we can be until they are pointed up by a child! And how purifying to the air and checking to the spirit it is to be submitted daily to this simple scrutiny!

"And whoso shall receive one such little child in my name receiveth me: but whoso shall cause one of these little ones that believe on me to stumble, it is profitable for him that . . . he should be sunk in the depth of the sea" (Matthew 18:5, 6, ASV).

"And the child Samuel ministered unto the Lord . . . . And Eli perceived that the Lord had called the child" (I Samuel 3:1, 8).

Big Cookies and Little Cheaters

"Once when we came home from school, we were astonished to see that the afterschool snack which Mother had prepared was very large cookies, as big as six ordinary ones," a grown-up daughter relates.

"Mother said, 'You children always take six before you are finished anyway; so why not make them big in the first place? Those little ones are little cheaters. You think you are just going to take one, but you are tempted on and on till at least six are gone. You might as well admit from the start that you are sitting down to a small sweet meal.' "

If the sins that so easily beset us were cookies, a lot of us would do well to make them big-sized too, so as not to fool ourselves when we start to indulge. Take, for instance, that little old conversational tidbit that starts with, "I really shouldn't say this, but—" And then we proceed to defame someone, simply taking one unintended little bite after another.

"The tongue is a little member, and boasteth great things. Behold, how great a matter a little fire kindleth" (James 3:5)!

"Let us lay aside every weight, and the sin which doth so easily beset us" (Hebrews 12:1).

"If any man thinketh himself to be religious, while he bridleth not his tongue but deceiveth his heart, this man's religion is vain" (James 1:26, ASV).

A *Child's Translation*

In one family the parents made a practice of reading directly from the Bible to their children each day, substituting simpler words for the children as they came to difficult expressions. One evening the group was discussing wishes. The six-year-old had been accosted by a student of child guidance earlier in the day who asked her what she would wish to be or to have if she had three wishes.

"So I told her I wanted to be God, and I wanted a horse, and I wanted a tricycle of my own," the child admitted simply. "What would *you* wish for, Mother?"

Some discussion of good and bad wishes followed. The mother admitted to wishing she could write a child's translation of the Bible.

"O Mother," instantly cried the ten-year-old, "you *are* a child's translation of the Bible."

"And they read in the book, in the law of God, distinctly; and they gave the sense, so that they understood the reading" (Nehemiah 8:8, ASV).

"And the Lord . . . said, Write the vision, and make it plain . . . , that he may run that readeth it" (Habakkuk 2:2).

"Even a child is known by his doings" (Proverbs 20:11).

Ants in the Kitchen

One morning a mother walked into her kitchen feeling

very well satisfied with its spotless condition, when her eye fell upon a line of tiny ants making a track like a thread across the floor to a crumb.

"They are like a conscience," she thought. "One little careless crumb, just one, but they have found it out.

"How clean do I have to be for them not to find anything to point out with their little searching fingers?"

As she picked up the broom and prepared to clean up the ants, she also searched her soul.

"There was that one little exaggeration yesterday," she remembered. "I failed to correct it and today the finger of conscience will not let me forget it.

"Thank you, God, for conscience. I will mind the pricks," she said, and began planning as soon as possible to correct the false impression she had given.

"Go to the ant, thou sluggard; consider her ways, and be wise" (Proverbs 6:6).

MAY 18

Finding Mother First

Two-year-old Annie wakes up in the morning and leaves her bed quietly to go to the place where she knows she will find her mother. This is always in the nook beside the east windows where Mother and her Bible are to be found at that hour.

One morning, however, Annie's mother hid herself in another spot so that she might enjoy her morning watch without the usual interruption. Annie climbed out of her crib that day and her feet were heard pattering confidently to the usual place. Then there was a little sound of dis-

141

appointment and the feet went running from room to room and a small voice was heard asking loudly, "Where's Mother?"

The interruption was as complete as if she had found her mother and settled herself directly within her arms. The woman said to herself in despair, "That child simply can't start her day right until she has located Mother." Suddenly her heart smote her with shame that she should have tried to hide.

"Is it not just like myself? I cannot start my day right unless I seek the Father's face. If I need to orient my world by my center and source of trustworthiness and love, so does she. I will not hide again."

"Oh satisfy us in the morning with thy lovingkindness, that we may rejoice and be glad all our days" (Psalm 90:14, ASV).

MAY 19

Grass, Fence, and Trees

One sunny afternoon a young mother spread a blanket out on the grass and lay down in the sunshine to play with her baby. With her head on the blanket she looked out across the field and was surprised at the perspective she got from that viewpoint. It was an ant's-eye view. From there the grasses near her face were taller than the fence posts and the fence posts were taller by far than the trees. She half closed her eyes and the sunshine made rainbows in her eyelashes, which made them even bigger than the grass.

She fell to wondering at such distorted proportion and

went to sleep still philosophizing about it. Why does the near seem so big? Why is the distant so small and unreal? Is it in the way they really are or is it in the way we see them?

Later in the house again she said to herself, "Why does the keeping of this house clean seem so important that I cannot keep from picking up a broom when something needs to be swept or from picking things up when I see them out of place? It is simply because they are near at hand staring me in the face. What right have I to clean house and busy myself with such absorption when there is work of far more eternal importance waiting for helpers? God forbid that I should go down to my grave with only a clean house to show for my life. Lord, give me more than an ant's-eye view."

"Pray ye therefore the Lord of the harvest, that he send forth laborers into his harvest" (Matthew 9:38, ASV).

"Then said I, Here am I; send me" (Isaiah 6:8).

MAY 20

Day After Day

"It has to be done over again so soon," a woman sighed to herself as she got down off the stepladder and surveyed the beautiful white woodwork she had been scrubbing.

"That certainly does look worth the effort, but if only it would *stay* done."

As she put away her ladder and poured out the water, she studied the problem of ever-present housework. Her joy at having finished the spring cleaning was tinged with pessimism.

"There is no future in it. Nothing stays clean," she said to herself. But at that point she stopped. There surely must be some answer. There was.

"I can become more efficient at this job of cleaning; for one thing, learn just what to reach for and just where to begin. The dirt is going to keep coming back, but I can improve my habits in meeting it.

"Like salvation, a daily thing, even a moment by moment act of faith . . . .

"Like the heart of love handling each vexing situation with patience and not with anger, keeping the personal relations clean and sweet . . . .

"Lord, there are situations which come up again and again," she finished with a prayer. *"Help me to stop fighting the fact that they are bound to come up (like the ever-recurring dirt in the house) and to become more skillful at reaching out to Thee for love to meet them every time."*

"Give us this day our daily bread" (Matthew 6:11).
". . . and take up his cross *daily* . . ." (Luke 9:23).

MAY 21

A Beautiful Old Face

My mother's was not the only face I remember with the light of heaven on it. One belonged to an old man. His name was Summers, and it did seem to be summer in his soul in spite of the snow on his temples. I met him at the breakfast table at a conference many years ago. My companion and I would not have intruded on him, but the cafeteria was full and there were no empty tables. Then we were glad because this old man was so pleasant and cheerful.

His open, humble face invited conversation. We found that he was a missionary, recently retired. When we asked, he told us how he came to enter God's service. It was a hard road. Though he had had a happy beginning with his young wife and baby, one tragic event after another had left him shorn of all worldly property. Even when he admitted God's call and embarked upon his mission to Africa, trouble did not stop. His baggage and food supplies were accidentally lost in a jungle river.

But his roots must have gone deep from all those storms, for he glowed with a humble, loving joy as he spoke of the yield of the years. He must be in heaven now. We never saw him again. But whenever I think of that face I think how the host of the redeemed must look gathered by the crystal sea.

"Let the beauty of the Lord our God be upon us" (Psalm 90:17).

MAY 22

The Sacrifice of Rising

"I have esteemed the words of his mouth more than my necessary food" (Job 23:12).

"Oh, if I could only sleep a little longer!" we groan to ourselves as the morning hour arrives.

But if I sleep I cannot pray, and if I do not pray I go in my own strength. And if I sleep I cannot read the Word which feeds my soul. I need the spiritual nourishment; and I do enjoy the fellowship with God when once I have it;

145

but oh, the sacrifice of rising, that is a hard price to pay.

Is this a universal feeling, that we should crave the food and loathe the price? Physical effort goes with all nourishment. The babe must suck; the housewife must cook and wash dishes; the man must pay with money, which is but trading one kind of work for another. How we do enjoy good food! But it does not come without hard work.

The physical price of getting up in the morning in order to be alone with God, like the effort connected with securing physical food, grows less with practice. When the habit is formed, it works for us. Then six is no worse than seven for rising, and the thirst for the Word entices more than food.

"Thou preparest a table before me in the presence of mine enemies" (Psalm 23:5).

*

MAY 23

Mother's Age

Mother never made a secret of her age, especially around those that were younger than she. "Let them have the fun of thinking how much younger they are," she said. And around older people she took pleasure in associating her age with theirs for the pure pleasure it seemed to give them to be classed in her age bracket.

In coming to this viewpoint about age, she recalled the story of a Chinese man she had known, who was converted well past the age of eighty. He heard the Gospel and his eye caught fire as his heart responded to the truth, but for a long time he refused to be baptized. When at last his struggle was over, he came to the church and gave his testimony. He said, "It was my age, my pride and my age. I was afraid I would have to confess to the lie which I have been telling all these years. I have said I was eighty-two, when the truth is I am eighty-three." He paused because it was hard even then to tell it. "It seemed such a small lie when I first deceived about my age long ago. But it had to be repeated every year and I did not want to lose face."

Unlikely as this appears, coming from a country reputed to respect old age, its revelation of the universal human heart helped to cure many who heard him of this common bane.

". . . who through fear of death were all their lifetime subject to bondage" (Hebrews 2:14, 15).

MAY 24

Tenement Room Church

"My mother has the oddest habit of picking up people," a teen-age girl apologized to her friend, as the car in which they were riding was slowed to a halt and her mother opened the door for an old woman carrying a heavy bundle.

That was the beginning of the little church of three that met in a tenement room. The old woman, it turned out, could not speak English. But when she was taken to her door, she made clear by motions that her friendly driver was welcome to come in and visit. The mother and daughter followed her up a rickety stair, through dark corridors smelling of immemorial cookery and close living, to her tiny one-room apartment.

On the table lay what was obviously a Bible though in a foreign language. Here was an instant point in common, and with joy the mother picked it up and exclaimed over it in tones that could be understood by the old woman. They sat down together on the creaking cot with the Bible between them. At the center surely would be Psalms, reckoned the younger woman, and using the numerals at the heads of chapters and fingering its lines she recited the words of Psalm 23 in English. The old woman beamed and followed in her own tongue. Then they knelt and prayed with clasped hands, each in her own language neither knowing the other's petition but sure of the same Listener above. They parted joyful friends.

"For where two or three are gathered together in my name, there am I in the midst of them" (Matthew 18:20).

✳

MAY 25

Invisible Proof

A woman was in the habit of praying by the window every morning, but this morning the going seemed heavy. There was no lightness of heart, no inspiration from reading a verse of Scripture, no feeling of having broken through in prayer. The names on her prayer list did not challenge her as usual. The clock was ticking away and the time would soon be gone for devotion; yet there was no experience of God's presence to lighten the day and no business accomplished before the throne of grace.

Aloud she sighed, "O God, I cannot pray. You must help me. I do not know what is the matter with me this morning."

Suddenly out of the storehouse of her memory He seemed to pluck this verse: "We wrestle not against flesh and blood, but against principalities, against powers . . . ."

"So that is it!" she said to herself. "This is a day when there is special need for prayer, and so Satan is trying to hinder me. It is not just myself. There is a power that does not want me to pray . . . . But God is on my side, and His power is greater." With joy she was able to pray again and was gloriously aware of the reality of God. The awareness of His presence never left her all day and she found herself praying at her tasks.

But what had happened at that window? Not one thing that could be seen. A woman knelt at a window and looked out and rose and went away according to a usual pattern. But the proof of God to her was stronger than a visible miracle.

"If God be for us, who can be against us" (Romans 8:31)?

"I love Jehovah, because he heareth my voice and my supplications" (Psalm 116:1, ASV).

MAY 26

Agony and Urgency

Have you ever felt the pain and pleasure of teaching a Sunday-school class, or leading prayer meeting or Bible study, or bringing a topic for your missionary society? Then you must sometime have shared this mother's feelings and found as well her reward. She writes:

"Yesterday was one perfect and glorious Sunday. The Lord helped me especially speaking to the group, though

149

in preparation I had been all but frantic! Oh, to what depths of despair I sink in being forced to secure God's Word for an audience. It is a cross between agony and urgency that cannot be explained. But, oh, thanks be unto God for His exceeding greatness in helping me to go into these meetings and not try to excuse my way out of them. Under the pressure of this heavy cross I have found a secret core of delight that surpasses anything I've ever experienced."*

"I was no prophet, neither was I a prophet's son; but . . . the Lord said unto me, Go, prophesy unto my people" (Amos 7:14, 15).

* From the journal of one long since in glory.

MAY 27

Treat Him Like a Stranger

"Treat him like a stranger." That was a mother's advice to her daughter who was about to be married. "If you ever feel like quarreling with your husband, treat him like a stranger."

"What in the world do you mean?" her daughter asked.

"How do you treat strangers? Do you not show them every courtesy, put your best foot forward to please them or to make a good impression? One never argues with a stranger. One does not disagree violently or speak rudely to a stranger. So when you become familiar with your husband, do not take his love for granted and take liberties with your speech which you would not even take with a stranger who means very little to you compared with the one with whom you have chosen to share your life. In fact that is a good rule for every member of the family. Treat them like strangers; take them in, show them love."

"I guess you are right, Mother. Few Christian families need to be reminded to show love to strangers, but most of us need to remind ourselves to show a stranger's courtesy and consideration to the ones we love."

"Forget not to show love unto strangers: for thereby some have entertained angels unawares" (Hebrews 13:2, ASV).

". . . who can bear gently with the ignorant and erring, for that he himself also is compassed with infirmity" (Hebrews 5:2, ASV).

MAY 28

Keep Us Humble

"Don't you ever feel tempted to be proud?" a woman asked another who was popularly in demand as a speaker and teacher and leader in church circles. "If you are, what do you do about it? And if not, how do you keep from it?"

"Well, I'll tell you," the other replied. "As long as we are human there is that danger, of course. Pride does rear its ugly head. But the Lord has a way of taking care of that. He just lets me fail often enough, and badly enough so that I can't forget it. I've made some awful flops. It happens often enough to remind me that it is just God's grace and not my cleverness when a message goes across. It keeps me depending on Him."

"Not by might, nor by power, but by my spirit, saith the Lord" (Zechariah 4:6).

A Mother's Regrets

"One afternoon I was walking along the sunny hill on KiKung Mountain in China with a dear child of God talking of heaven. I said, 'Well, it seems to me it would be heaven enough for me if I could get there without regrets.' She was silent a moment, then replied with great earnestness, 'Regrets! Who hasn't regrets? Plunge them in the fountain; that's what it's for!'

"As I pondered these words later, I saw more and more in them. Yes, that is what the Fountain is for, deliverance from our regrets, cleansing for our sins, freedom from our fears. Thank God! Glorious freedom indeed! And all purchased for us at such infinite cost upon the cross. Furthermore if it were possible for us to come to the gate of heaven with *no regrets,* would we not feel as if we had gotten there on a ladder of our own good works? And no one anywhere will ever reach that happy place except through the merit of that precious blood shed on Calvary for us. Glory to the Lamb alone forever and forever!"*

"All have sinned, and come short of the glory of God" (Romans 3:23).

"They . . . have washed their robes, and made them white in the blood of the Lamb" (Revelation 7:14).

* Quoted from Mother's diary.

A Blind Mother's Letters

One older mother, whose own children were grown and gone, still kept up a ministry of letter writing, the extent of which none of them knew until she went partially blind. She could still write, knowing the shapes of the letters and keeping the lines on the page, but she could not read the responses that came to her. It was only when the task of reading her mother's letters aloud to her fell to one of the daughters that she realized the hundreds of personal correspondents to whom she was a spiritual mother. For wherever she had gone, this mother had taken to herself the burdens and problems of others, had loved them too much to let them drift, and had followed them up with a mother's love and courage.

"I beseech thee for my son Onesimus, whom I have begotten in my bonds . . . . If thou count me therefore a partner, receive him as myself" (Philemon 10, 17).

Mother's Conversation

(An imaginary conversation suggested by Malachi 3:16)

Mrs. You and Mrs. I were visiting over a cup of tea. Our conversation did not turn upon gossip or trivia, but we spoke of our loving heavenly Father and His goodness. The Father Himself, leaning from heaven to hear the conversations of earth rising from the roofs of houses and the places where people meet, heard those who spoke with

153

11

gratitude and wonder of His love, and called an angel to Him.

"Write down what they are saying," He said. "Make a book of remembrance for them. They shall be a treasury of jewels to me, and I will save them when everything else is thrown away. For they are true children of mine."

"Then they that feared the Lord spake often one to another: and the Lord hearkened, and heard it, and a book of remembrance was written before him for them that feared the Lord, and that thought upon his name. And they shall be mine, saith the Lord of hosts, in that day when I make up my jewels; and I will spare them, as a man spareth his own son that serveth him" (Malachi 3:16, 17).

154

WITH FRENCH AND SPANISH WRITERS

Lois Gunden Clemens

JUNE 1

With French and Spanish Writers

Man has long been interested in understanding himself. This preoccupation has been nowhere better mirrored than in literature. When the literary artist has pictured his concept of man's essential character, he has often simply reiterated or graphically illustrated the concept of man's nature that is portrayed in the Bible.

When man attempts to understand himself, he examines his role in the larger scheme of values. He seeks to know the meaning of human existence. The meaning he attaches to life is determined by his concept of ultimate reality. Apart from God, he lacks wholesomeness and finds the problems of human life absurd; he attempts to incorporate into his being some other force as a substitute for the divine quality which he has refused to accept. He becomes the victim of his own passions. He is bored with life and tortured by fears. He makes a valiant attempt to appear something other than he actually knows himself to be. He becomes brutal and inhuman in his treatment of others. Although he may not label it as such, he is aware of the effects of sin and evil in his life. On the other hand, when

155

he has related himself to God he has found lasting values which provide him with a meaning for existence. He discovers serenity and satisfaction in the confusion surrounding him. He finds a new motivation in the spiritual force of love, and he knows joy in giving himself in the spirit of love.

The following series of meditations presents man's picture of the human condition as drawn from selected literary work written in the French and Spanish languages. These works illustrate the role of the literary artist in giving us a vivid picture of what man is.

Psalm 8:1-9

JUNE 2

The Plunge Downward

Racine was one of the great French dramatists of the seventeenth century. His tragedies are psychological analyses of the characters in intense moments of conflict.

The play *Britannicus* is the story of the sudden evolution from good to evil in the soul of the Roman emperor Nero. Nero, after having previously followed the advice of his mother and his tutors, is suddenly changed when he looks upon Junie. He is caught in the grip of his passion for her, and his determination to have her turns him into a monster. When he learns of the mutual love of Junie and his stepbrother Britannicus, his jealousy knows no bounds. Finally Nero's jealousy of Britannicus leads him to poison his stepbrother in a pretended gesture of reconciliation. In the end his passion brings him only despair, for Junie slips from his grasp by becoming a vestal virgin.

When Nero abandoned himself to his desire, he pushed aside all scruples and all good judgment, refusing the counsel of those concerned about his well-being. He was willing to pay any price to fulfill his desire, and he brought on his own destruction. James describes the process thus: ". . . each person is tempted when he is lured and enticed by his own desire. Then desire when it has conceived gives birth to sin; and sin when it is full-grown brings forth death."

Proverbs 4:23

Overcoming Evil

Anatole France wrote a novel about the French Revolution entitled *Les Dieux ont soif (The Gods Are Thirsty)*. In it he depicts the Revolution as something inspired by the idealism of liberty and justice, but which was soon transformed into a terrible disregard for human rights and even human life. He pictures some of the ordinary people who are caught and swept along in the events of the movement.

The novel presents various figures drawn into the Revolution by enthusiasm for its purposes. Gradually their idealism is replaced by an insidious degeneration of personality. Evariste Gamelin, the hero, illustrates such an evolution through participation in the Revolution. Before being appointed as a jury member on the Revolutionary Tribunal, he has a sensitive nature easily moved to pity and he loves justice. In this position, however, he is expected to be firm and pitiless, never showing any moderation or human weakness. At first he has a conscience against condemning an innocent person, but in the pursuance of his duty he gradually loses this sensitivity. He begins to regard the giving of punishment as an act having mystic merit or virtue. He now sends men to the guillotine in wholesale manner. He becomes insincere, inhuman, and ambitious. Although at a certain point he regards himself with disgust, he still believes in his cause and decides that there is no stopping for him. When in the end he too is destroyed, one of the other characters says of him, "Poor boy! He was sincere. It is the fanatics who have caused his ruin."

This novel is a clear warning against the danger of using evil to overcome evil. It is shown as a weapon that not only fails to accomplish its end, but which in the process also destroys the user.

Romans 12:17-21

JUNE 4

Man's Propensity to Evil

Baudelaire, a French poet of the nineteenth century, wrote a collection of poetry to which he gave the strange title, *Flowers of Evil.* For him life was only monotony and boredom; it was an evil to be somehow endured. His poetry presents sin in control of the human heart, and the wages of that sin ending in damnation. Like Dante, he has visited Inferno and he knows the bitter suffering of the sinner, but he is trapped in the horror of these lower regions. Unlike Dante, he cannot find his way to higher realms. Man's original sin continues its ravages in his nature, for while

158

knowing its suffering and the remorse brought by it, the victim still yields to the attractiveness of evil. His wretchedness is heightened by the awareness that what he is engaged in is evil and will bring him nothing but despair. The fact is that he simply must do something to deliver himself from boredom; this is why evil brings him a certain delight even though he is horrified by it.

In the opening poem of the collection, Baudelaire introduces to the reader this idea of the paradox of man's pleasure in doing evil. He states that Satan rules us and we delight in his rule; but he adds that evil is not an unmixed delight: it violates our dignity and makes us beasts. Throughout the work he gives poetic expression to these concepts in laments and maledictions, in blasphemy, in songs of ecstasy, in cries of anguish and grief. These are the flowers of evil produced by his own bitter encounter with it.

Baudelaire had real insight into the effect of evil as it feeds upon the lifeblood of man. He sensed that man knows his life to be empty as he pursues the evil he reaches after; nevertheless he cannot forsake it. This same awareness of the dilemma of the human condition is in the thinking of our confused world. It is at this very point that we have a responsibility. We must give perspective to this confusion by showing the reason and the remedy for man's spiritual disorder. We must bring within his perspective the new dimension found in the hope of his salvation.

Proverbs 10:2

159

Love Sees with Understanding

Colette Baudoche was written by Maurice Barrés, a Frenchman deeply rooted in the tradition of his native Lorraine region. This novel describes the feelings of the inhabitants of Metz as they watched their city being flooded by a continuous wave of German immigrants. They resisted this movement, which threatened to submerge their traditions and their existence as a people. All of the foreign usurpers were regarded with suspicion and were not generally shown much hospitality. When Colette Baudoche and her mother were forced by financial necessity to rent part of their house, they were dismayed at having a German accupy their rooms. However, they took him in. As time went on and they learned to know Frederic Asmus, he no longer seemed unworthy of their friendship. Eventually Colette realized that she loved him. She found herself understanding the culture he represented because she was interested in learning about it through Frederic. She, in turn, helped him to appreciate all that the people of Metz held dear. Both of them, in their respective circles of society, served as interpreters of each other's group attitudes. Thus a bridge began to span the abyss that separated the two hostile elements.

Where there is love, there will be understanding. The outreach of love can build mutual understanding between various elements in our communities. How far does our love reach on this front?

I Corinthians 13:4-7

160

In Search of Lost Time

Marcel Proust wrote a long novel entitled *In Search of Lost Time*. In the course of the narration he developed his own concept of how lost time can be found again.

The story consists of memories of the past recalled by the narrator. He places side by side events that come to his mind in succession rather than in chronological order. Certain occurrences involuntarily evoke memories of a living past that is still intact within him. From such experiences of "involuntary memory" he discovers that although certain experiences belong to past time, they are not really lost: they exist as part of his spiritual being that transcends time and matter. It becomes his purpose in writing his book to transmit to others this discovery that past time can be regained by its return to our consciousness in the present.

In a certain sense past time can continue into the present as its memory is recalled. But there is another sense in which past time is beyond recall, for its actions cannot be revoked or changed. Bossuet, in his meditation upon the brevity of life, reflected upon this matter. He found it frightening that what one does in time passes into eternity with time, forever to remain as his record before God.

In other words, when the moments of this life are past, one must answer for them as if they remained. He said, therefore, "It is not enough to say: 'They are past, I will no longer think of them'; they are past, yes for me, but not for God; He will demand an account of them from me."

Although past actions are beyond recall, God in His mercy offers to remember them against us no more. Because He forgives us if we accept His offer of redemption, we can forget the past and reach toward the future with confidence.

Philippians 3:13, 14

JUNE 7
Sincerity in Personal Relations

Martine is a play written by a contemporary French dramatist, showing the danger of trifling with affections. Martine was an attractive young peasant girl who ran errands for Madame Mervin, an elderly neighbor woman in her village. One day Julien, the grandson of Madame Mervin, returned to his grandmother's house after having lived abroad as a soldier. Impressed with the freshness and the naive quality of Martine, he showered his attentions upon her. She was completely captivated by his words of endearment and his interest in her. The romance was cut short, however, when Madame Mervin brought Jeanne back into the picture. Jeanne was the young city girl to whom Julien had been practically engaged before his departure. The grandmother hoped to see this friendship continued. Although she liked Martine, she judged Jeanne much more suitable as a wife for Julien. Julien soon discovered that Jeanne and he understood and appreciated the same things, since they had similar cultural backgrounds. Julien married Jeanne, and Martine married Alfred, the peasant boy who knew nothing of the ways of romantic love. However, Martine carried the memory of this experience with Julien throughout her life. Her suffering because of the unrequited love which his attentions had awakened in her is poignantly presented in a final scene when Julien returns after the grandmother's death.

Christians who have good consciences on other points sometimes show little conscience on the matter of trifling with the affections of another. Sincerity in personal relations is a basic Christian attitude which must be learned along with other attitudes. We cannot neglect to develop this ideal as we help to mold character in the lives we influence.

Ecclesiastes 11:9

JUNE 8

Meaning for Existence

Jean-Paul Sartre is a contemporary French writer whose works are an expression of the philosophy of existentialism. This vision of man seems to deny any value to human life. Man stands alone, abandoned to his liberty of action and responsible for choosing the action that will give meaning to the moment. He has no recourse to anything outside himself in making his decisions; he must exercise his freedom without being bound by any influence. Neither the moral laws nor the commandments of God, neither his past nor his passions, neither his concept of himself nor his social situation can dictate his action. His liberty consists in this absence of any outside factors determining the choice of his acts. Man is consequently free to give any meaning whatsoever to anything, but this freedom imposes upon him the awful obligation of continually giving meaning to something by voluntarily choosing his actions. The characters of Sartre's novels are forced to create for themselves a place in an absurd universe; they have no predetermined course to follow. Since they themselves are their own gods, the responsibility for finding any meaning to life rests ultimately and solely upon them.

Can one possibly imagine the anguish of a human soul who accepts such a responsibility without admitting any guide in the discharging of it? How different is the orientation of the Christian! He is freed from slavery to his own sophistication and pride in the decisions he must make. His life is hid with Christ in God, and he lives in the awareness of the help of an omniscient God as he faces decisions.

Ephesians 4:17-24

JUNE 9
Effective Witnessing

Chateaubriand was a French writer during the first half of the nineteenth century. He was interested in re-establishing the Christian theme in literature, after it had been quite thoroughly removed from it. He prepared a long work as a defense of the Christian religion.

René was a separate story inserted into the longer work to illustrate the harmony of life resulting from the acceptance of Christianity. The story is René's personal account of his unhappy life. After he explains the factors in his childhood and youth that are the reasons for his melancholy, he is rebuked by the missionary to whom he has been recounting all these details. The missionary upbraids him for having thought that man is sufficient unto himself and tells him that solitude is bad for one who does not live there with God. He further suggests that instead of pitying himself René should be using his strength in the service of others.

Although Chateaubriand's purpose was sincere, the value of *René* to show the strength of Christianity is doubtful. The outstanding impression it leaves is that of morbid pessimism. Chateaubriand's attempt to show the surpassing joy of the Christian faith was unsuccessful because he had not felt its harmony in his own life. He was trying to present as truth what he did not know in a first-hand manner; instead he wrote something of an ode to despair, since that was the character of his own living.

The Christian witness cannot be effectively communicated unless it is the expression of a personal experience that knows with certainty whereof it speaks.

Luke 6:39

JUNE 10

The Tortured Mind

Horacio Quiroga was a Uruguayan writer whose life ended suddenly in 1937. Tortured by ill health and preoccupied with the agony of death, he had developed a mental state of anguish and despair. Some of his tales indicate his grasp of a tortured mind in a most horrifying situation. After the death of his wife he was left with the care of two children. Living in constant struggle with the forces of nature in a jungle province, he became preoccupied with the details of their daily life.

In the collection of short stories entitled *El desierto*, Quiroga describes these experiences. He tells how a father

165

taught his motherless children to fear nothing except what he warned them to fear, such as the deadly vipers of the jungle. Thus they were perfectly at ease when their father had to be absent from them. All went well until the father was unable to cure an infection on his toe resulting from an insect bite. Finally the chills of a fever made him spend a sleepless night. As he grew worse, he called the children to him and told them that he was dying and that even though they would be left alone they were not to be afraid. Since they knew nothing of his fear of death, they accepted his explanation and quietly left the room. The father's agony in the impending tragedy is, however, vividly portrayed.

Horacio Quiroga lived and died haunted by fears and agonies of mind, unaware of the comforting presence of the One who casts out our fears and gives peace of mind amidst the uncertainties of life.

II Timothy 1:7

JUNE 11

Fearing Ridicule

Le Préjugé a la mode is a play criticizing the fashionable attitude which considered it ridiculous for a husband to love his wife. This was actually a rather widespread whim of high society in 1735, when La Chaussée wrote the play.

The story of this comedy revolves about Durval, who deeply loves his wife Constance, but who hides this feeling lest he appear ridiculous. He pays Constance only those attentions prescribed by custom and etiquette, and gives only cold and evasive responses to her expressions of love. Finally he tests his wife's loyalty to him by secretly sending her rich gifts, supposedly from a would-be lover. When she refuses to accept these gifts, he is finally convinced of her good character and of her genuine attachment to him. He recognizes the wrongs he has done her and the foolishness of his past conduct. At this point he is ready to brave any sarcastic remarks that his former companions may heap upon him, for he realizes that he was wrong in being ashamed of a love that was so well merited.

However foolish the theme of this play may appear to us, it illustrates the ridiculousness of slavishly following whatever is the fashionable thing to do. Fear of the disfavor of others can cause us to act according to the standards of those around us. This may well mean losing the integrity of our witness to the Gospel. We need still to be reminded that "the fear of the Lord is the beginning of wisdom."

I John 4:18

JUNE 12

Genuine or Counterfeit?

The Counterfeiters, a novel written by André Gide, seems at first glance to be merely a series of rather scattered incidents in the lives of the characters portrayed. According to the author, its subject is the struggle between what reality actually offers to the characters and what they would like to make of it. In keeping with this theme all of the characters are miserable because the real world in which they move is not actually what they want others to believe it to be. They are living in false situations, for each one tries to appear to be something different from what he really is. Mr. Vedel, for example, is a pious-appearing man who runs a boarding school, but there is no reality behind this religious exterior. One of his sons explains that his father has so fixed his role that he no longer has the right nor the power not to be in earnest in it. His life is nothing but a comedy, for it consists of playing a part which he has assigned to himself. No matter how sincerely and consciously he plays the part, his representation of himself is false. The emptiness and frustration of the counterfeit characters that people this novel are strongly stamped on all its pages.

Counterfeit Christians are no more attractive in their setting of religiosity than are any of the wretched persons pictured in the novel. Although made on the pattern of the genuine, they present a most distasteful representation of it. For the onlooker, such Christians are full proof that their religion is not what it claims to be. We cannot allow ourselves to be satisfied with what is only the outward label; we must lay hold of the glorious reality that is within our reach. For what shall it profit a man to profess godliness if he finds that his soul knows only emptiness?

Psalm 139:1-6, 23, 24

JUNE 13

Sublimation of Disappointments

Gabriela Mistral is a Chilean whose poetry gained international recognition in 1946 when she was awarded the

Nobel Prize for Literature. Her life was both intense and tragic, and her verses are a reflection of that life. After the loss of her beloved, she sublimated her grief and her maternal longing by giving of herself to others. She took upon herself the burdens and sorrows of others, first by distinguishing herself as a rural teacher and later in the consular service of Chile and in the League of Nations.

When Gabriela Mistral writes about the children of others, she voices her deep love and compassion for them, often with a certain poignancy. Her poem about the rural schoolteacher reveals how she regarded her responsibility as a teacher. Into her hands had fallen the care of little ones whose eyes and hands she must needs keep clear and pure. She found happiness in giving herself to them, even though her heart was still weeping. She realized that the humble peasants upon whose children she lavished her affections would never see how much deeper was the imprint in them of her own being than of themselves.

Disappointments and heartaches need not be tragedies; they can be made the means of understanding and sharing the suffering of others. The refining fires of such experiences may burn away personal ambitions and selfish motives, resulting in a purified love that reaches out in a wider embrace.

Hebrews 12:11-15

JUNE 14

Justice for All?

Various contemporary Spanish-American novelists have treated the Indian problem as it exists in their countries

169

today. One of these is the Mexican newspaper editor, Lopez y Fuentes.

His novel *El indio (The Indian)* has its setting in a remote mountain village. The arrival there one day of three haughty strangers in search of gold precipitates a crisis. They try to attack an Indian girl, and they cripple a young Indian serving as their guide. In bitter resentment the Indians crush one of the strangers by rolling a stone down the mountainside right into their path as they are making a hasty retreat. Knowing that they will be speedily punished by the law, the natives abandon the village and go into hiding. Although they mistrust the authorities who try to entice them with promises, they finally return. Revolution stalking over the countryside reaches them, and their food reserves must be given to the soldiers arriving in their village. A smallpox epidemic brings further catastrophe. A deputy of the new pseudo-democracy promises them help; however, he mobilizes their services for road building, for construction of a school and a church, and finally for fighting alongside their leader. In addition, their meager amounts of money are drained from them in taxes levied to pay for all this. As the story ends they are faced with the problem of hunger, since the men no longer have time at their disposal for tilling the fields. Justice seems to have abandoned them, and exploitation of them has been complete.

The reader of this novel is moved to deep sympathy for the victims of greed and thoughtlessness. But are there injustices which we fail to see in the communities where we live? How consistent is our outreach of love and compassion? What can we do to develop a sensitivity to such situations?

Leviticus 25:17

All Is Vanity

Bossuet was the court preacher at the French court during the reign of Louis XIV. He wrote a series of funeral orations pronounced in honor of distinguished personages of the period. Bossuet made these orations the occasion for preaching forceful sermons to the living.

The funeral oration of Henriette-Anne of England is based on the text from Ecclesiastes 1:2: "Vanity of vanities . . . all is vanity." Bossuet first reviewed her brief life. Distinguished as she was by her rank, and even more so by her merit, Henriette-Anne was suddenly taken from this life. Neither her royal splendor nor her youth protected her from the grip of death. Man's power and might are, after all, small things in the sight of God. The only factor that gave her any worth at the moment of her death was her acceptance of the salvation offered by the Lord in whom she had placed her faith. His concluding words directed the hearers to a consideration of their relationship to God. He told them that God in His providence could not have more clearly demonstrated the vanity of human things than He was doing in this event. He suggested that they should henceforth scorn the favors of the world and accept the glory of complete resignation to the commands of God.

Today, when we tend to base greatness and honor on possessing things and on the means for attaining them, it is easy to measure values by false standards. What values are commanding our attention day after day? What things are we striving for? Do they have lasting value?

I Timothy 6:17-19

171

Responsibility of Those Who Teach

Paul Bourget was a French writer who sensed the important role of teachers in the formation of the philosophy and ideals of their pupils. To warn teachers of the serious responsibility of such influence he wrote a story entitled *The Disciple*.

The novel centers about the philosopher Adrien Sixte, who taught freely his deterministic ideas and preached freedom from moral principles. One day he was informed of a murder committed by Robert Greslou, one of his former pupils. Surprised at this conduct by the promising youth he had known, he began to try to explain the crime. Robert's mother came to him, begging him to go to the prison and get Robert to talk, for he stubbornly refused to speak even a word in his own defense. She explained how much her son had revered his master, and expressed her confidence that his efforts would bring results. Then she handed to him a manuscript that Robert had asked her to bring. He had written these lines during his two months in prison and requested that no person other than Mr. Sixte should read them. The mother felt sure that here was to be found the proof of his innocence. The master began reading the manuscript, which was an analysis of how Robert had applied the principles of the master's philosophy to his own actions. In order to observe the laws of determinism in effect in human psychology he had courted a young lady, solely as an experiment. As the philosopher read on into the night, he realized more and more clearly his own part in the disaster which had resulted, and he was horrified at the havoc he had caused in this youth's life.

The molding of attitudes and the forming of basic principles of behavior are responsibilities with far-reaching consequences. Children develop their personalities as the result of what they have learned from the many who serve as their teachers. Parents and teachers together are responsible for what goes into this learning process. How faithfully do we serve as the guardians of upright character in those whom we teach?

I Timothy 4:15, 16

JUNE 17

The Sin of Self-Pity

Chatterton is a play written by the French poet Alfred de Vigny. It relates the story of a young poet who engaged in too much self-pity. Although born into a well-to-do family, he was now reduced to poverty. He felt unappreciated and misunderstood by a society which, in his opinion, ought to have supported him because of his contribution as a poet. He threatened to take his life. A Quaker who had befriended him tried to show him that he was taking an extreme attitude and that things were not really so hopeless as he thought. The final blow came when in response to his request to the lord-mayor for financial help, he received an offer to serve as his personal valet. This was too great an insult to his pride, and he felt that he could not go on living.

Indulgence in self-pity is not a mark of Christian maturity. It warps the outlook and blinds the soul to God's mercies freely offered anew each day. It gives wrong perspective to the individual's own experience. It is sin, for it fails to believe in the good hand of the Lord at work in the lives of those who trust Him. It will disappear as one focuses his attention upon the wonder of our God, who although He is altogether righteous, deigns to love us and to fellowship with us and to implant in us His being.

Psalm 42:5

JUNE 18
Love Purifies Selfish Motives

Alejandro Casona is a contemporary Spanish playwright whose personal suffering and loss in the Civil War have added to the maturity of his thought.

In Casona's *La barca sin pescador (The Boat Without a Fisherman)*, he pictures love as a purifying emotion able to destroy the evil plans of Satan in the character of Ricardo. The devil appears to him in a moment of despair, offering him the way out of the crisis. In order to regain his lost wealth and power, Ricardo signs a pact with the devil. The price asked by the devil is that Ricardo break the commandment: "Thou shalt not kill." He promises Ricardo that the killing need not be done by his own hands; it is enough that he is willing to murder. A victim is chosen in a faraway fishing village. The victim is Peter Anderson, and his death comes as he is triumphantly returning home after the purchase of a new fishing boat. The devil relates to Ricardo how Peter is pushed over a cliff just as he is raising his hand to greet his wife. Ricardo at that moment hears the heart-rending cry of Peter's wife, which thereafter continues to haunt him and to prick his conscience. Finally he makes the long trip to find the widow of Peter Anderson. He learns of the hardships suffered by the family of the fisherman whose new boat remains unused. He enjoys the hospitality of the home thus denied its livelihood. In the generosity and the warm spirits of the widow Estela and the grandmother, he discovers a new spiritual dimension. The power of the love he thus finds transforms him into a new man, and he renounces his former life in order to work by the side of Estela.

In his famous chapter on love, Paul reminds us that love does not pursue selfish advantage. Is this characteristic of love true of our family relationships? Is it true of our attitudes toward all those among whom we live and work? Does our love always look for a way of being constructive? Do we really believe that love works in all our person-to-person relationships?

Romans 13:10

JUNE 19

"Think on These Things"

In the novel *Madame Bovary*, Gustave Flaubert traces the downfall of a young woman who became bored with the uneventful life she was leading with her husband. Emma Bovary was the daughter of a rich farmer. Her father had married her to a widowed doctor, who deeply loved and adored her. She, however, did not share his feelings and found existence with him dull and monotonous. As time went on she concluded that her husband had nothing to offer her. One night she was invited to a party

175

in a nearby chateau. The attention she received again awakened in her the dreams of romantic love that she had cherished as a girl. Her dissatisfaction became so evident that even her husband noticed it. He moved to a larger town in an attempt to make her happy, but there Emma again found only mediocrity and monotony. Then began a series of episodes with two young men who easily won her affections. Finally, hopelessly in debt from her reckless spending and abandoned by her lovers, she took poison and died in agony.

This story indicates how easy is the path to ruin once the individual begins responding to temptation. And the process is the same regardless of what the temptation may be. This woman's downfall originated in her failure to center her thoughts on the right things. Feeling misused and discontent, she disdained her husband's love for her, and sought for happiness elsewhere. In the end this brought her only anguish and despair, and the bitter realization that the way of the transgressor is hard.

Placing our affections on things that will endure instead of on passing pleasures of the moment will insure us a purposeful life climaxing in great joy rather than one ending in despair.

Philippians 4:4-8

JUNE 20

Trust Brings Serenity

Amado Nervo is considered one of the great mystic poets of modern times. Although often troubled by doubts, in the poetry of his maturity he expressed serenity and confident trust.

Nervo's longest poem is "Sister Water." The idea for the poem came to him after he had listened night after night to the continuous dripping of water from a leaking faucet. That steady trickle of water taught him something of how man can attain happiness by accepting without complaint all the experiences that God may choose to bring into his life. He considers streams of water flowing along between flowery banks or dashing themselves down into some abyss, and he notices that the water never ceases sending forth its song; it even adorns the abyss with triumphant rainbow hues after its terrifying leap into space. The water's docility suggests faithfulness to the Creator. Another characteristic he sees in water is its adaptability to be used in a variety of ways. Always its form is determined by whatever vase happens to contain it. It is equally useful as holy water at the baptismal font or as waves on a lake gently rocking a canoe. In response to this observation he cries with the apostle: "Lord, what wouldst thou have me to do?"

The short poem "Optimism" radiates complete serenity in the midst of a world which still causes tears and pain. The opening lines give the key to its tone. Nervo says that he does not know if the world is good or if it is bad, but he does know that it is the form and expression of God Himself.

To face each day's perplexities and annoyances, there is abundant resource in a confident trust in the God whose love is our peace.

Isaiah 30:15

177

Sitting Where They Sit

Emile Zola wrote a series of novels describing the corruption and the ultimate collapse of the Second French Empire. These novels expose the poverty of the least privileged classes of French society and the misery resulting from this condition.

Germinal pictures the class struggle of an industrialized society. The central action is the great strike of the workers in a mining area. Deeply moved by the lot of the miners, Zola goes beyond the simple narration of a strike to create a work expressing both compassion and indignation. He shows the mining families living very close to the level of mere animal existence in a drab village completely devoid of any exterior beauty. Hunger is their close companion. Pleasures are almost nonexistent, and life is a wearisome burden for them. When Etienne Lantier arrives preaching deliverance through organized strikes, dissatisfaction with their misery causes them to follow him. The strike progresses from a calm and orderly beginning to a violent conclusion. This situation gives occasion for the expression of deep-seated hatreds of the "have-nots" against their overlords. Any possible occasion is utilized to get revenge, as daily the situation of the strikers becomes more desperate. In the end they are forced to return to work or to die from starvation.

It is a surprising experience to find oneself living in the world of "the other half" and to understand how life looks to them. *Germinal* depicts the complacency of those who selfishly enjoy their abundance viewed through the eyes of the hungry who cry at their gates. When once we understand what it means to sit where they sit, we will see our selfishness in its stark reality.

Ecclesiastes 4:1

JUNE 22

"Take Heed Lest Ye Fall"

The Pastoral Symphony, by André Gide, is the story of a pastor who brought unhappiness to his own family. During one of his pastoral calls, he found a blind girl who had been neglected and who was little more than a beast in her reactions. After many hours of patient teaching by the pastor, she finally learned to smile and to speak. More rapid progress followed, and in time she developed into a beautiful girl. All the while the pastor was becoming much attached to Gertrude. When his son returned from school and began to spend time with her, the father forbade him to have any part in her training. Jacques, now much in love with Gertrude, became aware that his father's jealousy was separating him from her. Eventually Gertrude's sight was restored through surgery. When she returned to the pastor's home after the operation, she saw what in her blindness she had never known. She sensed that her presence brought pain to the pastor's wife, and she finally learned that it was wrong for her to love the pastor. Crushed by this knowledge, she drowned herself in a pool. In the end there was only remorse for the pastor and unhappiness for the family.

This story illustrates the manner in which temptation may overcome even a highly respected person who fol-

179

lows the impulse of his wrong desires, no matter under what false pretense he condones his conduct. Happiness is most certainly not to be attained in this way, but godliness with contentment is great gain.

Psalm 119:1-8

JUNE 23

Kind Thoughts Are Not Enough

The Mexican Manuel Gutiérrez Nájera wrote a series of whimsical, highly colored sketches. Written with complete sincerity, they are intimate glimpses into the warmth of his reflective moods.

One of these delightful sketches presents some observations made during a ride in a streetcar. Since he was riding only to find diversion on a rainy day, he traveled in his "miniature Noah's ark" to parts of the city unknown to him. In an area where fine houses were lacking, he first examined what was to be seen along the streets. When he began to observe what was inside the car, he became interested in a poorly dressed old man leaning on the handle of his tattered umbrella. He wondered who this man might be. He concluded that he was a married man with daughters. Soon he was pitying the poor young girls, who undoubtedly were pretty, but were quite possibly suffering from hunger. He finally came to the conclusion that it would be a good idea for him to marry one of the girls; this would bring good fortune to the girl's family and would provide him with a good wife. Just as he was trying to decide whether he should marry the blond or the brunette, the man got off the streetcar and walked away. As he watched him go he was impressed with his pitiful condition and wished that he had done something for him, but he remained in his seat in the streetcar.

This sketch may not seem very striking in the retelling, and its solution may appear unrealistic. After all it was only a fanciful imaginative process for whiling away the hours of a dreary afternoon; there was never any intention of carrying out the idea. Nevertheless, is it not a parable showing how easily one may see with the eye and grasp with the mind, but still fail to feel deeply enough in the heart to act?

James 4:17

JUNE 24

Real Worth Is in Being

Moliere's comedy *Le Bourgeois Gentilhomme* depicts the actions of a newly rich industrialist who tries to play the part of an aristocratic gentleman. He hires various masters to make him proficient in their fields. This group of private teachers includes a music teacher, a dancing teacher, a fencing teacher, and a philosophy teacher. As he attempts to perform for each of them, it becomes obvious that he can never possibly become the polished gentleman of culture which he aspires to be. His teachers try to please his every whim, for although he is a ridiculous learner he is a source of good income for them. The master tailor he has hired delivers a ridiculous outfit in which our gentleman Jourdain struts about feeling that now he will be admired by everyone. Throughout the play he becomes the dupe of anyone who offers to give him importance or honor.

Man often makes a fool of himself in pretending to be what he obviously is not. Although he may think that he is making the desired impression, those who look on can usually determine his true nature. How much more is this true of God's appraisal of us! Making a pretense before God is of no avail, for God knows even our innermost thoughts. We can, however, come to Him in humility, asking Him to create in us new hearts and a right spirit, for He is willing to accept us as we are and to make new creatures out of us.

Psalm 139:1-4, 23, 24

JUNE 25

Discerning Reality

Many Spanish writers have tried to explain the philosophical concept of reality; they have portrayed man seeking to understand the meaning beyond the facts of his everyday experiences. Calderón de la Barca, a famous dramatist of the Spanish Golden Age, used such a theme in the play *Life Is a Dream.*

Segismundo is a prince exiled by his father to live in a dungeon in order to prevent the fulfillment of an astrologer's prediction that his evil impulses will cause him to be a bad ruler. He knows nothing of his royal lineage. One day he is drugged and carried to the palace, where he finds himself a prince. Then just as suddenly, and again in a drugged state, he is returned to the dungeon. At that point he is confused; was he dreaming when he was in the palace or is he dreaming now? What is his real situation? Although puzzled concerning the answer, it seems to him that everything in this life happens as in a dream, and that the real world must be what will come with the waking. His conclusion is that whether it is real or not, the important thing in this life is to accept the responsibilities which come with it; thereby man will find happiness when he awakens in the real world.

What is the real world for us in our daily, busy living? Do we not often become so engrossed with routine and so busy with necessary duties that we become overly concerned with the doing of them? Their immediacy easily dims our vision; we forget that they are but passing things. With Mary of Bethany we must choose not to allow their pressing demands to crowd out of our lives the better part. After all, what is there of greater importance for this passing life than actually possessing those unseen things which are eternal? Are we now preparing ourselves for the awakening in the real world when this transient life has run its course?

II Corinthians 4:17, 18

JUNE 26

"He That Loseth His Life . . ."

The French poet Paul Claudel was profoundly changed at the age of eighteen while listening to the singing of the Magnificat at Christmas time. This marked the beginning of his strong belief in God, which remained as a powerful certainty throughout the succeeding years of his life. His literary works express the radiance and joy that filled his being; they are also his attempt to sing the Magnificat for those who have not yet received its message.

183

In the play *L'Announce faite a Marie (The Annunciation to Mary)* he shows how ultimate happiness is achieved by Violaine, the heroine, through self-sacrifice. She embodies the Christian virtues of faith, hope, and charity. Because she gives the kiss of charity to a poor leper, she loses the love of her fiance Jacques. She allows him to believe her unfaithful in order that he will marry her jealous sister Mara. Having contracted leprosy, she spends her life in poverty and desolation. Then one night Mara seeks her out, clasping her dead child and begging Violaine to restore her to life. Violaine accomplishes the miracle. She explains that the suffering which she has voluntarily accepted in her living death is powerful. In the end all the others, including Mara, are saved through her self-sacrifice. The theme of the play is best summarized in the father's words when he states that Violaine has wisely recognized that the aim of life is not to live by remaining attached to this miserable earth, but to die by mounting upon the cross in order to give what we have.

Family living provides a magnificent setting for learning the way of self-sacrifice. This kind of lesson is undoubtedly learned by discovering its expression rather than by precept. Do the activities in which we spend our energies day after day indicate a spirit of sacrificial giving of ourselves?

Romans 8:12, 13

JUNE 27

Christian Love in Action

In *Candide,* as in several of his other works, Voltaire made reference to Anabaptists. He related how Candide arrived in Holland after having fled from the horrors of a country carrying on a brutal war. Since he had heard that everybody in that country was rich, and Christian as well, he had no doubts about his being well cared for. He asked for alms from several rather serious-looking people, only to be told that if he continued to beg he would be shut up in a house of correction. Next he addressed himself to a man who had just lectured for an hour concerning charity before a big assembly. This Protestant minister, looking askance at Candide, asked him if he represented the right cause. Candide explained that he had nothing to do with the causes that impelled him to beg for his bread until he could earn it. The man then wanted to know if he thought the pope was the Antichrist. To this query, Candide replied that he had not yet heard, but that whether the pope was or was not the Antichrist, he needed bread. He was promptly and mercilessly sent on his way, being told that he did not merit having any bread to eat. It happened that a good Anabaptist named Jacques saw the cruel treatment given to one of his human brothers having a soul; he took him to his home, where he most kindly cared for him. Jacques also befriended Pangloss, the sick friend of Candide, and provided him medical care at his expense.

This account of Christian charity as practiced by "the good Anabaptist" coming from the pen of Voltaire is quite significant, for he usually finds little to be commended in what he sees of Christianity. It indicates that sincere Christian discipleship can be recognized by even the unbeliever. How much Christian love is being demonstrated in our treatment of the unfortunate?

I John 3:17, 18

185

For Such a Time as This

The play *Esther,* written by Jean Racine, is built upon the Biblical account of Esther's risking her own safety to save her people. The opening scenes set forth the very real danger that threatens the Jewish nation. Mordecai comes to inform Esther of the decree that Haman has influenced the king to make. When he presses her to intercede for her people, she hesitates, knowing that this might incur the king's disfavor. Mordecai pleads with her, suggesting that she ought not consider her life as her own. He asks her whether it is not possible that God may have brought her to the throne expressly for the purpose of saving His people. He climaxes his plea by saying that if this is God's intent she need fear nothing; all the kings of the earth would prove powerless against Him, were He to rely upon even the weakest hand in the whole world to accomplish His purpose. After Esther considers the matter and makes her decision, she calls for the prayers of all the Jews. Then, alone on the scene, she prays to God in deep humility, calling upon Him to accompany her as she goes before the king. The remaining scenes show how forcefully God moves in the succeeding events to save His people. In fact, God seems to be the principal character of the play, for He in turn inspires, sustains, and softens the hearts of the main characters.

Do we find ourselves shrinking from a difficult situation calling for sacrifice, dedication, or surrender? Might we not do well to consider whether God may have placed us in that situation for the very purpose of saving His people through us? And if this is God's intent, like Esther, we can count on His help.

Esther 4:14

186

I Will Fear No Evil

The Infernal Machine, one of the plays of Jean Cocteau, deals with the problem of human liberty in choosing between good and evil. The character of Oedipus is the central figure of the play. Oedipus tries heroically not to commit the two crimes that have been foretold for his life. He feels that he is free to choose between good and evil, and is confident of his victory. However, everything that he does in order not to commit the crimes becomes another step leading him toward them. It becomes increasingly obvious that since he is only a man, he can do nothing against the gods and their infernal machine. In the end he falls victim to this machine constructed to destroy him.

The fatalistic philosophy thus picturing man's defeat in spite of his will to conquer stands in sharp contrast to the triumphant note of the Christian's testimony. In his Galatian letter, Paul speaks of Christ "who gave himself for our sins, that he might deliver us from this present evil world." Instead of a god who destroys us in an infernal machine, the Christian serves a God who is for him a good shepherd, who leads him in paths of righteousness so that he need fear no evil.

Romans 8:26-28

Our Triumphant God

Athaliah is one of the late tragedies of Jean Racine and is based on a Biblical theme. It is a powerful portrayal of the triumph of God, who avenges Himself of those who fail to recognize Him. He accomplishes this through His faithful servants. The story is that of Jehoiada and his wife putting to naught the plans of the wicked queen Athaliah in the crowning of the boy Joash, whom they have reared in the temple. Racine represents most effectively the feelings of the Israelites through the use of a chorus of Levite girls. This group sings words of either supplication or praise to God as demanded by the situation. When Jehoiada's confidence in God is rewarded, honor and glory are duly ascribed to the God who has heard the cry of His people. One of the most impressive scenes is the one in which Athaliah finds Joash in the temple and questions him. The protecting hand of God is evident in the way in which the young boy wisely answers her questions without revealing any of the information she is seeking.

The play leaves the reader with an overpowering impression of the greatness and goodness of the true God, who can triumph over the wickedness of men. This is a picture of the God whom we serve. He is still the same. He stands ready to make us to triumph always whether it be in victory or in defeat. Can we be mindful of this fact in all the little defeats and victories that are a part of the routine of our days?

Psalm 149

KEEPER AT HOME

Elaine Sommers Rich

JULY 1

Morning Prayer

Lord, Thou art the water of life.
  As this day begins, I am an empty pitcher before Thee.
    Fill me, O Lord.

Thou art the light of the world.
  As this day begins, I am an unlit candle.
  Thy light can never shine through me to others unless
    Thou dost shine in my heart.
  Thou art the true light that lightest every man
    that cometh into the world.
    Light me, O Lord.

Thou art the true vine.
  Unless I dwell in Thee this day,
    I can bring forth no fruit. My leaves
    turn brown, shrivel, blow away, and I die.
  Let Thy life always flow into me, Thy branch, O Lord.

John 15:1-11

189

Before an Unmade Bed

One woman said, "I always pray before an unmade bed. For if I make the bed first, I also pick up clothes. I go into another room to put something away. There I see things that need doing. And before I know it, I am well into my morning's work and have not prayed. So I always pray before an unmade bed."

Another said, "As I use the gifts given to us at our wedding, I remember the givers in prayer."

A college teacher said, "As I call the class roll, I lift each student to the Lord in prayer."

A homemaker said, "I am a peacemaker. My heart aches when my country prepares for war. When I hear jet planes overhead, I pray for the young men piloting those planes."

Sadhu Sundar Singh said, "Prayer is as important as breathing, and we never say we have no time to breathe."

The Apostle Paul said, "Pray without ceasing."

1 Thessalonians 5:17

JULY 3

On Greatness

Helen remembered spirited discussions she had once participated in about why there were so many fewer women than men among the "great" in history. She had felt called upon to defend and vindicate her sex. If only society down through the centuries had permitted women in all fields, there would be more women on the pages of history, she had asserted with fervor.

Why had she been unable to see that, after all, the creativity of women has gone first of all into the creation of other people? The lending of one's body to a force much greater than oneself. The nurture of children. The guidance of young people.

Why had she swallowed whole the unchristian values about her? Why had she been so conformed to the world in her thinking? Christ taught clearly that the greatest person is the one who serves. Is it necessarily greater to compose a symphony than to care for a newborn baby in the wee small hours of the night?

Is it greater to win a battle recorded on pages in the books than to teach a child to read?

Luke 22:26

JULY 4

Laboratory of Love

The home is one place in society where it is not considered wrong to practice complete love in human relationships. Competition can be completely eliminated in the home. Here life is conceived and the tiny baby is lovingly cared for and cherished. Here we always try to "build up" life. We are interested in providing a wholesome, nutritious diet for our children. We want them to have constructive attitudes.

In some institutions the goal of "building up" human life is also accepted, e.g., in hospitals, schools, recreation councils, libraries, and others. In these institutions Christian love in human relationships may be practiced. But com-

191

petition and jostling for position are still too common. God grant courage to all Christians in these fields!

In business and politics it is much harder to practice complete love. The philosophy is still too much "dog eat dog." Profit and personal gain rather than love are too often the motives for action of any kind. God grant courage to all those endeavoring to serve Christ in business and government. They have a difficult job.

At the far end of the scale are organizations that apparently don't care at all about "building up" life, e.g., the crime comic and liquor industries, atomic missile programs.

Christian home builders can thank God that they are pioneers for all of society in a way. Theirs is a laboratory of love. They can set up patterns for all of society to emulate and for home members to carry into all fields.

Matthew 6:10

JULY 5

Evening Prayer

Dear Father,

Tonight I come to Thee filled with joy and knowing that Thou art the source of joy. I thank Thee for the love which surrounds and fills me, for my husband, for our children, for our parents, for Christian brothers and sisters around the world. Thou art the source of love and of all these blessings.

I pray especially for all who are bereaved and weeping on this night. Comfort and sustain them. Grant to them deep inner peace even in the midst of their sorrow.

Increase my faith to believe that as Thou hast guided in the past, Thou wilt lead in the future also.

Into Thy hands I commit my work of this day and myself this night. Amen.

Psalm 4:7, 8

JULY 6

Gifts

"Now there are varieties of gifts, but the same Spirit; and there are varieties of service, but the same Lord; and there are varieties of working, but it is the same God who inspires them all in every one."

These different spiritual gifts are given to different ones of us in the church so that we may all be perfect in the work of the Lord. To one is given the ability to speak wisely. To another, the gifts of healing.

Helen thought of the beloved minister in her own congregation whose words were always helpful and upbuilding. She thought of her Aunt Hannah, a nurse, whose very presence seemed to enable healing to take place.

Was there perhaps also the same diversity in the lesser gifts? Helen wondered. Is it right to expect all women to conduct business meetings or bake pies equally well? Should we not be more appreciative of gifts that differ from our own? Piecing beautiful quilts, singing the soprano solos in "The Messiah." Cannot both contribute to the upbuilding of the church?

I Corinthians 12:4

JULY 7

In Praise

"O taste and see that the Lord is good!" No one can tell you how good He is. You must taste Him yourself.

"Rest in the Lord, . . . wait patiently for him . . . and he shall give thee the desires of thine heart." Do not rush and hurry in the Lord. Rest in Him. Do not rush ahead of Him. Wait patiently for Him and truly He shall satisfy the deepest desires of thy heart.

"Great is the Lord, and greatly to be praised, and his greatness is unsearchable." If I could understand the atom, if I could comprehend the space in the universe, if I could fathom that God Himself became Man for our sakes, His greatness would still be unsearchable to me. "My mouth will speak the praise of the Lord, and let all . . . people bless his holy name for ever and ever."

· *Psalm 51:15*

JULY 8

Preparing for Sunday

Sunday morning! "O day of days the best!" thought Helen, as she did each week at this time. "I was glad when they said unto me, Let us go into the house of the Lord," she said with the children as she dressed them.

Sunday had always seemed special to her. As a child she had loved the vivid Bible stories her grandfather told in his sermons. She could still see Gideon wringing water out of the fleece. And she could see Peter, Grandfather's favorite character, walking on the water so long as his

194

eyes were fixed on Jesus and sinking when he looked at the water. As a child she had also enjoyed Sunday visiting with relatives and friends.

How would her own children think of Sunday as they grew older? The answer, she realized, lay largely in her and Hal's hands. It did take effort to get the preparation done on Saturday so that the house was in order and the clothes ready for church. It took effort to get up in time to have breakfast together without rush. It took effort to begin study of the Sunday-school lesson early in the week instead of on Saturday night, but it was well worth it she knew.

Psalm 122

JULY 9

As a Grain of Mustard Seed

Sometimes we cannot see at all through the murky fog around us. Then we must remind ourselves that we walk by faith, not by sight. We keep on believing, no matter what happens.

Why, thought Helen in almost despair, does evil seem so strong and powerful and good so weak? Was Machiavelli right when he said, "A man striving in every way to be good will meet his ruin among the great number who are not good"? She thought of a few women like herself trying hard to teach children the way of peace, and the tremendous propaganda they are subjected to via radio and television. She thought of a small group of nonresistant Christians in a world that seems to become more and more militaristic. A few missionaries among millions who do not believe.

A machine gun pointed at a Christian preacher. Which is more powerful? The community of Christian Indians at Schonbrunn, Ohio, in earlier days or their marauding destroyers. Which was stronger?

Helen thought ultimately of the Son of God, nailed to a cross by Roman soldiers. Which was stronger?

Luke 17:5, 6

JULY 10

Wings Like Eagles

"They who wait for the Lord shall renew their strength, they shall mount up with wings like eagles, they shall run and not be weary, they shall walk and not faint."

Women down through the generations have proved the truth of this verse! And the words and wings are ours also.

When the children are sick, these are words to think of as we take temperatures, prepare special meals, give medicine, or get up at night to soothe an aching child. *Wings like eagles!*

When a new baby joins the family and the ordinary tasks of the household seem unending because of our limited strength, these are words to think of. *They shall renew their strength.*

When death comes, and there are relatives to notify, funeral arrangements to make, others to comfort, plus all the responsibilities of daily life, these are words to remember. *They shall walk and not faint.*

Muriel Lester was to speak to a group one evening. She looked tired, for she had had what would be a busy day

196

for a woman of thirty, and she was more than twice that. She asked for fifteen minutes alone. And when she returned she looked completely rested and spoke with vitality.

Surely the Lord does not wish us to abuse our bodies by overwork. But He does promise to those who wait on Him this blessed renewal of strength in time of need.

Isaiah 40:31

✳

JULY 11

Absent Grandparents

One feature of modern life which Helen disliked particularly was the number of miles that frequently separated the generations. Children needed their grandparents. Of that she was sure. And she suspected that grandparents also needed their grandchildren. How fortunate little Timothy was to be able to benefit from the spiritual wisdom of his grandmother!

Of course, Helen reflected, parents could not accompany their children to distant mission and other fields of service far from the "home place." She wondered what she and Hal could do about it.

They could make the most of infrequent visits. For them this was once or twice a year. For many of her friends on mission fields, it was only once in many years. She could try not to envy those who could be with their parents every week or oftener.

And she could perhaps be a kind of bridge between her children and their grandparents. She could speak often to the children of Grandfather and Grandmother, showing them pictures, helping them to write letters or to send little homemade gifts. And she could try to write detailed homey letters to her and Hal's parents about such tremendous trifles as the baby's new tooth or what her toddler said about the butterfly.

And finally she and Hal could help their children "adopt" grandparents in their congregation and community, especially those who had no grandchildren of their own. And since the church is made up of brothers and sisters in Christ, thought Helen half whimsically, children of churchgoing families certainly need never lack uncles, aunts, and cousins!

II Timothy 1:5

JULY 12

A New Day

"The steadfast love of the Lord never ceases, his mercies never come to an end; they are new every morning; great is thy faithfulness."

The sun rises on a new day. For a few moments the eastern sky is a kaleidoscope of delicate color, ivories and mother-of-pearl pinks. Or perhaps the east is dimmed with heavy clouds. But the steadfast love of the Lord which has strengthened us through the night of sleep now accompanies us into a new day.

What will this day bring? Many small tasks to do? A surprise which we cannot even guess in the morning? A letter from a long-silent friend? A moment of perfect beauty? An opportunity to speak to another of Christ?

What do we take into this day? Worry? Faith? Discouragement? Joy? A resolve to give every moment of the day to the Lord?

However much our patience may be tried on this day, the Lord's mercies will not come to an end. However weak our love for another may be on this day, the Lord's love for that person and for us will remain strong and steadfast. No matter how ungrateful we may be for health, for clothing and shelter, for our easy access to the Bible, for freedom to assemble for worship—no matter how ungrateful we may be to God for all the good gifts, He will continue to shower His blessings upon us all day long.

This is a new day. The Lord has given it to us. Let us rejoice and be glad in it.

Lamentations 3:23

JULY 13

All Men Everywhere

When shall I pray? All the time.

For whom shall I pray? For all men everywhere. For Africans. For every person in Sierra Leone. For those who govern in Nigeria. For Mau Mau in Kenya. For Afrikaners in Johannesburg. For Christians in Belgian Congo. For Moslem women in Egypt. For Coptic Christians in Ethiopia. For missionaries.

When shall I pray? All the time.

For whom shall I pray? For all men everywhere. For my children. For my husband. For the people in my block or section. For our Sunday-school superintendent. For members of my Sunday-school class. For public school teachers. For the President of the United States. For all delegates to the United Nations. For clerks in the dime store. For generals in the army. For all who own stock in liquor companies. For the pope.

For all men everywhere. We ought always to pray.

I Timothy 2:1

JULY 14

A Narrow Way

Helen felt demands of her congregation and community pressing in upon her. Would she help clean the church? Would she roll bandages for relief? Would she bake a cake for the bake sale? Would she help the PTA raise money? She found herself parodying "Old MacDonald." "Here a committee, there a committee, everywhere a committee-mittee!"

"No," Helen said, knowing that she would be misunderstood at times. "No, I cannot do these hundreds of good things without crowding out the greatest one thing. My obligation is first of all to Christ, to my husband, to my children, to my home. What if I should do 'many good works' and my own children be lost to Christ and the church through lack of teaching? What if I should be 'very active in the community' and my own home become a madhouse instead of the outpost of heaven I wish it to be? No, I will try to do whatever the Lord calls me to do, whether inside or outside my home. But I cannot do all that everyone else thinks I should do."

Lord, help me to say "no" only in love. Help me to walk the way to which Thou hast called me. Help me to add

200

what you wish me to add and to cut off what you wish me to cut off. Amen.

Matthew 7:14

JULY 15

Paradox

"The most unfree people," Helen mused, "are those whose lives go off in three dozen directions at once. They are slaves to what other people will think of them. They are slaves to their own contradictory standards and desires. They are caught in a tornado of forces which nearly tear them apart. And I tend to be this kind of person."

"And the freest people are those whose lives are ordered by one principle, by one person, Christ. They can say, 'This one thing I do.' They can say, 'My eye is single.' And I want to be this kind of person."

Dear Father, help me daily to give up everything, everyone but Thee only. In this is my freedom. Amen.

Matthew 6:22, 23

JULY 16

A Mother's Prayer

Lord, I thank Thee for the many opportunities family living provides for teaching me to be unselfish. Help me to place the welfare of my children and husband above my own selfish desires. Help me to give ungrudgingly and with joy.

Let the roof of our home stretch out over the earth. Let our walls extend to include the friendless and loveless.

With gratitude I remember that Thy Son humbled Himself to become like one of us. That all through His life He healed and taught, pouring forth love and compassion. That He gave His life on the cross for our sakes. That He conquered death for us.

Though it seems almost impudent to ask, for I am all unworthy, let the same Spirit that dwelt in Him, dwell in me also and in all thy church.

Romans 8:9

JULY 17

The Church in Thy House

Helen set the table for the evening meal. The extra plate was for a Christian student from a far country. Or he had come to a far country, depending on one's vantage point. Just today he had landed in the capital, and Hal was bringing him along home to share their evening. The missionary letter that preceded him had called him "a precious jewel in Christ."

And so he was! The little boys responded immediately to his warm smile. No race prejudice in children! Later in the evening Hal and Helen helped him get accustomed to U.S. postage stamps and coins. They learned about the complicated alphabet in his country. Then the three opened the Bible and read together favorite passages of Scripture.

Now, months later, the memory of that precious Christian fellowship was still warm and glowing in Helen's mind. And it was only one bead on a long strand of similar memories. The experience seemed symbolic to Helen. However important the church building and assembling there may be, much, perhaps most, of the activity of the church—fellowship, evangelism, counseling, teaching—still takes place in homes.

I Corinthians 16:19

JULY 18

Crowned with Glory and Honor

What is the most important piece of equipment in the home? The range? The washing machine? Certainly if Helen's washing machine needed repairing, she had it repaired right away and had no guilt feelings about it!

Yet Helen herself, in charge of the washing, felt uneasy sometimes when she sat down to repair her own mind and spirit. An inner persistent voice, perhaps the legacy of pioneer forebears, scolded, "Should you be reading that book for your own pleasure when the ironing isn't done?" Yet Helen knew that if busy young mothers waited until all the housework was done, they would never get to the reading, poetry, music, painting, flowers, or whatever else gave them renewing pleasure.

Our Master in His life recognized the necessity of [coming] apart . . . [to] rest a while." Helen realized that she could not go away from her home very often to renew her mind and spirit. But she could "come . . . apart . . . and rest" through a change of activity. She could "come away" from the routine of necessary household tasks.

"After all, my washing machine was made by man,"

203

Helen reflected. "Am I not more important than inanimate objects? Was I not created by God to glorify Him forever?"

Psalm 8

✳

JULY 19

Eternal Companion

Loneliness can be like sharp teeth gnawing into one's stomach. The loneliness of the city. Millions of faces in crowds rushing in and out of subways, in shops, on streets. And not a familiar face among them. Proud, self-sufficient houses in the suburbs. And no one with whom the young bride can share in conversation. Loneliness of the missionary or student in a foreign land where even the speech and customs are alien. Loneliness of having no one who understands.

To whom can we pour out our hearts? Who will understand us? With whom can we share? Where can we find much-needed courage?

Surely Jesus Himself was the supremely lonely person. How He longed to share with His disciples, but they were "not [yet] able to bear" what He had for them. In Gethsemane He was alone.

Yet there was One to whom He could and did turn. And that One is our Father also. The Lord is always near us. His ear is always ready to listen, and His wings are ever covering us.

He enables lonely people to pray with St. Francis: "Help me long not so much to be understood as to understand, to be loved as to love; for it is in giving that we receive, and in dying that we are born to eternal life."

Psalm 16:7-11

JULY 20

Small Endless Affairs

". . . The humble life of tiresome and easy achievements; this life, which, precisely on account of monotony and lack of great things to be done, exacts so much charity, so great a power of seeing God's eternal will back of the whole mass of small endless affairs, so as every day to live in the Sunday's Spirit."

These words by a biographer of St. Francis might well describe the life of today's homemaker, Helen reflected. Always there are the small endless affairs. Dishes to do. Picking up in the living room. Shoes to polish. A grocery list to make out. And an A in Latin is not required for the doing of these tasks.

Yet much grace is required. And much love. "For it is God which worketh in you both to will and to do of his good pleasure" (Philippians 2:13).

JULY 21

The Children Lead Us

Can we ever praise the Lord enough for our children! What hard work and joy they bring into our lives! How often they bring us to our knees in humility! What laughter they sprinkle through our days!

"Muzzer, I can't find my tricycle. Oh, its wheels are peeking around the corner."

"Is Mommy sad?"

"Muzzer, may I help you?"

"Thank you for grandpas, and for Mommy and Daddy, and for Rosie and Debby, and for my teddy bear, and for my books, and—"

Luke 18:16

JULY 22

Faithful Today

Immediately after persecutor Saul became Paul, the Lord gave him something to do. The Lord did not immediately ask Paul to testify before King Agrippa, to present the Gospel to the Gentiles, or to be imprisoned in Rome. He asked him to go to the next city and wait for further direction. Yet Paul's later assignments would probably not have come to him if he had been unfaithful in this first simple one.

As Helen thought of Paul and his assignments she wondered. And she found some of the answers: "What does the Lord ask of me today?" Teach your children and your neighbors' children diligently. Encourage your despairing friend. Open your home to the stranger in your midst. Exercise faith. Remember the hungry and the illiterate. Study to show yourself approved unto God. Whatever your hand finds to do, do it with your might.

What does the Lord ask of me today? Unless I am

faithful in insignificant-seeming tasks today, I cannot be assigned to what the Lord wishes me to do tomorrow.

Acts 9:6

✳

JULY 23

Query

An old Quaker query asks, "Are you endeavoring to make your home a place of friendliness, refreshment, and peace, where God becomes more real to all who dwell there and to those who visit it?"

Helen remembered a home she used to visit each Friday afternoon after a busy week of teaching. The minute she stepped inside the door of that home all hustle and bustle, all tension, melted away. The air itself seemed pervaded with a deep peace. Much far-reaching work for the church had its origin here. But the atmosphere was always fun-loving, easy, deeply aware of God.

"And what about our home?" Helen wondered. "Is it a place of friendliness, refreshment, and peace? The peace here is certainly not synonymous with quiet. It is often a place of noise and scattered toys. Is it a place where the children learn as naturally as breathing to love God and the brotherhood? Is it a place where they learn to share the Gospel with others, where they learn to feed the hungry and clothe the naked? Is it a place where others are welcome? Is it a place where God becomes more real to us daily? Is it a place where God becomes more real to each visitor?"

Cleanliness, order, efficient scheduling help much. But prayer is absolutely necessary.

II Chronicles 6:2

JULY 24

Mastering One's Body

"But I keep under my body, and bring it into subjection: lest that by any means, when I have preached to others, I myself should be a castaway" (I Corinthians 9:27).

One would think that after twenty or thirty years of being a Christian, one could relax the battle against sin and feel secure. But no. Life remains for the Christian a battle, a struggle, a vigorous, victorious wrestling with sin. Even after years of service to Christ, it is possible to slip in a moment.

If it becomes impossible for me to say "no" to a piece of chocolate cake, then my appetite rather than Christ is master of my body at that time. I never reach the place where it is not possible for me to fall even into gross sin.

Prayer, fasting, Bible reading, service, fellowship with one another are techniques that God's people in the past have found necessary. Each day requires vigilance. God forbid that after many years of living for Christ, I should become a castaway.

I Corinthians 9:27

Giving Up Isaac

Renunciation for Christ's sake seems to be a principle of the Christian life. Like Abraham of old, we must come to the place where we are willing to place our dearly loved Isaacs on the altar of God. One person's Isaac may be a cherished gift. After anguish of soul Gerard Manley Hopkins was able to give up writing because God called him to something else. Isaac may indeed be a son or daughter. Isaac may be a pathway.

After agony and inward turmoil we finally climb the mountain to say, "Here, Lord, is Isaac." There follows the surge of joy. Lo, Isaac is restored to us! We see Isaac with new eyes. Isaac is never the same again, for we are never the same again.

Genesis 22:16-18; Matthew 10:39

JULY 26

Praise and Prayer for Guidance

Almighty God, our Father, Thou art great. Thou art good. Thou art love. Thou art Creator of the Milky Way, of the unknown reaches of the universe, and of the wayside wild flowers, goldenrod and Queen Anne's lace. Thou art Creator of many-tasting foods. All that we see and touch is a window through which we may see Thy greatness and glory.

Let me now align my little life, my plans and purposes

with Thy eternal plans and purposes that we may all be
one in Thee. Amen.

Psalm 146

JULY 27

Is Not Life More Than Food?

"Is not life more than food, and the body more than
clothing?"

We cook. We set tables. We wash dishes. We plan
menus and buy groceries. We can or put food into the
Deepfreeze.

We wash. We iron. We mend.

Do we pray? Do we read the Scripture? Do we take
time for rich fellowship with our friends? Do we play with
our children? Do we spend time with those we love?

Do we open our lives to those in need? Do we share
Christ with others?

"Is not life more than food, and the body more than
clothing" (Matthew 6:25)?

JULY 28

Praise for Fellowship of Saints

Dear Father,

I thank and praise Thee for the fellowship of the saints.
For those who have so often shared my joys and comforted
me in sorrow. For those whose words have encouraged me.

For those who have given me wise counsel. For comrades in prayer. For brothers and sisters in Christ whose love has often covered my bleak failures.

I praise Thee for strengthening times of shared worship —on beaches, on hillsides, in quiet rooms. Help all of us to keep the solemn promises we have made to Thee in these moments. Let us remember this strengthening brotherhood when we seem to be alone in the fray. For every one of this great company of fellow believers around the world, I praise and thank Thee, Lord. Amen.

Philippians 1:3-5

JULY 29

Prayer of Intercession for Friends

To Thee who healest broken hearts I commit these friends. I cannot understand. But Thou art all understanding. I cannot comfort. But Thou art the great Comforter. I pray for

Annetta, whose husband has not lived to see their children out of baby days,

Charlotte, who has heard the words, "You will never be able to have a child of your own,"

Betty, who has wanted a child so badly, and time after time has been unable to see her baby reach its birthday,

Lois, whose long-awaited child is a Mongoloid,

Barbara, who never mentions at all that her husband is cruelly unloving and unsympathetic,

Ruth, who knows firsthand ill health and economic reverses,

211

Nancy, whose young fiance has been suddenly taken away.

We thank Thee for the tears of Thy Son with Mary and Martha when their brother Lazarus had died. Enable us all to trust Thee in dark hours as well as in light and to praise Thee in sorrow as well as in joy. Amen.

John 11:35

JULY 30

Keeper at Home

This week Helen's mail had included two attractive job offers. As she reread them, trying to phrase answers, the lure of the classroom was strong for a moment. Yet she had no doubt about her answer. There would come a time when it could be "yes." But now it was "no." Her children were young. She was certain that to turn them over to others every day was not God's will for her. God had given them to her to mother, teach, and enjoy.

"You put various things on a scale," Helen mused. "More income, more stimulating contacts with adults, seemingly more status, opportunity to contribute in a small way to the lives of many people. Physical tiredness through trying to do two jobs, resultant irritability and increased possibility of family disharmony, being away from the children in these wonderful years, missing the joy and golden opportunity of contributing much to a few people, 'long-range contribution to the kingdom.'"

Helen could not and did not wish to make other people's decisions. But she knew that for her a full-time job outside her home during these years would cost too much. Her husband and children would pay for it. And she would have to give up that priceless treasure of inner peace.

No, it wouldn't be hard to answer the letters.

Philippians 4:20

Dear Lord, we pray for those women who must earn a living for their families. For widows. For those whose husbands are ill. Grant to them wisdom, courage, and energy. Help us in love to fulfill our obligations to them.

We praise Thee for the good and perfect gifts that are ours through Thy hand. For salvation in Christ. For fellowship in the church. For joy in simple living. For the hope of glorious things to come.

Grant to all of us guidance as we attempt to find our places in our homes, churches, and communities. May Thy Son always be glorified through us. Amen.

JULY 31

A Prayer

Giver of joy, we praise Thee.

We praise Thee, for Thou art pure beauty, unadulterated holiness.

We praise Thee, for Thou art unending love and unlimited forgiveness.

May our hearts and homes glow with Thy presence.

May our daily lives be anthems of praise to Thee.

May our sons and daughters in the flesh and in the faith grow strong in Thee.

Enable us to count everything joy, even suffering and testing, until that glorious day when our knowledge of Thee becomes complete and we know even as we are known. Amen.

Titus 2:5

SO GREAT A CLOUD OF WITNESSES

Miriam Sieber Lind

AUGUST 1

Only One Sorrow

"I'm no saint!" she laughed ruefully. And so badly has this good word suffered from misuse by thoughtless people that behind the admission one senses a further boast—"And I wouldn't want to be one."

But what *is* a saint?

Thomas Kepler, in his Preface to *The Fellowship of the Saints,* suggests that the life of each Christian saint is conditioned in ten ways, a number of which follow:

First of all, he sees Christianity as the answer to his problems of adjustment to himself and to society, and as such he is lovingly loyal to it. He lives joyously, with an air of freedom, recognizing that he is completely dependent on God. He attempts to imitate Christ in all he does. He is wide open to receive the love of God, and as a result he gives himself freely in love to the unfortunate and loveless about him. He believes that Christianity, far from being an impossible ideal, is a practical necessity in living in an unchristian society, and that God has actually worked and does work in history. He acknowledges all races and classes and creeds of men as potential Christian brothers.

He practices devotion, not to be removed from the world, but to be more truly fitted to help better that world. Finally, he is a *radiant* person. He is, Kepler says, using the definition of a child familiar with the figures on stained glass windows, "a man the light shines through."

She read these conditions, and she remembered the words Maritain used in speaking of Leon Bloy; that there is only one sorrow—not to be a saint. She felt the sting of that sorrow as she prayed: *God, I'm no saint—but I want to be one. I want to be a woman the light shines through!*

"Look to him, and be radiant" (Psalm 34:5, RSV).

AUGUST 2

Surrounded!

She wanted to be a saint—but only seconds after she had prayed that the door of her lips might be kept, she lost her patience upon discovering that her child had emptied the entire bookcase in order to have a "nice smooth super-highway."

She wanted to be a saint—but her neighbor made a remark, a designed remark, she was sure, and the cold fingers of unlove tightened about her heart.

She wanted to be a saint, but even when she did what seemed to be a good thing, her motives rose up inwardly in silent damnation of the deed.

She wanted to be a saint—but it was one of those days—oh, it was hopeless, all she had to put up with inside herself and outside. No one could be a saint!

No one? Composing herself before God, she had to

216

admit that she was surrounded with saints. There were voices from the dim mists of beginning time, speaking to her of faith. There were echoes from the dank cloisters of the Middle Ages, speaking to her of devotion. There were the radiant faces of contemporary saints, speaking to her of the reality of the kingdom of God on earth. Few were men and women of intellectual genius, she knew. There were "not many mighty." They were simply ordinary people like herself who opened their lives to God and found themselves saved from themselves and joyously enslaved to God. They were people of the single eye, the pure in heart, who—having caught a vision of God—saw nothing, and meant nothing, but God. She read their story in Hebrews eleven and twelve, and prayed with the writer:

"Since we are surrounded . . . let us also . . . run" (Hebrews 12:1, RSV).

AUGUST 3

Take Up and Read

The children's voices across the wall came to the struggling Augustine in his own garden of agony, "Take up and read . . . take up and read." He, interpreting this as the very voice of God, opened the copy of the Scriptures beside him and saw the answer to the last doubt that was keeping him from his "rest in God."

For Augustine, ever a reader, to turn to a book for answers to problems, for growth, and for enlightenment was the natural habit of a lifetime. He was not one to dismiss lightly, with a "haven't time" shrug, the opportunity for fellowship with the great minds of the ages whose

217

words and works again spring to life on the printed page.

She thought back on her own tortuous path upward. She saw that many of the signposts which had guided her were books—the voices of those living and dead, who had been over this particular way before her. And she was glad—glad that though she had made many wrong choices along the way, and would make more, she had often chosen to leave the unwashed windows of her house to wash the windows of her soul through the reading of a book.

"Take up and read," the Voice comes to her; again it comes quite clearly, "Tell *them* to take up and read." And she knows that a part of her life's task is to obey those words. "Tell them—the women so careful of houses and health, yet so careless of cobwebs in the mind and malnutrition of the soul—tell them to take up and read. Read the clean, pure Word of God. Read also the testimony of those who have tried to follow and interpret that Word. Make the acquaintance of the saints living in time and beyond time, who are speaking. Hear them—from Paul to Augustine to Underhill. Take up and read!"

"Bring . . . the books, and above all the parchments" (II Timothy 4:13, RSV).

AUGUST 4

The Speaking Dead

When she was a child they always told her that Abel's sacrifice was acceptable because it was a lamb, a type of Christ; Cain's unacceptable because it was grain. Though she never said so, that story always made her feel vaguely

218

uneasy. God was a stickler for details, and—when it came right down to it—rather arbitrary. Abel never spoke to her as long as this interpretation prevailed.

Years later a friend went over the story with her. "Look at this carefully," he explained. "The Lord had regard for *Abel* and his offerings but for *Cain* . . . . Do you not see that even the finest of the flock would have been unacceptable to God, had Abel himself been unacceptable?"

She will always be grateful to the man who switched on the controls so that the voice of Abel could come to her, distinct across the centuries:

It is the motive that makes the sacrifice acceptable.

It is the life that hallows the deed.

It is the being that consecrates the doing.

She thought, Abel is dead—and he is speaking to me! And she prayed: *God of all time and eternity, open my inner ears to the voices of the sainted dead. They were human—even as I; they made mistakes—even as I. But they heard you speak, and they listened with the whole man. They heard you speak, and they answered in lives of freely given obedience, even though that obedience meant physical death. In return you have ordained that their mouths be not stopped by death, but that their words should go out "unto the ends of the world"—even to me, at this time, at this place!*

"He died, but through his faith he is still speaking" (Hebrews 11:4, RSV).

Make It Easy

"I wanta die easy when I die . . . "

"Don't we all?" she used to think as she heard the plaintive tenor of the *Wings over Jordan Choir* in the lovely old spiritual.

"Make my journey ea—sy when I die. . . ."

And whenever she read in the Bible the thumbnail biography of Enoch, she was touched with the simple eloquence of the words, "and he was not; for God took him."

Who has not wished that his crossing "from out our bourne of time and place" would be that easy? But even if we knew it would be—would we be satisfied? No, she thought. We not only "wanta" *die* easy—we "wanta" *live* easy too. We want to be eligible for the pure garb of the saints without scrubbing behind the ears—and elbows too. We want to be on the winning side without having to lift a finger in the fight. We want a magic religion—rabbits out of a hat, the flying carpet, Open sesame!—just say the right words and the grace of God will set us afire!

We are inflamed by the beauty of "and he was not; for God took him"; we would rather ignore the implications of "Enoch walked with God." We want the pleasures of sainthood without the bitterness of discipleship.

Sören Kierkegaard doubted that there is such a thing as being a Christian and not a disciple. Dietrich Bonhoeffer, who was later executed, wrote in stark simplicity that when Christ calls a man to be a disciple He calls him to die.

O God (she prayed), *seeing I am surrounded, I can ask neither to live easy nor to "die easy." Only this—in life and death, I would walk with Thee.*

"Whoever loses his life for my sake will find it" (Matthew 16:25, RSV).

*

AUGUST 6

Not Knowing, But Going

Abram, I read your story in Genesis, and its commentary in Hebrews, and you speak to me. You speak to me—a child of the twentieth century, set down in a bustling, harried civilization where the whirring machines and tight schedules all but eliminate the chance for such meditation as you must have known on the wide, barren plains toward which you set your face. In my time there are watchwords like "security" and "plan for the future" and "retire on so many dollars a month."

Such are my times, and the temptation is to think of myself as a child of my times rather than a pilgrim of eternity. Where will we be in five years? How will our children turn out? Will the money stretch for the needs of a growing family? What about the fear, the want, the unrest in the world?

But you speak to me, Abram, and the voice is still and small, like the gentle rain dripping after the confusion of the electric storm. You speak—confiding to me the secret of the conservation of soul energy: "Look to the future, not knowing, but going. This is the very glory of the walk with God."

O Expansive Adventurer, it is your secret that enables me to refrain from fretting to know what lies ahead. "How can we know the way?" cried Thomas, symbol of the millions of anxious humanity from your time to mine, who have chosen to walk by sight, not by faith. But I will

221

follow you, Abram, willingly leaving all my tomorrows in the hands of your God. And I am joyously assured that, though this road be "uphill all the way," yet with God it will be a way strewn with surprises and splendors.

"Commit your way to the Lord;
trust in him, and he will act" (Psalm 37:5, RSV).

AUGUST 7
God and the Impossible

From the beginning of her existence life had imposed upon her certain limitations. At the moment of conception her features, her sex, and many of the factors of her life in the world were determined. As a child, however, she had naively interpreted "With God nothing shall be impossible" as meaning that if she only prayed, her dead father would be waiting at home for her when she came in from her paper route. Or her stringy yellow-white hair would suddenly be black curls. God was the Master-Magician—a magician, however, who never seemed to pull out of his bag of tricks any that would benefit *her*.

When she was a child, she thought as a child.

But she was to discover and keep discovering more fully all her life, that life "with God" could be a continuing Miracle of Grace. She kept seeing Insurmountables and Unthinkables and Impossibles disappear as mountains moved before her very eyes—"with God." She saw one who was dear to her "himself receive power" to rise and shine out of a situation so desperate that she had believed it almost useless to pray. And one day—after she had prayed that she "herself might receive power" to love someone whom for years she had politely resented, the Miracle happened again. And again it happened, and again.

After which she concluded that in comparison, the fact that Sarah "herself received power" to bear a child even when she was "past the age"—was a minor miracle indeed!

"You shall see greater things than these" (John 1:50, RSV).

∗

AUGUST 8

God Meant It for Good

I have taken up and read the story of Joseph and his brothers. Still, as in childhood, the unfolding drama grips me, and I cannot bear to stop reading until I have finished the story.

I follow Joseph from his beginnings—his birth into a divided home which sets the stage for the jealousies and violence to follow. Here is Joseph, the precocious dreamer bating his brothers. (As I read I want to restrain him with a little motherly advice: Joseph, Joseph, there is no need to tell your brothers of your dreams—don't flaunt your superior powers—whether they be of God or of your own arrogant imagination!) Here is Joseph, the forlorn youngster stripped and sold as a slave. (Your poise, young Joseph, will stand you in good stead here!) Next, Joseph, the upright servant of Pharaoh, chooses integrity and prison rather than compromise. Now Joseph, restored to court, proves a faithful ruler of Egypt, putting his insight and wisdom at the disposal of his adopted country. At last comes the heart-rending, yet beautiful scene where Joseph,

223

the forgiving brother and compassionate provider, is re-united with the ones who long before meant to kill him—and he becomes their savior.

One by one the pictures of this Prince of God flash upon the inward eye. And as they do, I think wistfully—what a sweet fresh air would be in the world if all the wronged of all nations should say to their enemies, with tears, "You meant to do us evil, but God meant it for good."

"In everything God works for good with those who love him" (Romans 8:28, RSV).

Seeing the Invisible

("Speak to me, Moses. Speak to me out of your experi-ence, that I may see if there be any word of yours that is for me—at such a time as this.")

O child of the twentieth century—what have I to say to you? To you who are bedded down in comforts; who accept your winter homes and your summer homes as your due; to you who, when among your women friends, can-not carry on a conversation about any but corruptible things: meals, clothes, colors, draperies, conveniences, houses, budgets. How can I speak to you?

For I confess that I was only a stranger, an exile, a pilgrim on the earth. True, even in my time there was the glitter, the shine and the show, the illusion of reality. And as with you, the choice was before me to settle down and enjoy a *lifetime,* or on the other hand, to be satisfied with nothing less than Life itself. But I sensed that the pleas-ures of a life at home in the world are fleeting, and that there is a wealth more real than the treasures of Egypt (Egypt in my day, or America in yours)—a wealth of the Spirit to be had for the taking.

By faith, I chose the way of the greater treasure, though for a time it meant abuse and ill-treatment. Yet I saw what you hardly can see, wearing, as you do, your possessions and your at-homeness like blinders. I saw clearly that what is seen with the physical eye is temporal; but that the vistas open to the spiritual eye stretch on into eternity. To possess this eternal perspective was to be able to count my sufferings as light indeed. Truly I set the Invisible One always before me, and seeing Him, I was not moved from a straight course through Time to Life.

"I keep the Lord always before me" (Psalm 16:8, RSV).

AUGUST 10

Make Way for Harlots

"Christ came," a Christian writer has said, "to save men from religion." It is an arresting experience to read the life of Christ in this light. To whom was Jesus most gentle, understanding, forgiving? And who was it that brought the fiery words of condemnation from the "gentle" Jesus?

I have taken up and read the Gospel story again today, and all too clearly the pattern envolves: He was the friend of the outsider, the adulterer, the mistaken, the skeptical seeker, the hated tax collector, the sinner! It was the "Pillar of the Church" who tried His patience, and brought from Him some of the most terrible denunciations recorded in the Bible.

O Rahab, today I have taken up and read *your* story, too. I do not know what forced you into the evil of selling your body for a few pieces of silver—but I know that "good people" may have been responsible. Yet by a simple act of goodness performed in faith, you have been chosen to the list of the immortal faithful, a list from which many "better" women are omitted!

Thank you, Lord Jesus, for being a lover of sinners— that leaves room for me. Thank you for coming to save us from the holier-than-thou stance, the shell of godliness, the glib "spiritual" vocabulary, the "right" clothes and the "right" people and the "right" side of the tracks. Accept the gratitude of sinners for saving us—Rahab and the rest of us—from "religion"!

"I have not come to call the righteous, but sinners to repentance" (Luke 5:32, RSV).

AUGUST 11

I Acknowledge

I have taken up and read the story of David. It is not a pretty story. There are unglossed details which, if written today of a prominent church leader, would not be printed by our religious publications. There is war, revenge, lust, contempt, downright murder. And there is more.

Yet of this David it was said that his heart was perfect before God. Could it be, I muse, that part of the explanation may be in these two words—"I acknowledge"? For, oh, how devious and versatile is pride! How deeply its texture is ingrained in our nature! How frantically we will scramble and scrape the Scripture for texts to justify our own wrongs and the wrongs of those we love! How hard it is to say, even to our little children, "I have done wrong. Forgive me"! How tearing it is to admit that another has surpassed us in our own field!

David, king of Israel, surrounded with riches and honor, could have followed in the steps of his predecessor, refusing to see himself as only "a king under The King." But it was David the king who reiterated, "Thou art my Lord; I have no good apart from thee. . . . The Lord is my rock . . . my stronghold . . . his kingdom rules over all. . . . I acknowledge."

But if it was greatness in a powerful king to acknowledge the King above all, perhaps it was even a greater virtue that such a famous leader should so freely acknowledge his sin. It may be that the heart of David was never more perfect before God than in that moment when Nathan dramatically pointed to him, "Thou art the man!" and David cried in answer the poignant "Have mercy upon me, O God. . . . For I acknowledge my transgressions: and my sin is ever before me. . . ."

O God, my King, I desire a heart perfect before Thee. Help me to open the unyielding doors of pride, that I may fully and freely acknowledge my sin and my salvation!

"My Lord and my God" (John 20:28).

AUGUST 12

Under the Fig Trees

"Can there any good thing come out of Nazareth?" retorted Nathanael when he was told of one Jesus of Nazareth. Perhaps it was with a wry yet affectionate smile that Jesus welcomed this outspoken man with the words, "Behold an Israelite indeed, *in whom is no guile!*" Ah, these Nathanaels—so honest that they do not consider it right to withhold an opinion—kind or unkind, solicited or not! But if Nathanael was quick to blurt out an opinion (before "observing with care" of whom he spoke, to whom he spoke, and how, and when, and where), he was just as quick to acknowledge that something good *had* come out of Nazareth, something Supremely Good.

I have taken up and read the story of Nathanael's first encounter with Jesus; it moves me newly, deeply. And I think, as with Nathanael, so it is with us. The Eternal Christ has seen each of us under our own fig tree—and He has marked us for His own. He has perceived our weakness, probed our potential, and accepted us—all that we are, the whole package:

> . . . all, the world's coarse thumb
> And finger failed to plumb,
> So passed in making up the main account;
> All instincts immature,
> All purposes unsure,
> That weighed not as his work, yet swelled the man's
>   amount:
> Thoughts hardly to be packed
> Into a narrow act,
> Fancies that broke through language and escaped;
> All I could never be,
> All, men ignored in me,
> This, I was worth to God, whose wheel the pitcher
>   shaped.

From "Rabbi Ben Ezra" by Robert Browning

O Thou Discerning Christ, I am aware that Thou hast seen me under my fig tree; hast weighed me; and hast accepted me for what I am and what I can be. May I be eager to rise up, courageous to follow.

"Thou dost beset me behind and before, and layest thy hand upon me" (Psalm 139:5, RSV).

AUGUST 13

To Keep and Ponder

Blest as she was above all women, there was much that she could keep and ponder: The birth of the Child, under strange and haunting circumstances. The visit of the Personages from the East. The voice of old Simeon as he held her Son and quavered, "Now lettest thou thy servant depart in peace." And all the treasures of the hidden years at Nazareth, about which we can only guess, but which were hers to keep.

Then there were the puzzling and hurtful memories. Her Child looking at her with that odd, ancient look of one seasoned in living and wisdom—"Do you not know that I must be about my Father's business?" And even this was nothing compared to that later time when with one stroke He seemed to brush away His entire family—"My mother and my brothers? He who does the will of God— *they* are my mother and my brothers and sisters!"

In that instant Mary must have realized, if she had not done so before, that her Child had never been hers. It was one of those sayings which was thrust into her heart to keep and ponder, whether or no.

I have taken up and read the story of Mary's mother-hood. I see how similar to those of every mother were the memories given her to keep and ponder; from the shining treasures of babyhood to the puzzling shapes of adolescence, to the painful thorns of maturity when she must realize that the child, now man, is not a possession of hers, nor indeed ever has been.

As I read and meditate, I pray that I may sense the real relationship between my children and me. And I hope that when we are no longer parent and child, but brother and sister in the kingdom of God, I shall joyfully relinquish each child to God.

"And a sword will pierce through your own soul also" (Luke 2:35, RSV).

AUGUST 14

Bread—or Hyacinths?

"A whole year's wages! It could have been sold and the money given to the poor!" Even as the whole house was being filled with the sweetness of the ointment—and more, the fragrance of a deed unsurpassed in its reckless beauty—even then, the crass Judas mumbled his complaint.

The spirit of Judas' "It could have been sold" is still being echoed in our churches and their charities today, I reflect, as I have taken up and read the striking account of Mary's devotion. There are always those who will dampen a giver's enthusiasm by saying or implying, "You shouldn't have—you can't afford it!" Or, "It should be something *practical*."

"If thou hast two loaves," says the Eastern proverb, "sell

230

one and buy hyacinths to feed thy soul." And, we would add—to feed the soul of another!

God, grant me this grace, that I may be numbered among the Marys of the world—the foolhardy givers, the openhearted lovers, the buyers of hyacinths for the soul, even at risk of starvation for the body. Let me not finger the price tags, nor haggle and strain; nor give with my hands only to recall the gift a thousand times in my heart. Let me be one of Thy fools—opening myself to others without hesitation over propriety or presumption. This I would do—this I would be—for have I not an example in Thee— the most carelessly reckless lover of all, and the most extravagant of givers?

"For God so loved the world that he gave his only Son" (John 3:16, RSV).

Of Friendship

She had taken up and read the *Confessions* of Augustine. And when she came to the account of the death of his friend, behold, it touched a tender sore within her.

Now this was a friendship "sweet above all the sweetness of life," and when it ended in death, the young Augustine was in black grief. Whatever he looked on, he says, had the air of death. "My eyes sought him everywhere, but he was not granted them." He wondered how it could be that others should live when such a one was dead! He recalls vividly the torments of grief—"I bore about a torn and bleeding soul, yet where to repose it, I found not." Only years later, after finding his repose in God, could he

231

evaluate that first terrible experience of grief. Then he observes that it had pierced so deeply because he had "spilt out his soul, as on the sand" in loving a person as if he were never to die!

As she read this, she thought of her own grief over losses. She thought of the quality of her present friendships. She remembered the words she had read somewhere: "He only is fit for friendship who can get along without it." She recalled what Thomas Kelly wrote—that friendships which do not have their source in God are incomplete, open-ended. And she prayed with Augustine:

"Blessed is he that loveth Thee, and his friend in Thee, and his enemy for Thee. For he alone loses no dear one to whom all are dear, in Him who is never lost."

"In life and in death they were not divided" (II Samuel 1:23, RSV).

AUGUST 16

A Long Time in the Way

(At the close of the fourteenth century, there sprang up in Holland a spiritual group called the Brethren of the Common Life. These laymen, under the preaching of one Gerard Groote, gave themselves to the living of the intense life of discipleship. Some formed lay brotherhoods; others later established religious houses, taking on particular rules and disciplines. From this background came Thomas a Kempis, who actually issued the famous Imitation of Christ, *though the contents are thought to be the words of Groote.)*

I have taken up and read the *Imitation of Christ,* and as

I read I think, "Stop, a Kempis—you are probing too deeply! Too much of what you say finds a target in my own lazy will, in my own wayward affections, in my own uncommitted mind." Yet I read on, knowing that God, who at different times and in different manners has spoken to His people, is today speaking to me through Preacher Groote. I write down one line on which I meditate:

"Thou hast good cause to be ashamed in looking upon the life of Jesus Christ, seeing thou hast not as yet endeavored to conform thyself more unto him, though thou hast been a long time in the way of God."

And I pray with the Preacher:

Speak Thou unto me, to the comfort, however imperfect, of my soul, and to the amendment of my whole life, and to thy praise and glory and honor everlasting.

"Let us leave the elementary doctrines of Christ and go on to maturity" (Hebrews 6:1, RSV).

AUGUST 17

Lord, Have Mercy upon Us

(It is 1498, and in a prison in Florence, Italy, Girolamo Savonarola awaits death on the false charge of heresy. As Psalm 51 opens to his inward eye in the darkened cell, he pours forth his soul in a great "Miserere"—excerpts of which follow.)

Have mercy upon me, O God—"Have mercy upon me, O God. Not according to a small measure of Thy mercy. For this is the small measure of Thy mercy, when Thou deliverest men from their bodily woes. But Thy mercy is great when Thou liftest men above the heights of the earth. . . ."

Wash me throughly from mine iniquity, and cleanse me from my sin—"I confess, O Lord, that once Thou hast put away mine iniquity. A second time hast Thou put it away. Thou hast washed me a thousand times. Wash me again from mine iniquity, because again I have fallen. . . . Wash me, that Thou mayest take away, not the crime and the guilt alone, but likewise the fuel of my sins. . . ."

Create in me a clean heart—"Create such a heart in me, O God, . . . that, such as it cannot be by nature, such it may become through grace. . . ."

Restore unto me the joy of thy salvation; and . . . [establish] me with thy free spirit—"Who, therefore, asketh of Thee carnal things asketh small things. But whoso demandeth spiritual things verily demandeth great things. But he who asketh the joy of Thy salvation asketh the greatest of all."

(In closing, Savonarola breathes the prayer of all martyrs from the catacomb Christians of the first century to the Kikuyu Christians of the twentieth century:)

"Establish me with Thy free Spirit, that I may be able to persevere in Thy obedience, and to give my life for Thee."

(Following his imprisonment, Savonarola is hanged, and his body is burned and thrown into the Arne.)

Lord, have mercy upon us.

Psalm 51

Angels Abroad—Devils at Home

It was a celibate French bishop who, in 1609, was responsible for one of the greatest devotional books ever addressed to women: *Introduction to the Devout Life.* Although Francis of Sales helped to found a contemplative order for women, his spiritual exercises are addressed to women who, being in the midst of secular life, yet desire to commit themselves more deeply to God.

It was not Francis' aim to encourage a "convent piety" in these women, nor the sort of glib religiosity whose addicts are, as he says, "perpetually interlarding their conversation with pious words and sayings." He keeps reminding those who come to him for counsel that only the piety which is united with good works is attractive.

Sick people, he declares, will recognize that piety as genuine which cares for them and comforts them in their need. Children will recognize that which makes a gentler, more understanding mother. Husbands will know that their wives are truly growing in the matter of religious devotion when these wives show a greater love and sweetness to them.

Francis urges upon Philothea to learn to live without being angry and instead, to lay up a store of meekness and kindliness. This stored sweetness is to be used, not primarily among strangers, but with one's own neighbors and household: "a sweetness," he says, "terribly lacking to some who are as angels abroad and devils at home. . . ."

She took up and read *Introduction to the Devout Life,* and repeatedly was she smitten, and repeatedly did she question, "Francis of Sales, are you speaking to *me?*"

"Walk in love" (Ephesians 5:2).

Spoken to My Condition

From *The Journal of George Fox* I have taken up and read: "When all my hopes in . . . all men were gone, so that I had nothing outwardly to help me, nor could I tell what to do; O! then I heard a voice which said, 'There is one, even Christ Jesus, that can speak to thy condition.'"

Father of us all, I thank you for revealing in Jesus what God is and what man can be. I thank you for the insight of such saints as George Fox to whose condition Jesus spoke, just as He does to mine. I thank you for filling the "God-sized hole" in our hearts by means of one Christ Jesus. I thank you that He is constantly speaking to my condition, answering needs, uncovering uglinesses, revealing Truth, to the comfort—and, yes, to the discomfort and the conversion of my life. Amen.

"This poor man cried, and the Lord heard him, and saved him out of all his troubles" (Psalm 34:6, RSV).

Confidentially Yours

Into my hand has been given a small book—*Maxims of the Saints,* by Francois Fénelon. I take up and read:

"I think you cannot treat God with too much confidence. Tell Him all that is in your heart, as one unloads one's heart to a dear friend of all that gives it pain or pleasure. Tell Him your troubles, that He may comfort you; tell Him your joys, that He may sober them; tell Him your longings, that He may purify them; tell Him your mislikings, that He may help you to conquer them; talk to Him of your temptations, that He may shield you from them; show Him all the wounds of your heart, that He may heal them. . . . If you thus pour out to Him all your weakness, needs, and troubles, there will be no lack of what to say; you will never exhaust this subject, it is continually being renewed. People who have no secrets from each other never want subjects of conversation. . . . The heart of each speaks to the other; they pour out, so to say, one into another. Blessed are they who attain to such familiar, unreserved intercourse with God! . . .

"In proportion as you talk to Him He will talk to you; and often you should be silent and let Him speak, so that you may listen in the stillness of your heart . . . (and) the Spirit of Truth will teach you inwardly all that Jesus Christ teaches you outwardly in the Gospel."

"Let us then with confidence draw near to the throne of grace, that we may receive mercy and find grace to help in time of need" (Hebrews 4:16, RSV).

AUGUST 21

Dominus Est

A friend writes to me: "I find that when I am open to God He speaks to me in the most ordinary circumstances, and through the most common people!"

Lewis Sherrill in *The Struggle of the Soul* suggests that the circumstances of life which surround us and require of us a decision to grow are the very "garments of God" in which He confronts us. I like that. I like to know that God has a word for me, that He is active in every occurrence of my life . . . that He stands under the guise of this sorrow, that joy; this dryness, that consolation; this duty, that pleasure; to teach me, to convict me, to make me aware of Himself, and to lead me ever into fuller Truth.

The seventeenth-century saint, Jean Pierre de Caussade, reminds us that the same Jesus who walked with the unknowing two on the road to Emmaus and who cooked breakfast for the disheartened fishermen still surprises undiscerning souls.

"At every occurrence," he suggests, "we should say: *Dominus est*—it is the Lord; and in all circumstances we should find a gift from God."

Lord—what is Thy gift for me—at this difficult, or dry, or exalted instant? Open my eyes—that I may see!

"And their eyes were opened and they recognized him" (Luke 24:31, RSV).

AUGUST 22

These Absurd Characters

I have taken up and read William Law's *A Serious Call to a Devout and Holy Life,* where I have met:

Caelia. Caelia is always talking about her troubles—her poor health, how rudely she is treated, how much she must spend on medicines and doctor's calls—how *miserable* she is most of the time. Of her, Law says that the only real tormentor she has is her own spirit, and that a little Christian humility would take care of all her aches and pains.

Flavia. Flavia, Law says, would be "a miracle of piety" if she paid half as much attention to her soul as to the occasional pimple appearing on her face. She speaks warmly against heretics, is a regular church attendant, and is always quick to commend the minister for a sermon—when she thinks it particularly fits certain other women in the church. Her conscience is very tender on the matter of giving "amiss." She will not encourage people to continue in their evil, shiftless ways by means of *her* charities!

Mundanus. Mundanus, a born promoter, can't look at the smallest trifle without studying how it could be improved. He figures out ways to better almost everything he lays his hand on. Everything, that is, except his devotion. That, says Law, is in the same state as when he was six years old! After all, why should he read a book of devotion, any more than a spelling book? He learned all that at his mother's knee!

Caecus. Caecus hates pride and loves humility—in everyone but himself. He might have been a religious man, says Law, if he hadn't always thought he *was!*

Law sums up: "I have just touched upon these absurd characters to convince you. . . ." I close the book and consider some of my own absurdities. . . . I accept the challenge of *A Serious Call.*

"Examine me, O Lord, and prove me" (Psalm 26:2).

AUGUST 23
"I Feel a Concern"

I have taken up and read the *Journal of John Woolman.* The last word is read and I can say, "I have walked with a child of God." Along our journey I was overwhelmed with the humility, yet the fearlessness; with the earnest warmth, yet the boldness, of this Quaker saint.

"I feel a concern," he would say, and beginning with himself, he courageously followed the implications of such a concern. He felt a concern when he saw that children of God could subjugate and enslave other children of God. So he went about, approaching slaveholders in the spirit of Christian love, speaking on street corners, and calling everyone to stop and listen to the Voice within them. For he believed that if they did, they would know that slavery could not be tolerated.

He "felt a concern" about the accumulation of possessions. Beginning with himself, he curtailed his tailoring business, accepting only enough orders to answer the necessities of life, thus being free to spread his concern to others. That concern took him on the road many months out of a year, and all along the way he entreated others to free themselves of the entanglements of riches. He pleaded with parents to be less anxious about the farms and riches they would have to leave to their children, but rather to strive to leave them the legacy of a godly home and an example of good works to the needy of the community.

To a woman of today—who often has conflicts about how many duties to take on outside the home, the Quaker has something vital to say. Your chief concern may not be mine—"God does not burden us equally," suggests Thomas Kelly. But he goes on to say that He does put upon each of us a few central tasks which are our particular responsibilities.

O Thou who speakest within, I would develop a listening ear that I may "feel the concern" which is particularly for me. Then help me to curtail the many good activities that I may be faithful to the few responsibilities.

"Lord, what about this man?"

"What is that to you? Follow me" (John 21:21, 22, RSV)!

AUGUST 24

"God Deny You Peace and Give You Glory"

These are the words of Unamuno, used by Douglas Steere to sum up the message of a man designated in the annals of church history as "the gloomy Dane."

Sören Kierkegaard died in 1855 at the age of forty-two. In less than ten years of writing he had produced many books. Yet in his day he was not popular; his writings even cut him off from the state church—which was his target because of what he felt was its acceptance of easygoing Christianity. All through his works there runs a refrain like a cry—the need of complete abandonment to God, of genuine faith, of mature commitment, of action, here and now.

Most people, he says, really believe that Christ's commandments are meant to be oversevere, like setting the clock ahead half an hour so as not to be late to work.

To those of us who sit passively "at ease in Zion" Kierkegaard comes with his uncompromising *Purity of Heart* and asks us where we are in our commitment. He demands of us a decision to act, and he makes it plain that if we are going to see God with a single eye, we shall surely suffer.

I read *Purity of Heart,* and whether or not I agree with, or understand, the whole of Kierkegaard's theology, I know that never again will I be able to sing quite so glibly, "It is well with my soul."

God, God, deny me any cheap peace—only give the glory that arises out of the suffering of commitment!

"I consider that the sufferings of this present time are not worth comparing with the glory that is to be revealed to us" (Romans 8:18, RSV).

$*$

AUGUST 25

He Taught Us to Care

"Last night I invited her to supper," she wrote. "In spite of all the raised eyebrows when her name is mentioned. I got out my best dishes, silverware, Christmas tablecloth, and lit my priceless candles. I wanted her to know she counted. You see—no one, absolutely no one loves her. They are sick of her worthless promises and her binges. . . ."

"I wanted her to know she counted," wrote that bright saint, a friend of mine whose life is constantly being poured out in making people feel "counted." And while the rest of us sit back and watch, and predict that for all her pains there will be nothing "to show"; while we carefully dole out our charities to those people and causes which we think will bear the most fruit, she continues to scatter her love abroad recklessly.

Thinking of her, I can only remember and repeat what that great soul, Friedrich von Hugel, is reported to have said shortly before his death:

"Christianity taught us to care. . . . Caring is the greatest thing in the world. . . . Caring is all that matters."

"And he had compassion on them" (Matthew 14:14, RSV).

∗

AUGUST 26

My Life a Miracle

(Thomas Kelly died in 1941 at the age of forty-seven. Years before he had confided to Rufus Jones that he wanted, in some way, to make his life a miracle.)

She held in her hand a small book, *A Testament of Devotion*. It was a worn book, lined and underlined and full of marginal symbols. As she thought of the words its author had spoken, she communed with him inwardly:

Yes, Thomas Kelly, and your miracle continues. It continues in the lives of your family and friends and students, no doubt. But also, in a way remote from them, yet near—it continues in the life of this ordinary woman here on this hill, and many like me. This woman goes about her work—washing dishes, cooking, cleaning, laundering—and yet, and yet the miracle of your life has touched her, too.

For she has read this small book many times—and each time she feels the warm radiance of the saintly heart out of which the strong and tender words have flowed. Each time she finds herself again inflamed by a vision of what life can be, lived from the Center: "Simple . . . serene . . . amazing . . . triumphant . . . radiant." Each time she reads it she prays that she may be more firmly attached to That Center, less fussy about peripheral matters. Each time she makes new discoveries of the possibilities for the simplification of her life, of new commitments of Holy Obedience.

And as she is inflamed, as she prays, as she discovers, as

she commits—behold, Thomas Kelly, the Miracle of your life is also at work within her.

"Thanks be to God, who . . . through us spreads the fragrance of the knowledge of him everywhere" (II Corinthians 2:14, RSV).

AUGUST 27
The Most Dangerous Prayer

All her remembered life she had prayed "prayers." Following the sing song years of "Now I lay me down to sleep" were growing up and grown-up versions of the same. Praying prayers was a thing good people did.

One day a book was given her—Albert E. Day's *Autobiography of Prayer*. As she began reading, first casually, then wonderingly, then hungrily, she found herself making the most dangerous request she had ever made of God: "Lord, teach me to pray."

It was a dangerous prayer, for when she honestly asked to be taught, she discovered that prayer was, as a friend had written, "not the kindergarten activity" she had thought. She discovered that prayer was not a recital on a "victorious living" theme, not just a session of reading back the Bible to God—"We know that Thou hast said. . . ." It was not a mere ventilation or a safety valve, let alone a blank check or an order to Sears Roebuck.

She discovered that prayer is a *relationship*, its function being, as Albert Day says, not to bring her to God's attention, but to set God squarely in the center of *her* attention. She discovered this to be a dangerous relationship, for in proportion to the degree to which her consciousness

was aware of God, she was laid open to the demands of
God for purification, for annihilation of her ego, for clarifi-
cation of her desires and fears. As Day predicted, she
found, and continues to find, that a vivid consciousness
of God can be had only at a price—the price of commitment, abandonment to God's will, discipline. And this discipline could be no less rigorous than Jesus said it must
be—the daily denial, the daily shouldering of the cross, the
daily following.

Abandoning herself more and more to the dangerous life
of prayer, she knew that she could never return to the
comfort and safety of "prayers."

"Abide in me, and I in you" (John 15:4).

AUGUST 28

Taken by Violence

I have taken up and read from Evelyn Underhill's *The
Essentials of Mysticism* and have been rewarded by a
variety of surprise insights. Today I have picked from the
garden of my meditation this flower:

"Grace presses in upon life perpetually,
   and awaits our voluntary appropriation of it."

How much "loose talk" there is in religious circles concerning this word—grace! Yet how little of it there is
evidenced in our lives—this rich "inflow of spiritual vitality," as Evelyn Underhill calls it; this unmerited, all-out-of-
proportion response of the Divine to our feeble human
attempts of love and adoration. And when we do not
have it, is it not often because we ask in words only, ex-

pecting words to bring a shower of blessing, while we withhold the will to reach out and take? We are like the would-be dieter who "wants" to lose weight, but does not *will* to put forth the disciplinary effort necessary to achieve that slim image of her imagination.

"The kingdom of heaven is taken by violence," we read in the Gospel. Evelyn Underhill believes that this implies effort, courage, willed action, not great knowledge nor high emotions.

Lord, I would violently lay hold on eternal life. I would appropriate Thy waiting grace. Strengthen my will that I may truly deny myself. Whet my courage that I may joyously shoulder the cross. For ah, Thou hast said it, and it is true—that the road is difficult and the gate is narrow, and there are few who will persevere!

"To him who knocks it will be opened" (Matthew 7:8, RSV).

*

AUGUST 29

The Sea of Silence

"Back of language and clinging to it, when it is real, is the receptive sea of silence," writes Douglas Steere in his exhilarating little book, *On Listening to Another.*

How few of us women have explored the possibilities of silence, even when we are alone! "I can't bear it," says one. "I turn the radio on, just to keep me company." Yet, how infinitely richer than the trinkets of radio entertainment are the treasures of silence! How clearly we might see ourselves, the person we love, and the one we resent; how much more efficiently we might order our days; how certain we might be of just what is the One Thing Needful—if we would oftener withdraw to that Place where words are no longer necessary. Here the Eternal Listener hears all that the heart has to say, and replies with a surer guidance than the daily schedule on the bulletin board.

O my God, it is morning and I am waiting.

I am waiting as a child waits by his mother
To be washed and clothed for another day.

I am waiting as the tools of the artisan lie waiting
To be sharpened and oiled for another day of use.

I am waiting as the servant stands waiting
For the daily orders from the lips of his master.

I am waiting as the empty cup waits, inert,
To be filled from the outpouring stream.

O my God, it is morning and I am waiting.

"For God alone my soul waits in silence" (Psalm 62:1, RSV).

AUGUST 30
What More Shall I Say

"And what more shall I say?" For time would fail me to recount the lives and the words of the Biblical saints who lived by faith, and of all those who came after: of Justin Martyr, searching in Plato and Socrates for the answer, finding it in Jesus, and dying because he could not keep That Answer to himself; of Francis of Assisi, wedded to Lady Poverty, ministering a lifetime to the poor and sick of the cities; of John Bunyan writing the great Christian allegory in a prison cell; of the Reformation leaders, who were willing to accept exile and death rather than compromise. And of our twentieth-century saints: the Hindu, Sundar Singh, who met Christ on his own "Damascus Road" in India—and thereafter took Christ with him, trudging all his life the dusty roads from village to village, radiating the presence of his Silent Partner; of Frank Laubach, radiant experimenter through whose efforts thousands have learned to read and write, but more, to experience God; of John Baillie, whose prayers reach deep into the hearts of those of us who are less articulate, to our inspiration and comfort; of modern Assisis—like Toyohiko Kagawa and Philippe Vernier—pouring out their lives in love for the poor and unfortunate.

"Time would fail" to tell of all these—and the host of others whose names, not written in this book, nor in any published book, are yet assuredly written in the Book of Life!

And the world was not, is not, nor ever will be worthy of them.

"He who sits upon the throne will shelter them with his presence" (Revelation 7:15, RSV).

Looking to Jesus

I have taken up and read the lives and the words of saints, of a few of the great cloud of witnesses surrounding me. They have spoken to me in words and in works, and my days have been lit up by their radiance, my life warmed by their fire.

But, as one has said, even the saints have their blind spots, and at best theirs is only a reflected radiance, a radiated warmth.

I would look full into the Sun himself. I would not be warmed only, but *inflamed* by the very fire of God. I would join the company of those who, in the words of Allan Hunter, "Say 'Yes' to the Light."

I have read again Hebrews eleven and twelve, the basis for my meditations of this past month, and in these words I read the secret of myself joining the fellowship of the saints:

"Looking to Jesus . . ." (Hebrews 12:2, RSV).

O God, who in Jesus hast made Thyself tangible, I want to go forward, laying aside the gross flesh which has weighed me down, and the clinging, tangling sins. As I run, urged on by the cloud of witnesses, let my eyes be single, let my heart be pure, let me see and mean and desire God and only God.

17

THE GREATEST IS CHARITY

Grace Wenger

SEPTEMBER 1

Charity Defined

"This love of which I speak is slow to lose patience—it looks for a way of being constructive. It is not possessive: it is neither anxious to impress nor does it cherish inflated ideas of its own importance.

"Love has good manners and does not pursue selfish advantage. It is not touchy. It does not compile statistics of evil or gloat over the wickedness of other people. On the contrary, it is glad with all good men when Truth prevails.

"Love knows no limit to its edurance, no end to its trust, no fading of its hope: it can outlast anything. It is, in fact, the one thing that still stands when all else has fallen."*

"Love is patient. Love is kind. Love does not envy; love does not boast, it is not vain. Love does not look down upon others; it is never rude. It does not insist upon having its own will. It does not get angry at little things; it does not nurse hurt feelings. Love is not glad when others do wrong. It is glad when they do right. Love stands true through every trouble, believes the best always, always hopes for the best, is always patient."†

I Corinthians 13:4-8

* Phillips, J. B., *Letters to Young Churches,* The Macmillan Company, New York, 1950.
† Laubach, Frank C., *The Inspired Letters,* Thomas Nelson and Sons, New York, 1956. Used by permission.

The Debt of Love

All of us dislike debts. Paying off the mortgage or the school debt is a milestone. We are embarrassed to have to ask, "Lend me a dollar—or a dime."

Some people hesitate to accept even a favor. When you give a gift, you get a bigger one in return. You do a kind deed and receive an offer of payment. It seems as though the recipient, wanting never to feel under obligation to another person, prefers to keep others under a sense of obligation. To be in debt to no one, to feel an obligation to no one, must be a comfortable feeling—comfortably selfish. There is one obligation that we Christians cannot escape. There is one debt that can never be paid in full—the debt of love which we owe to all men. Do you wonder why this unending obligation? Take time to think about the limitless love of God to you and the impossibility of your ever paying it back. Then instead of feeling the obligation to love a bond to hamper your freedom, you will rejoice in every opportunity to pay back through others, small though the measure may be, something of His measureless love to you.

Romans 13:8

The Test of Love

Mrs. Miller said she almost hated to pick up the daily paper because there was so much in it about accidents and disaster. When she read descriptions of world needs in the church papers, she talked much about how sorry she felt for the poor sufferers. After a relief worker had given a talk at her church, Mrs. Miller said she lay awake a great many nights, thinking about the poor hungry children. But Mrs. Miller went on living as comfortably as usual. She continued her plans to redecorate her house, and in her spare time she crocheted a lovely lace tablecloth.

Mrs. Benner didn't talk a great deal about her concern for the needs of the world. But she decided that she would enlarge her gift to the mission board even though it meant using her old washing machine for a few more years. She took an active part in the canning-for-relief project and in her spare time knitted sweaters for war sufferers.

Mrs. Benner's only son decided to go abroad for voluntary service. Mrs. Miller came to comfort her and asked, "How can you bear to see him go?"

1 John 3:17, 18

✳

SEPTEMBER 4

The Witness of Love

It is not by pulpit eloquence that men are convinced of the truth of Christianity. Neither is it essential that we be prepared to explain all of the mysteries of God's plan. Not even miraculous demonstrations of the power of faith are sufficient to arouse the faith of others. All of these, it is true, may challenge men's intellect or awaken their wonder; but they may also merely mystify or confuse.

A life of rigid self-denial will not suffice to teach men the power of the cross. Even the triumphant courage of the martyr in the flames is not the most effective witness to

252

the love of God. For these may excite admiration for the ascetic and the martyr without leading men to a personal response to their God. Observers may fail to understand or not even care to understand.

There is only one message which all men can understand—the witness of love. A group of Christians loving one another and stretching out generous hands to those about them—this witness cannot be misunderstood or ignored.

The testimony that counts is a testimony that every Christian can give. Only a chosen few can speak with golden tongues, understand all knowledge, or move mountains. To live as an ascetic is impossible for most Christians, and comparatively small is the number of those who are called to the martyr's death. But the witness of love can be given by the humblest believer in the remotest place.

John 13:35

SEPTEMBER 5

The Seasoning of Love

Excellent food, soft lights, brilliant talk—the banquet of the professional organization was a success. However, to the plain country schoolteacher who wasn't trying to be brilliant, all of the sparkling conversation seemed to have only one purpose—to advertise the importance of the person speaking. Translated bluntly, it seemed to say, "I know a lot of distinguished people," "I have been to the most interesting places," "I hold a very important position," or "I am terribly clever."

A few weeks later in her own home she paused for a last-minute checkup before Sunday dinner guests arrived. Living room spotless and furnished in faultless taste; table a work of art with the best linens and china; and the food being prepared, she was sure, would please the most critical tastes. Her guests, who were full-time homemakers, wouldn't be able to find any fault with her dinner.

A sudden question jolted her: "Who's trying to show off now?" Her bothersome conscience persisted: "What is your motive—concern for the comfort of your guests or desire to display your ability as a hostess? Love or pride? Have you considered the preferences of your guests? Wouldn't the mother of two little boys feel more relaxed if plastic replaced your best linen cloth? Wouldn't all the ladies enjoy helping you with the dishes if the china were not so expensive that chipping a cup is a minor tragedy? Have you forgotten that good food is less important than good fellowship?"

Proverbs 15:17

SEPTEMBER 6

The Courage of Love

Should courage be linked with love? We speak of humility and love, of gentleness and love, of peace and love. But courage—does love take courage?

Ask the Apostle Paul. That tireless messenger of the love of God replies: "In journeyings often, in perils of waters, in perils of robbers, in perils by mine own countrymen, in perils by the heathen, in perils in the city, in perils in the wilderness, in perils in the sea, in perils among false

254

brethren; in weariness and painfulness, in watchings often, in hunger and thirst, in fastings often, in cold and nakedness."

Does love take courage? Ask the missionary who decides to stay when war threatens the people he loves or the nurse who risks her own life to save that of another.

Does love take courage? Ask the teacher who refuses to exclude a pupil because of the color of his skin. Ask the girl who tries to make a place in her social circle for her refugee friend. Ask the young man who faces the charge of cowardice because he refuses to kill.

Does love take courage? Ask anyone who has ever turned the other cheek: "Was it easier than striking back?"

Kagawa, who had experienced the perils of daring to practice love, wrote:

> "Not fighting only—
> Love, too, means adventure."

II Corinthians 11:23-28

SEPTEMBER 7

The Miracle of Love

> I marvel at God's miracles:
> That kindly He enshrouds
> In strength more calm than solitude
> The spirit thronged by crowds;
>
> That beauty shared with myriad lives
> And laughter scattered free
> In rainbow splendor glorified
> Are mirrored back to me;

That joyous labor done in love
  Is richer than repose;
That as I joy in others' gains
  My chalice overflows;

And when I stoop to lift some heart
  Bowed low beneath life's pain,
I feel the cool white wings of peace
  My spirit strength sustain.

Matthew 10:39

SEPTEMBER 8

Moved with Compassion

We are created to love. Each heart finds its center in something or somebody. Our affections may become attached to things; so that it becomes all-important to have hearty meals, fine clothing, a beautifully furnished house, a two-tone car with an excess of chrome. Training may raise the level of our sensory enjoyments; so that we find delight in beautiful music, in masterpieces of art, or in the magic of words. However, a life lived solely for the love of beauty does not satisfy. We need to love persons, not mere things.

There are those who seem perfectly content to pour out all of their love in the snug coziness of the family circle. Others enlarge their affections to include the immediate neighborhood or the fellowship of the home congregation. The Christian may be satisfied with no less than a world-wide compassion. Such compassion is touched by the starvation of an orphan in the Orient as well as by the suffering of a child in one's own home. It is a compassion which embraces the untidy, complaining old woman down the street as well as the chubby innocent baby next door. This compassion does not stop with sentimental feelings and talk; it moves to action.

Would you widen the circle of your love and deepen your compassion? Draw close to Christ; His love will become yours.

Matthew 9:36

SEPTEMBER 9

The Second Commandment and the First

You remember the story of *Silas Marner*. As long as he loved his gold, his life was shrunken and self-centered. He was hard as the coins he loved to touch and insensible as they to the joys and sorrows of those about him. After his gold was stolen and a little child came to his hearth, Marner's life was completely changed. The child he loved drew him into the stream of human life again. With her he learned to enjoy the companionship of the neighbors whom in the past he had avoided. Something of the innocent trustfulness of the child became his.

It is a common belief that we become like the person or thing we love. A pupil acquires the mannerisms of his favorite teacher. Husband and wife develop a marked resemblance to each other. Therefore, we are told, we should love the good, the noble, the true, and the beautiful so that we too may become good, noble, true, and beautiful.

Does it follow, then, that if we love the unlovely we are

endangering our own characters? Are we to limit our association to those whose lives are exemplary lest we become corrupted? Shall we draw the cloak of righteousness tightly about us and shrink from the touch of sinners?

We need have no fear in keeping the second commandment if we keep the first and great one. When the dominating passion of our lives is love of God, love of others will not draw us away from Him. Instead, our love will lift them to God.

Matthew 22:37-39

SEPTEMBER 10

Who Is My Neighbor?

"Every person in the world is your neighbor," someone answers. Yet this enlarged vision of your responsibility presents a new conflict. Being preoccupied with needs in distant places, you may fail to see the need next door. Doing big tasks for God may crowd out time for the little kindnesses to your fellow man. You may become so bowed down with concern for the wide world that you become a most unpleasant person at home.

Instead of closing your eyes to the world's problems when they almost overwhelm you, open your eyes wide to the bigness of God's plan. He does not expect to do all of His work within the span of your threescore years and ten, neither does He expect your little person to encompass the globe. "His state is kingly," wrote the blind poet who was tempted to fret about his own apparent uselessness. "Thousands at His bidding speed and post o'er land and ocean without rest."

258

Your responsibility, then, is not to try to do all of the world's work, but to discover which tasks are yours to do, and to do them with all your powers. You may help other causes with prayers, gifts, and good will; but concentrate your energy on your specific service. In order to be delivered from the busyness of trying to do the work for which some other Christian is responsible, consult God before you agree to help in even the most worthy efforts. Lest in trying to love everybody else's neighbor, you neglect your own, you must continue to pray, "Lord, who is *my neighbor?*"

Luke 10:29

SEPTEMBER 11

The Gift and the Giver

"Though I bestow all my goods to feed the poor . . . and have not charity, it profiteth me nothing."

But perhaps there is profit to the one who receives the gift. James Russell Lowell thought not. In *The Vision of Sir Launfal* the leper to whom the young knight tossed a piece of gold in scorn said:

"Better to me the poor man's crust,
Better the blessing of the poor,
    Though I turn me empty from his door;
That is no true alms which the hand can hold;
He gives only the worthless gold
Who gives from a sense of duty."

Then Sir Launfal dreamed that after a long fruitless search for the Holy Grail, he returned as an old man and again a leper asked for alms. Sir Launfal had little to give.

259

"He parted in twain his single crust,
He broke the ice on the streamlet's brink,
And gave the leper to eat and drink.
'Twas a moldy crust of coarse brown bread,
'Twas water out of a wooden bowl—
Yet with fine wheaten bread was the leper fed,
And 'twas red wine he drank with his thirsty soul."

Then the beggar was transformed into the glorified Christ and spoke the well-known words:
"Not what we give, but what we share,
For the gift without the giver is bare;
Who gives himself with his alms feeds three,
Himself, his hungering neighbor, and me."

I Corinthians 13:3

SEPTEMBER 12

To Get or to Give

Some love is like that of a kitten. It wants primarily the snug satisfaction of being loved in return. Such love finds its happiness in receiving. Because it expects others always to give, it is sensitive, jealous, and often resentful. Really this is not love, but self-love.

True love loves as Christ did. It does not seek to satisfy self but rather to serve others. Such love finds its joy in sacrifice. Because it demands nothing for itself, it is long-suffering, tolerant, and ready to forgive. It is love for Christ which finds expression in love for others.

Life's paradox is that, as we give, we gain that which

we had surrendered, and that, as we refuse to give, we lose that to which we had been clinging. The one who seeks merely to surround himself with love, who tries to bind others to himself, who dominates others for his own emotional satisfaction, risks losing the ones whose affection he values most. On the other hand, the one who chooses not to please himself not only discovers the joy of sacrificial service but also finds that the love he has given freely is returned to him as freely. "Good measure, pressed down, and shaken together, and running over, shall men give into your bosom."

Romans 15:2, 3

✳

SEPTEMBER 13

Simple Addition

The self-pitying patient who makes unreasonable demands of a busy nurse, the pupil who tries constantly to be the center of attention, the exacting customer whom nothing will please, the filthy tramp at the back door—how, we ask, are we to love persons like these?

All of us know the futility of trying to stir up warm feelings toward those who rub us the wrong way. Almost in despair we look at the matter-of-fact command, "Add . . . to godliness brotherly kindness; and to brotherly kindness charity." The Scripture makes it sound as easy as the simplest mathematical process. To us it seems difficult, almost impossible.

Our problem is that we fail to understand that love—like faith—is an act of the will rather than an impulse of the heart. In this the great saints agree, that charity is not a

261

sweet emotion but a sincere determination. Therefore, instead of puzzling about how to develop a certain feeling, we should rather devote ourselves to doing good to others and to praying for them—not forgetting to deal with our own sins of anger, criticism, and resentment.

As we refuse to pamper our own malicious feelings and as we carry out our determination to make the well-being of others our chief concern, we will discover that the emotion follows. God will see to that.

A matter of mere human effort? No, the command is only to those who are "partakers of the divine nature."

II Peter 1:4-7

SEPTEMBER 14

Walking in Love

Pray for the people you meet. Not only your family, friends, and neighbors need your prayers, but also the agent at your door, the lady beside you on the bus, and the person who stops to ask you the way to Centerville.

Never allow love for things to supersede love for persons in your life. Your family is more important than your furniture; hospitality is a greater virtue than is perfect housekeeping; efficiency on the job is less significant than human relations.

Deny yourself when there is a conflict between your personal wishes and the good of another person. It's an excellent discipline in charity to give a stranger your turn at a busy counter, to adjust your own schedule to that of other members of your household, and to throw yourself wholeheartedly into activities suggested by others when they interfere with plans of your own.

When tempted to discuss the faults of other persons, speak of their good points instead. No one who gossips about another can ever expect to help that person to a better way of life.

If you discover that you are secretly wishing ill to anyone, do that person a favor immediately. You will find ill will gradually being replaced by concern as you willingly do good to him.

Refuse to let your mind dwell on annoying personal traits of others. If another's habits, speech, or conduct irritate you, the wrong that you must right is not the other person's offense but your own irritation.

Ephesians 5:1, 2

SEPTEMBER 15

Love Does Not Condemn

To the lady standing in front of the small town store, the two crying children in the parked car were ill-behaved youngsters who should have been taught to wait quietly while their mother was getting groceries. The lady did not know that just a few weeks before, the father of the children had been killed in an accident and that now, when their mother did not return immediately, they concluded that she too had gone away and would never return. Because the lady did not know of the frantic fear that prompted their crying, she shook her head and muttered something about "spoiled children."

263

Not until summer vacation did Carol learn of the difficult personal problem that had been bothering her roommate during the last weeks of the school year. "I was annoyed at her because she seemed so grumpy," Carol said regretfully. "If I had had any idea of what she was going through, I'd have been more patient."

Eileen had shocked parents and teachers and even friends of her own age by her apparent flippancy toward sacred things. Years later they learned that during that time she had been in deep despair. "I thought I had committed the unpardonable sin," she explained. "I was scared stiff at the thought of death and of Christ's return. I determined to have some fun out of life since I was doomed for eternity anyway."

Jesus understood perfectly all who came to Him. He could see that the life of the rich seeker was dominated by love of possessions; but He could see, too, that back of the question was a sincere hunger for something more satisfying than things. Jesus knew the intensity of the conflict in the young man's soul. "Jesus beholding him loved him."

(Mark 10:21)

SEPTEMBER 16

Charity Covers

Miriam, who taught crafts in a mental hospital, commented on the reactions of visitors: "You'd think people would be glad to see their sick relatives and friends getting well enough to do something constructive, but some of them just point out the flaws they see in each piece of work. They don't seem to realize that it represents the best effort of which the sick person is capable."

Love always rejoices in the best efforts of another and does not fix its attention on flaws. A primary teacher does not count the number of times the crayon of a six-year-old strays across the outlines of a picture. No mother rebukes her little child for stumbling when he is learning to walk. Both have confidence that growth will bring more strength and skill. As Christians, shouldn't we exercise a similar confidence in our dealings with one another?

The person who sees the mote in the eye of his brother is not commended for his perfect vision. There is no beatitude for those who have eyes trained to observe the faults of others. That we are quick to point out spiritual shortcomings is an indication—not of our superior insight—but of our spiritual need. To display a critical attitude is to admit a lack of fervent charity.

I Peter 4:8

SEPTEMBER 17

Considering Thyself

A fellow Christian is overtaken in a fault. Before you fix your eyes on the guilt or on the guilty one, take a good look at yourself. Let God's Word penetrate beneath the surface and reveal all your own hidden soul stains. Only if you find yourself without sin may you start to hurl the stones of condemnation. When you really see yourself, you will want to steal away silently in the condemnation of your own conscience, leaving the sinning one alone with the Saviour.

265

God's Word, however, directs you not to sit meditating on your own failures but to return to help the fallen. Now you can do it in the spirit of meekness because, no matter how vile the sin, you know that you too apart from the grace of God might have yielded to that temptation. It humbles you to know that you can rely on no merits of your own, that only the power of God can keep you. Your own sense of unworthiness gives you a feeling of kinship with the one you have come to help. You feel that if any stones are to be cast, your place is with the sinner, sharing the condemnation.

To love mercy and to walk humbly with your God—even the Old Testament prophet saw that the two are inseparable.

Galatians 6:1

SEPTEMBER 18

Love Does Not Boast

"I don't want to gossip, but it's the plain truth that she's a poor housekeeper. Any time of the day you drop in there's a sinkful of dishes and her living room's all cluttered up and, likely as not, she's sitting down with a storybook reading to the children. Now don't get me wrong. It's not that I consider myself better or anything like that. Only I can't see how anyone can stand to live like she does."

"I don't want to be a snob, but she and I just don't have anything in common. She spends her whole life fussing about details and talking about things. She never gets into the realm of ideas. I wonder if she opens a single book from one year's end to another. Music and art are a waste of time, as far as she's concerned. Of course, I know that in the sight of God she's just as good as I am, only I do think she's the most uninteresting person I've ever met."

"I don't want to be critical, but the people back home do bother me. All they ever seem to think about is clothes, and cars, and comfort. Of course, I don't regret any of the sacrifices I've made for the Lord. I *want* to work for Him. Only when I see how complacently my old friends live—calling themselves Christians but feeling no obligation to do anything for Christ—I'm tempted to lose patience. Don't they have any vision? Can't they see the needs of the world? Haven't they any concept whatsoever of consecration?"

Philippians 2:3

SEPTEMBER 19

Love Is Not Jealous

A mother is told by her small daughter, "That's not the right way to make an 'r' because Miss Smith makes it like this."

A minister watches his congregation flock to a visiting evangelist for the counsel which he himself would have been only too happy to give.

A tired teacher who has worked for a year, with little success, to get the confidence of a class of teen-agers sees a lively young colleague win their loyalty within a few weeks.

At some time all of us face a temptation to envy the success of another. We may yield to the temptation and thus destroy the effectiveness of our own efforts. Or we may drive the poison from our hearts by examining the quality of our own love.

If I really love, I will be happy to see others helped—no matter by whom. It is not so important that I be the person to give help as that the needed help be given. The work of the kingdom is a co-operative venture, not a competitive one. If you and I were operating rival dime stores, your success might indeed be my failure. In the labor of winning souls to God, your success can never be a hindrance to mine. Instead, we are helping each other in a cause so great that it is petty to think in terms of mere personal achievement.

I Corinthians 13:4

SEPTEMBER 20

Love Is Courteous

Courtesy is more than the practice of a set of rules for correct behavior; it is the golden rule in action.

A visitor in a college dining hall found herself at a table with students who were strangers to her. When the hostess asked her to pass the first dish, the visitor started passing it to the right, not knowing that in this dining hall the custom was to pass to the left. The student to her right, instead of accepting the dish and passing it on, said stiffly, "The other way, please."

An old man arrived at a meeting after the building was already crowded. His friends were pleased to see that he had found a seat because they knew him to be in poor health. Later they noticed him standing. When they questioned him afterward, he explained, "Well, a woman with a baby came in, and there was no seat for her. None of the younger men seemed to notice; so I gave her my seat. I knew she couldn't stand through the whole meeting with a baby to hold."

The young lady in the college dining hall had a profound respect for Emily Post; the old man at church had, I am sure, never heard of her. Yet he did the correct thing because he did what his kind heart prompted him to do.

Luke 6:31

SEPTEMBER 21

Love Is Not Possessive

Self-love is possessive. Selfishness would keep the object of one's affection always dependent. True love rejoices to see the loved one find wings.

The first day of school had come for two six-year-olds. Ellen was up early, chattering eagerly about going to school with the "other childrens." When her next-door neighbor—a big girl in second grade—stopped for her, Ellen went dancing down the street, pigtails flying, with hardly a backward glance at her mother. For Mrs. Good had successfully hidden her twinge of reluctance at seeing her little girl begin to grow up and had talked often about the good times children have in school.

Mary Jane's mother drove her little girl to school. Mary Jane entered the first-grade room shyly, clinging tightly to her mother's hand. Mrs. Martin introduced her child to the teacher and then asked in a whisper if it would be all right if she sneaked into the cloakroom and waited there until school had begun. "I think I ought to be here in case she begins to cry," Mrs. Martin explained. "The poor little dear is very much frightened at the idea of being away from her mother for a whole long day."

Now which of these two mothers loved her daughter the better?

I Corinthians 13:5

SEPTEMBER 22

Rejoicing in the Truth

Surely no Christian would rejoice to see anyone do wrong. Sin grieves us. We rejoice to see sinners repent of sin and come to Christ—that's our purpose in life. We rejoice to see Christians grow in grace—we pray for it often.

Yet some of us good Christian women dearly love the excitement of holding a circle of friends spellbound with a recital of amusing, exciting, or shocking events. How often such recitals become chronicles of another person's follies and sins! If the one at fault had been a member of her family or a dear friend, would the teller enjoy telling the story? Would the rest of us care to listen if the story were about someone we really loved?

Can we truthfully say that we do not rejoice in iniquity when we feel scornfully superior to the new neighbor who does her family washing on Sunday morning or when we avidly watch the course of the wild party across the street? In prayer meetings is it honest concern that prompts us to recount at length the evil deeds of the one for whom we request prayer? We would be indignant if anyone suggested that when others do wrong we feel a secret satisfaction because of our own carefully concealed love of sin. Is it then more virtuous to feel the secret satisfaction of "God, I thank thee, that I am not as other men are"?

I Corinthians 13:6

SEPTEMBER 23

Love Never Fails

Some three hundred years ago an English philosopher wrote, "Charity will hardly water the ground where it must first fill a pool." Francis Bacon knew a great deal about many things—in fact, he had taken all knowledge for his province—but he failed to comprehend the resources of Christian charity.

Of course, he had a point in that one may selfishly limit his affection to "me and my wife, my son John and his wife." However, one's supply of charity cannot be exhausted by "us four and no more." Caring for one's own intensely need not disqualify the Christian for loving outsiders. Rather, it may make him more ready to respond to all those who need his love.

A mother whose daughter was a victim of cerebral palsy became active in an effort to help all similarly afflicted children. A fond grandmother developed a concern for hungry, homeless children in distant countries as she tried to visualize her own healthy grandchildren in such a plight. A relief worker who was especially attracted to the old women among the refugees explained that they made her think of her own mother. All of these loved others better because they loved their own well. It is doubtful whether anyone who has not learned to love those near to him is capable of loving those at a distance.

Perhaps Francis Bacon would have been nearer to the truth if he had written, "Charity will hardly water the ground unless it can first fill a pool."

I Corinthians 13:8

SEPTEMBER 24

Love Heals

Poet Peter Viereck was admiring the landscape near Massachusetts State Hospital. With him was his three-year-old son who knew certainly that a kiss drives away the pain of a hurt. As he looked at the hedges surrounding the hospital, the poet found himself agreeing with his small son's philosophy: it is "lack of a kiss" that makes a place like this necessary.

Is the poet right? Are the people in mental hospitals there because there was no one who loved them when they needed love? Is physical recovery delayed when care is adequate medically but lacking in the personal touch? Do babies fail to grow when every need is supplied except the need to be loved? How many children fail in school because they sense that no one honestly cares whether they achieve or not? What about moral failures? Would we need jails if there had always been an abundance of love?

If the poet is right, then none of us may pass these orderly piles of brick and stone that we call "necessary institutions" with no more than a smug prayer of thanksgiving for one's own healthy body, sound mind, and clear con-

science. Each one should rather examine his own conscience to ask whether it was his lack of love that caused
any person to be here. However, such questioning will be
useless, even harmful, if it drives us only to self-punishment
for past failure. It should lead us to a new determination
to practice in the contacts of each day the healing love of
Christ.

John 15:12

SEPTEMBER 25

A Real Interest in Ordinary People

Ann was a teacher—plus. To the high-school freshmen
she was a combination of pal, big sister, counselor, and
"next-thing-to-mother." Other teachers wondered at the
confidence she inspired in her pupils. Nearly every noon
groups of boys and girls dropped in just to chat. Often a
lone pupil sought her out to air his personal problems.
When several fellows became involved in a destructive
prank, they went first of all to tell Miss Moore about it.
"We aren't asking you to get us out of trouble," they explained. "We just wanted you to understand how we happened to get into it."

Most pupils would not have been able to explain exactly why they liked Miss Moore. They might have said, "She
knows her subject and makes it interesting to us," or "She
takes part in our activities as though she really enjoys
them," or "She has a lively and attractive Christian personality." Yet they would not have fully explained the reason
for their feeling toward her.

Ann did not pamper her pupils. She pointed out their

faults more frankly than did most teachers. When they deserved praise, she gave it without gushing. There was nothing sentimental in her approach to students. Yet somehow each person in her class knew that she loved him.

A fellow teacher was in her office one day when a timid ninth-grade boy hesitated at the doorway. Ann's face lighted and her eyes sparkled as she asked, "Is there something I can do for you?" Her facial expression added, "I'm delighted to be interrupted. You are every bit as important as this grownup, if not more so."

Romans 12:16

SEPTEMBER 26
Burden-Bearers for Others

Often the burdens of others seem too heavy to bear. We are grieved as we see neglected little children or lonely old people or patient sufferers from incurable diseases. We read of the agony in war-torn countries, of famines and disasters. Others bring us their personal troubles—unhappy homes, rejected loves, disheartening defeats, hopeless situations of all kinds. We feel powerless to help. We are tempted to feel that we can shoulder our own burdens but those of others will eventually get us down. Almost we shrink from the responsibility of loving; we would avoid the pain of caring deeply for those who suffer.

Then we remember, "Cast thy burden upon the Lord, and he shall sustain thee." We begin to understand that, just as we take our personal problems to the Lord and trust Him for the solution, so we must learn to take to Him the

274

problems that others bring to us. If we who love in a limited way are capable of caring deeply, how much more care will be shown by our God, who is love? He is not powerless to help. Only as we learn to trust to God the burdens of others, can we learn to love intensely yet without tension.

Galatians 6:2

SEPTEMBER 27

Builded Together

We call the medieval hermit sincere but misguided. We brand as queer the person who worships alone because he cannot find a church to suit him. Yet all of us have within us some temptation to be rugged individualists. Some prefer to initiate their own service projects rather than be part of the group work. Others are tempted to withdraw from the fellowship whenever details don't suit them. Still others seem to consider themselves detached observers with no responsibility for the welfare of the Christian community.

If Christianity were only a matter of one's personal relationship to God, isolation would be an aid in living for Christ. But the New Testament teaches otherwise. We are no longer foreigners, but fellow citizens; not strangers, but friends. We are members of one body, living stones in one holy temple, branches of one vine.

Because of this oneness no Christian can isolate himself without hurting both himself and the entire group. All of us need one another. This mutual dependence means that no one person's function is more important than another's, and that no one has a monopoly on truth.

When we really understand this, each of us will make his contribution with humility, performing his own service without complacency and offering his own suggestions without trying to urge them on others. Harmony results as each one gains a vision of his relationship to the whole.

Ephesians 2:21, 22

SEPTEMBER 28

The Cup of Cold Water

"What has *this* to do with building the kingdom of God?" It is a question which nags the teacher starting to correct a mountainous stack of papers, the nurse endlessly changing linens, or the mother facing a sinkful of dishes for the third time in one day. Many of us who started out with visions of doing great things for God find ourselves caught in an everyday routine of tasks that seem altogether insignificant. We envy those who are called to more exciting service.

Love sanctifies the common tasks and makes them of high worth in the sight of God. Giving the cup of cold water can be a way of showing God's love to one who does not know Him. Or it may be that some other disciple can preach the Gospel more effectively because an unknown Christian cared enough to give him the drink.

In every great work for God there are those in the background who work at seemingly mundane tasks; and in doing their work well, they make it possible for someone else to do the front-line heroic deeds. It is not which task we do, but the fact that we do it for Christ, that matters. The

worth of a life is not measured by the sum total of great
deeds done. We can rejoice in routine tasks when we do
them as part of a total life of loving service to God and
man.

Matthew 10:42

SEPTEMBER 29

Coals of Fire

We thrill to the stories of the conquering power of Christian love. In Anabaptist literature we read of the Swiss
Mennonite minister whose kindness and prayers shamed
into restitution the young men who had torn the thatch
from his roof. An early American tradition pictures aged
Peter Miller, after securing General Washington's pardon
for the man who had mistreated him, walking away hand
in hand with his former enemy. Sometimes we hear miraculous stories of how modern missionaries, facing dangers
in the wilds of pagan lands or in the slums of civilized
countries, have won their persecutors by meeting violence
with positive love.

But what of the stories in which good does not triumph
over evil intentions? What of the five men who lost their
lives in a mission to the fierce Aucas? What of the Amish
family which was massacred by Indians because the father
refused to kill? What of Dirk Willems who turned back to
rescue his pursuer from drowning only to be captured and
put to death at a lingering fire? What of Stephen whose
enemies continued to hurl stones although he cried, "Lord,
lay not this sin to their charge"? The pages of church his-

tory are crowded with stories like these. Should we conclude then that good does not overcome evil?

Does love really have power? For the answer faith looks to eternity.

Romans 12:20, 21

∗

SEPTEMBER 30

Channels of His Love

Lord, make me a channel of Thy peace
    That where there is hatred—
        I may bring love,
    That where there is wrong—
        I may bring the spirit of forgiveness,
    That where there is discord—
        I may bring harmony,
    That where there is error—
        I may bring truth,
    That where there is doubt—
        I may bring faith,
    That where there is despair—
        I may bring hope,
    That where there are shadows—
        I may bring light,
    That where there is sadness—
        I may bring joy.
Lord, grant that I may seek rather
    To comfort—than to be comforted;
    To understand—than to be understood;
    To love—than to be loved;
        For it is by giving—

That one receives;
It is by self-forgetting—
That one finds;
It is by forgiving—
That one is forgiven;
It is by dying—
That one awakens to eternal life.

—*A Prayer of St. Francis of Assisi.*

John 17:26

AUTUMN LEAVES

Minnie Swartzendruber Graber

OCTOBER 1

Autumn Leaves

A tree in autumn is an awesome thing. Two trees make you stop to wonder; many trees transfix. Spring is lovely with new life surging up, with gracious warmth, with new leaves. But comes October, Mother Earth has fully fruited. There is impending change. The tiny leaf that was to be, is; it can never be more. And it has turned to gold. There are many leaves, golden, red, brown, on many trees. All are here today, but what of tomorrow?

There is that which speaks of sadness, but not of sadness more than joy. No wonder the soul stirs to this scene so symbolic of its own change.

Life has its seasons. There will always be leaves, tender and green, somewhere; green spreading branches somewhere. But in October God speaks of change, the change of the leaves and in our lives and of His own unchangeableness. "I am that I am." I shall dwell safely with Thee who abideth forever.

Exodus 3:11-15

280

Saved from Willful Striving

Have you ever been saved from yourself and your own willful strivings? Then you know the relief it is to rest once again in the knowledge that He has charge of your life. Therein is security and peace.

Grandmother sat in her rocker facing the bedroom door. Jane had been put to bed twice, each time climbing out with the uneasy consciousness that she was acting counter to Grandmother's wish. The bed creaked; there were sounds of climbing out the third time. Then Grandmother saw an amazing sight—a little white-gowned figure backing ever so slowly into the hall, cautiously peeping to see if Grandma was looking. Finally with one last careful backward peep, Janie settled down to a box of blocks, every moment quiet and restrained.

All Grandmother would have needed to do would have been to say "Janie" in the right tone of voice and Janie would have been in her arms, so happy, cuddled up close to her chin. How cute she was sitting there all absorbed in her big idea!

But Grandmother read on—one page, two pages.

Janie played, covertly glancing back to check. This block, that block, this one, that one. Grandmother kept reading—three pages, four pages. Nothing made sense with those little eyes peeping ever so slightly.

Suddenly Grandmother was there. In one big swoop Janie was lifted into the air, given a warm tight hug and kiss, and settled definitely and finally upon her bed.

A long sigh of relief escaped Janie. She was sound asleep in two minutes. Grandmother had saved her from herself.

Psalm 32:6-11

When I Remember upon My Bed

They say older people do not require so much sleep. Many a grandfather and grandmother say, "I wake up at three o'clock." A goodly number actually get up and putter about, eating an early breakfast, as if hauling hogs to Chicago or spading the garden before dinner were the next obvious duty. Occasionally, young or middle-aged people also turn night into day for one reason or another.

It is not a calamity to miss a few hours of sleep unless we worry and fret and toss about in a frustrated and unhappy way. God can speak reassurance and peace to us in the wee hours of the morning when the world sleeps. Time becomes part of eternity as it truly is; and He speaks His message. There is no hurry. We are quiet.

We see in panorama His dealings. How could He have loved so small a bit of His making? To be a child in such a family! What a luxury! O Lord, thank you. Help me to live royally. Let there be no meanness, no littleness. Let love be unfeigned.

What greatness is Thine! Thou hast order and plan, though I do not understand. Today the darling child of my dear friend was accidentally killed. This is plainly a time and space act in purpose and love. Open my faith faculty, I pray. Without faith it is impossible to please Thee.

Thou art my Hope. I know little of the mystery of life, but Thou hast given me a little light, enough by which to walk. It is sure knowledge that Thou hast somehow linked me with Thy life and purpose. My hope is in Thee. Thou art with me. I shall not be baffled or confused.

Is that the dawn—so soon? I have understood better by night than by day. Thank you.

Psalm 63:1-7

Blessing of Being Grandparents

By the time men and women have lived long enough to be grandparents, they have reached a new vantage point in life. From this point other people's situations are better observed and evaluated. Mellowed by their own experiences and those of others, they are more ready to attribute good motives and honest efforts to people about them. Friends and acquaintances become more interesting; there follows a deeper sympathy and understanding. Grandparents see young men and women in their community dream dreams and toil to bring them to fruition. When these dreams in some measure come true, when they see their own children and the children of their friends developing in Christian stature and usefulness, it is for them the glad occasion to say, "Thank God." Grandmother is a true stand-by and her grandchildren her great enjoyment. Danny, Johnny, Kathy, Ann, Robert, and their mothers and fathers are being blessed all along the way by these God-fearing grandparents.

Dear Father of us all, we thank Thee for the family:
For grandmother and grandfather with their
sympathy and understanding enriched by experience;
For parents, who bring love, strength,
and safety into family life;
For children and grandchildren to adorn our homes
and bring joy to all.

May our hands minister to the necessity of each one.
May we remember in our family and community circle
"the words of the Lord Jesus, how he said, It is more bless-
ed to give than to receive." Amen.

Acts 20:32-38

Grandmother, You Are Needed

Thirty years ago there were few grandmothers in the Dhamtari, India, Church. I missed them. My earliest recollection of worshiping in God's house was that of making my way first of all into an anteroom filled with older women. I searched for my own little friends in that maze of full dark skirts. Then I sat among them with my mother. They were kind to me. They became a part of my worship experience. Later as a young girl I saw them in their corner so quiet, sweet, and serene—my mother and her friends, Carrie, Nannie, Fannie, Mary, Lydia.

The whole bearing and appearance of a good Christian woman who has grown older in faithful service is of inestimable value. It is difficult to realize how important the influence until one witnesses a social life in which Christian grandmothers are all but absent.

The Christian faith requires a becoming conduct even to the observance of small details. Older women are encouraged to be examples in such a life of faith.

Dear Grandmother, if you are tempted to question the use of a life physically weakening, remember that little girls see and will remember; young women see and take courage. Life to its last days holds a great responsibility for the kind, sweet, charitable grandmother.

Titus 2:1-5

The Story Must Be Told

The whole town of Dhamtari was agog with the happening of Saturday night. An Indian Sadhu had been buried alive, secret precautions having been taken in covering the grave to insure a sufficient amount of air for relaxed breathing. Sunday morning the grave had been uncovered; the man revived. Much money had been thrown at his feet in worship.

Monday morning I opened the compound gate, joining the stream of wayfarers traveling south. I fell behind two women engaged in honest conversation, one a Hindu, the other a devoted Christian woman. Bits of their conversation reached my ears:

Christian: ". . . did only good continually, kind to children . . . ."

Hindu: "Yes, yes."

Christian: "He patted them on the head . . . took . . . His lap."

Hindu: "Yes, indeed."

Christian: "Wicked men seized Him . . . a cross . . . suffered . . . ."

Hindu: "Alas, alas, wicked men!"

Christian: "Not overnight . . . the third day . . . alive . . . heaven forevermore . . . Son of God, Jesus Christ!"

The story is being told by His true devotees.

Dear Lord, help me to share the story of Thy unselfish love. Let the wonder of Thy power to change and control the wayward be made real in me. To the glory of Thy name. Amen.

Acts 8:26-40

*

285

All One in Christ

It took place in an Indian jungle village, far from any trace of modern life. We had traveled many miles to worship with a small group of Christian people. It so happened that a government inspector on tour of his district had arrived at the rest bungalow the day before. He was an elderly Christian man, known for his integrity, devout in his worship of God. He knew of the Christian fellowship and joined us in the morning service.

What a precious fellowship that was as we sang, read the Word, and prayed together. It was after the communion, in the observance of feetwashing that our guest brother, who had never witnessed the rite before, rose without a moment's hesitation to lead a poor illiterate Christian by the hand to the place of washing. He knelt humbly before him and washed his feet.

Thank you, Lord, for the world-wide fellowship of the church. Thank you for the stalwart, faithful Christians of every land who take note of their brethren, who sacrifice for the Gospel. Help me that I may not despise the poor and underprivileged. Give me, O Father, the grace of kindness to all who are weaker than myself. Let the mind of Christ dwell in me richly. Amen.

Philippians 2:1-11

". . . Publicly and from House to House"

We veered our bicycles in and out and around protruding rocks on the open plain, occasionally going through small jungle tracts, on and off cart trails until we reached a certain Indian village. It was Dora's idea to take that early Sunday morning ride. But it was more than her idea of how one might spend an exhilarating hour. It was her morning's task, accepted as naturally and definitely as the manner in which she had asked me, "Would you like to go along?"

Once in the village we went through devious alleys until we reached the one small, mud house which was our destination. Dora called to the mother, and the two stooped to enter the door that led into a small dark room. I waited outside. In a few minutes they came out—Dora carrying in her arms what must have been a nine-year-old girl, although her emaciated body belied the fact. Tenderly she laid her on the rope bed in the sunshine and began the tedious work of dressing the many burns. I have never forgotten the mother standing there by her uncomplaining little daughter and the nurse bringing so much of healing, courage, and comfort.

Today let us pray for our missionaries around the world —for preachers, teachers, doctors, nurses, relief workers, for all of them at home and abroad. The Gospel must be preached "publicly" and translated into loving deeds "from house to house."

Acts 20:20, 21

OCTOBER 9

Burnt Toast

You can never tell what will be used by the Spirit to convince a soul to accept Christ. The marvel is that God can use such small, inconsequential, ordinary happenings to bring about His will. And He does it through people like you and me. Take, for example, the conversion of Ma Haider.

Ma Haider was employed as a cook in the home of mid-India missionaries. She was Mohammedan, a widow, a woman of commanding personality. The missionaries expected her to attend morning worship with others about the place. She had no intention of doing so. She was again asked to lay aside her morning duty and sit quietly with them while the Word of God was being read. She had excuses, the chief being that it was at this time she needed to finish preparing breakfast. She had to make toast. When the missionary said the breakfast was not so important, Ma Haider said no more, although inwardly she fumed. Being creative, she quickly formulated a plan.

Next morning Ma Haider attended worship. Afterwards she very promptly served breakfast. In my imagination I can see her march in, setting down the platter of toast with a thud, as much as to say, "There now; eat your burnt toast." And this is exactly what the missionaries did. There followed mornings of the same procedure, and there was never a word of complaint on their part. By this time Ma's mind was in a tempest. Gradually it subdued. In the end her curiosity, as much as her admiration and sense of fairness, caused her to listen to a Gospel that would make people bear such retaliation.

Ma Haider became a Christian. A precious memory of my own early days in India is accompanying Ma Haider in Bible women's work. She was a fearless soldier of the cross. Interestingly enough, I also remember her as an excellent cook, presiding at big church fellowship dinners. No burnt food! What a small thing it was for the missionaries to eat burnt toast! Suppose they had not done so. Suppose they had dismissed her for her obstinacy.

OCTOBER 10

By Preaching

While I was calling in a friend's home, my gracious hostess said, "I've often thought I'd like to, but—well, we've never done it. I'd be so embarrassed and at sea in knowing how to do it." And what do you suppose it was? They had never had a preacher as an overnight guest! (I almost offered to come with my husband that she might practice on us.) A mature woman who presided at beautiful teas was afraid to entertain a minister.

Some people are shy of preachers. They somehow have come to consider preaching outside the range of ordinary Christian experience, while in truth preachers are humble servants of the Lord and His people, committed to proclaiming His Word.

There are also those at the opposite pole in their attitude toward preaching and the preacher. Their condescending manner and remarks show they lack understanding of this, one of the greatest forces for good in the history of mankind. It is by the preaching of the Gospel that men will hear about and accept Jesus Christ, though the preaching is foolishness in the eyes of the world.

I thank God for my preacher—brother, pastor, evangelist. Let me not withhold for some selfish or foolish reason my prayer support, my share in burden-bearing, even that invitation to the minister for fellowship in our home.

Prosper, dear Lord, the preaching of Thy Word by faithful saints around the world. Amen.

Romans 10:13-17

✳

OCTOBER 11

Unfinished Business

"And Paul dwelt two whole years in his own hired house . . . no man forbidding him." So ends in this clipped-off, abrupt, unfinished manner the account of the early church in action. And with good form, for the task was and is yet unfinished. The Lord must have said at that point, "It is enough for the Book; we will hear of others in the years to come."

And the story continued—but not in the Book—tells us how Monica interceded for her wayward son; how John Paton risked his life among the cannibals to bring them the Gospel; how a robber chief in mid-India led a whole village to Christ; how Franca from her Sicilian balcony recognized and welcomed men of God to her home and was baptized; how Jiwanhal suffered rejection of his family to become a Christian.

What a privilege it is for us today to continue the writing of the story of the church, to co-operate with our Lord in His purpose and plan, to identify ourselves in this great movement of His Spirit!

You are in the midst of Christ's wonder-working. He is ever at work, today as yesterday. There is no past tense in His saying, "My Father worketh hitherto, and I work." What a privilege it is to do even a small, seemingly insignificant task for Him!

John 20:19-23

290

"... These Things ..."

This morning I straightened up the room where last night I had been measuring a skirt length. The skirt marker was one I had received from a friend. She, in turn, had received it from the husband of one of her friends who had passed away. As I wiped up the chalky dust, thinking the while of the little convenience that made putting in a hem so much simpler, I wondered also of the woman before me, who probably like myself had used and thought kindly of the glass of powder and the rubber bulb. Then it was hers, now it is mine—for a short while.

And then whose shall these things be? Set your affection on things above, not on the things that perish. Seek ye first the kingdom of heaven. Things shall perish, but Thou and Thy kingdom shall abide forever. Thy Word is established in the heavens. From everlasting to everlasting Thou art God.

Electric sweepers, mixers, yes, even skirt markers are to be used and appreciated, but not to be hoarded and gloated over. How insignificant such things must appear in the light of heaven and all things eternal!

O Lord, Thy kingdom, Thy praise, Thy will, may these be my deep concern as through life I wipe up chalky dust. Stir me by the knowledge of Thy greatness that I may rightly understand that it is Thee and not things that I worship. Amen.

Isaiah 40

291

Rupee for Christ

Isabux lived in the orphanage. But he was not an orphan, not quite. During the great famine his mother and he had wandered about in search of food, finally arriving at the camp in a mango grove. There for some days they shared with the hundreds of others food from the great kettles and slept in improvised huts. The time came when his mother returned to her old village, leaving Isabux in the care of the missionary. On occasion she would come to see him, never failing to bring him some small memento of her love—a bit of bread she had made, or some trinket a child would like. One day she put into his little hand a rupee, a big shiny silver rupee. He could scarcely believe his eyes. It is doubtful that he had ever held a rupee before; certainly he had not owned one.

But owning a rupee presented a problem. What to do with it! Peanuts, hair oil, a new pencil, sweets, marbles—what should it be! Several days he struggled, trying to come to some decision.

Sunday morning found him seated on the floor in church among several dozen of his friends, who like himself were orphan boys. When the offering plate appeared before him, without a moment's hesitation he placed the shiny rupee upon it!

Today, dear Lord, what may I give Thee in such lavish fashion, for I too love Thee. Amen.

Matthew 26:6-15

OCTOBER 14

We Accept Failure

Dear Mary,

Esther tells me you are discouraged because you and Bob have experienced failure. I am not in a position to discuss whether you have failed or whether you haven't. Let's say you have, since that is the worst construction we can put on this happening. Do please read Matthew 10. Jesus indicates that we will fail, and He says we should acknowledge it and move on: "Whosoever shall not receive you . . . depart . . . shake off the dust." His meaning is that we don't stay with the failure, downcast, bemoaning our lot—in their case insisting on over-proselyting. We're not to say, "Poor me! See what I must bear for Christ's sake." Don't blame the people or yourself. Shake off the dust; depart.

While there are times to persevere, to work ahead in spite of hardship, there are also times when we need to disengage ourselves, recognize God's call, do something new and hopeful. This philosophy of Jesus is not only operative in a crisis in life but can also be applied to experiences in which we are oppressed by our inadequacies, our imperfections and mistakes. We leave them and press on. *(continued October 15)*

Matthew 10

OCTOBER 15

Success Through Failure

(Mary's letter continued)

Have you ever considered that we fail more often than

we succeed? This should not keep us from setting our goals high or encourage us to set them low so that we might succeed. It is in the realism of Jesus for us to recognize failure and yet not let it prevent the measure of success that still is in store for us. The seed falls on the ground; some is snatched away. Other seed is choked; seedlings are withered. Much fails; only some yields and produces the good harvest. Yes, we fail. But take heart; honest failure keeps us humble; it mellows our lives, makes us wiser, more sympathetic. No one likes that eminently successful, cocksure person going around clearing the decks anyway! Mary, we have watched you and Bob struggle. We love you the more for it, and do take God at His word, "I will never leave thee, nor forsake thee."

Now I must close. You know those greeting cards we send sometimes? Only success, all joy, every day of your life, wonderful? They just aren't realistic, are they?

God will bless you,
Dora

Psalm 55:16-23

✳

OCTOBER 16

On Simple Things

Life seems too complicated, too cluttered. We lose our way. This is because there is too much of everything, too much room, too many things in the room, too many meetings, too much machinery, too many gadgets, too many clothes, too many toys. In the maze we lose our capacity to appreciate simplicity, a most precious possession.

I said to myself, "Tomorrow we will have dinner in Mary's home. I want to take something for her dear children." I ended up buying two tiny frying pans, one for Ruthie, one for Kathy. "These," I thought, "will please them; they have been taught to appreciate simple things." I was not mistaken. While grownups sat visiting, two little girls could be heard saying, "Do you want one egg or two eggs?" "We like ours soft." "I'll set mine here." I shall not forget their childish, wide-eyed acceptance of the frying pans.

God's purposes—His glory is more easily perceived in the simple than in the confusion of much. Indeed, God has chosen the simple to confound the wise.

Dear Lord, let the gentle, cooling, refreshing breezes of Thy Spirit's presence make my anxious mind to know that Thou wouldst have me be a simple child of simple faith, of simple love and wonder. Free me from the pursuit of much; let me seek first Thy kingdom, that all these other things may fall into their true perspective. Amen.

I Corinthians 1:18-31

OCTOBER 17

Sober?

Rebecca was deeply in earnest about her religion. Her elongated face with the pathetic drooping eyes, the corners of the mouth also curved downward—weren't they good proof that she was sober-minded? (John was not a drunk; so he was counted sober too.)

I am sure the Apostle Paul had neither Rebecca nor John in mind when he used the word "sober" in his writings, and he used the word often, especially in insisting that older men and women be examples of sobriety.

The Greek meaning of "sober" refers to a sound mind, showing itself in discreet conduct, particularly in the matter of self-control. Self-control, far from being merely the curbing of sensual, physical impulses, has also to do with controlling our spiritual impulses. It is possible for a Christian to be careful about the former, only to be lax about the latter.

Yes, older women are to be examples in avoiding spiritual excesses. How important it is that we be women of the Word if we are to have good judgment! Lydia, Dorcas, Mary, Priscilla believed full, loved lavishly, but it was a simple faith, a deep-seated love. We never see them usurping places in the church, disturbing the peace of the fellowship. (Paul reprimands unnamed ones who did so.)

The Word has definite teaching on how we can ascertain the will of God. It is no secret how a Christian filled with the Spirit will act. Teaching on divine healing, on the "gifts," it is all there. We need not be "carried about with every wind of doctrine."

Help me, dear Father, to be reverent of behavior, to live a spiritually controlled life. I thank Thee that joy is the possession of all sober-minded women. Amen.

Titus 2:3-5

OCTOBER 18

Yes, Sober

A steadfast, temperate, spiritually controlled woman will recognize that hers is a walk of faith; she will not seek emotionally loaded experiences as the highly desired ends of Christian experience. It is true we have "mountaintop" experiences which are given us for our encouragement to help us through difficulties or crises, but they are the unusual, not the usual. To have them is not even desirable unless they are controlled so as to strengthen character and lead into more exemplary conduct. Religious emotions should not evaporate into nothingness or give way to a self-complacency that is satisfied with the past or the *status quo*. We should have a deep desire within us for a steady growth of the spiritual in which there is little need of the tumult upheavals. Certainly we are not encouraged to seek after highly emotional experiences as the ultimate in Christian experience.

Forgive me, Lord,
> *for undisciplined thoughts and desires,*
> *for every failure of self-control.*

Help me
> *not to rely on the laurels of past religious experiences,*
> *not to seek the exciting and demonstrative.*

Save me
> *from frittering away the value of high moments of spiritual*
> *exhilaration when Thou dost see fit to give me such.*

Teach me
> *to live spiritually by faith, not by feeling,*
> *to seek a steady growth in grace and knowledge.*

Accept my thanks
> *for every means of grace,*
> *for Thy Spirit, Thy Word,*
> > *Through Jesus Christ, my Lord.*

Titus 2:4

A Stranger in the Midst of Love

She wore a brown fur-trimmed hood, a long, green velvet skirt, a purple blouse, a red jacket, heavy boots, and thick gray woolen stockings. Our attention was caught by her wrinkled face, her long blue-veined hands joined and extended imploringly, the rosary in her lap, and her lips in whispered prayer. She was definitely different in that Protestant congregation. As was she, so was I, a stranger in their midst. But I forgot myself in wondering how she would be received.

I thanked the Lord for what I witnessed at the end of the worship service. Several women gathered about her, and I found myself among them. They spoke kindly to her and to me and to one another. The old lady's face lighted up in smiles.

O wondrous love of Christ, that flows through our beings to bless strangers and makes of us common children of Thine! Grant that we who worship Thee in Thy house may never lack that love which proves us truly Thine. Amen.

I Corinthians 13

Personnel Problems

Lettie had trouble with her neighbors and acquaintances; even her nearest friends fell short of her requirements. She attributed inferior motives, questioned their acts. Half the time she lived in quite a self-righteous frame of mind; the other half she spent depreciating herself, for Lettie was conscientious too.

One day Aunt Sally happened in. Aunt Sally understood Lettie better than Lettie understood herself. Gently but firmly, she suggested the solution for her difficulty in public relations. This is the verse Aunt Sally shared with Lettie: "And the Lord turned the captivity of Job, when he prayed for his friends."

Through intercession for our friends, both we and they are blessed. Differences, misunderstandings, jealousies, rivalries resolve themselves and disappear. Through honest, sympathetic prayer for others, God's love can be realized in ways and in fullness otherwise impossible for us. How this can be, we do not undertand, but it is true, thank God!

The Lord does not intend any of His children to live ill-adjusted lives. He wants us to live victorious, free lives. He will turn our captivity into freedom when we intercede for others.

Job 42:10

OCTOBER 21

Fourscore and Four Years or Thereabouts

Maggie, 75 years old, was taking care of Anna, 93 years old.

Bits of conversation with Maggie come back to me.
On the church steps:

"Tell your husband I thank him for that good sermon. It is good to have men of God bring us such messages."
On a busy street:

"I'd like to know about India. Tell me, are the Christians making progress? Are they getting along all right? Being a missionary is a great work. I couldn't go, but I pray for the work."

In my living room:

"I think the best thing I did in my life was to take care of James. He was so helpless and crippled and needed love so much."

At the church door:

"Do come and visit Anna. She needs encouragement."

It was not unusual for Maggie to give an occasional gift, some little thing she had picked up—a small glass dish, a granite cup, a head scarf. It was all so spontaneous, so un-called-for in my way of thinking. It takes so little to prove so much and raises the question, "What kind of person will I be at 75, if 75 I come to be?"

Luke 2:36-38

OCTOBER 22

Modern Priscillas

Aunt Sally is much like Priscilla of New Testament times. Aquila and Priscilla had no children of their own, but their home and hearts were open to others. Priscilla was that hospitable, homey sort of person. The church met in their home. Apollos, the eloquent young Christian from Alexandria, must have made his home with them for some time.

Besides managing her household and helping to weave tent cloth, Priscilla found time and interest to be a student of the Gospel. Just as Aunt Sally helped Lettie to a Christian way of solving her difficulty, so although Priscilla appreciated Apollos' zeal and his remarkable abilities, she

300

sensed that he had a superficial knowledge of the new faith. The fact that Aquila and Priscilla took him aside and taught him had an important bearing on the development of the church. Apollos became a well-informed exponent of Christianity.

At a certain point in the life of a younger person the direction and explanation given by a God-directed woman can be of inestimable value. The young man that lingers just outside the church door needs Aunt Sally's smile and Christian greeting. The young mother who doesn't understand why her children are the naughty ones needs a word of encouragement. The frustrated, the wayward need the Gospel interpreted for their particular need, not insinuating gossip for their despair.

I thank Thee, Father, for the church whose fellowship abounds in such rich relationships; for the host of faithful ones who lived in the past, for those living in the present, for Priscilla of yesterday and Aunt Sally of today.

O Lord, make us particularly sensitive to each other's need.

I bless and adore Thy name that Thou hast called me to be a member of this church. Let the consciousness of this high calling comfort, sustain, and encourage us to all good and fruitful living. Amen.

Acts 18:24-28

OCTOBER 23

Come to My House

Lydia's invitation to Paul and his companions is a fine example of Christian hospitality. " 'If you have judged

me to be faithful to the Lord, come to my house and stay.'
And she prevailed upon us" (RSV).

A man is said to be friendly (if he *is* friendly), but rarely
is a man called hospitable. This is a lovely word reserved
primarily for woman. And what more attractive characteristic is there for the keeper of the home, for the one who
most often opens the door to friends and strangers!

Lydia's invitation was based on a sense of her responsibility to God. If she could be judged faithful, which she
much desired, then she would count it a great privilege to
entertain God's ministers. What a fine dimension for entertaining people, a sense that the visitor, the hostess, and
faithfulness to God are all interrelated. Such a visit will
never be a failure.

Have you ever examined your reasons for entertaining
or not entertaining your friends or the visitor at church?
Has it ever occurred to you that your oft-given invitation
couched in "sometime," "come sometime" is just a way of
"signing off" before you part? Have you been troubled by
the stingy feeling that crops up at the thought of giving
time and energy to entertainment? Is it possible you may
have something in common with Mrs. Blaine whom you
criticize because "she somehow makes me feel very uncomfortable"?

What individuals or families should do depends on circumstances. We judge not. But this must be said, though
it is shocking to us all: Selfishness runs counter to hospitality. Selfishness is at the root of the matter. A generous
Christian woman will share her home as unselfishly as she
does herself. That Christian love of which she cannot convince another on the sidewalk or in a church aisle she can
enact in kind hospitality within the familiar walls of her
own home.

302

Dear Lord, help me to be like Lydia. I want to be faithful to Thee, that I might be faithful to those who cross the threshold of our home. Take away all selfishness, that I may be truly hospitable. Amen.

Acts 16:14, 15

✳

OCTOBER 24

Teach the Younger Women

Do you mean to say that Mary, married to John five years, needs to be encouraged to love her family? I recall their wedding day.

Today divorce grants are as prominent a part of the daily paper as marriage announcements. People think lightly of divorce. Romantic love is played up; society as a whole moves with little regard to the sanctity of the marriage relation. Yes, Mary needs every encouragement for keeping her marriage one of commitment, sanctity, and love.

Christ's love for the church is the parallel of a husband's love for his wife. Because John is human, Mary, in the days of adjustment that follow their wedding, must be encouraged to consider John's love her most precious earthly relationship and to exult in it. She can safely give herself in submission when John loves her. So much depends on Mary's response.

The example of an elderly couple who have lived together for many years "in submission" and "in love" has great value in society. It is as beautiful as first love, having the added attraction that it has proved itself; it has lasted.

The older woman who has had a happy marriage can encourage Mary. Mary must be reminded to look to the real values of life, to her partnership with John. The older woman can share in the enjoyment of Mary's children. For this she needs an open mind. To her the past should not be so dear as to make it impossible to be tolerant of new ideas and ways of doing things. She must be ready to acknowledge, in some cases, the superiority of newer ways. Her attitude as much as anything makes it possible to encourage Mary to love and appreciate her husband and children.

Ephesians 5:21-33

OCTOBER 25

God Setteth in Families

Dear Mother and Father,
    John and I think the family arrangement you helped us to is of the Lord. Why didn't we think of it before!
    (A description of the church services, a neighbor's visit, a quiet Sunday afternoon, hours at home with children followed.)   *Love, Mary*

Dear Mary,
    Thanks for your reassuring letter. We shall miss not seeing you every Sunday, but we know it is for the best. Those precious Sunday hours will mean even more as the children grow up.
    Tell Kathy Grandpa's birdhouse is up. . . .
    I'm glad Johnny apologized and paid for the neighbor's basement pane. That's the man!
    The God of peace be with you.

                                                    Love, Mother

And this is the story behind these notes:
    Mary was an only child. She felt her responsibility to

304

her parents keenly. After her marriage she and John spent their Sundays with them. Even after the babies came, Mary and John faithfully drove the fifty miles to cheer Grandmother and Grandfather. With the years it became more of a burden to both the grandparents and the parents. The preparation, the trip, the aftermath, the hurry were tiring. The little family was robbed of its own birthright. Both were relieved to know that the weekly visit would be more acceptable if reserved for somewhat less frequent and more special occasions.

Dear Father, we thank Thee for our family. Make our home a place of joy and encouragement for our dear ones. We remember those family circles broken by death. Bless them, we pray. Amen.

Psalm 68:6; Ephesians 5:31

OCTOBER 26

Love Lifted Me

A Hindu man of high caste spent a long period of time in the spiritual struggle that finally brought him to accept Jesus Christ as his Saviour. The morning following his decision he stepped into the open street. In the glaring light he saw a poor low-caste man coming toward him. He was altogether unprepared for the impact to which his commitment to Christ now led him. So real was the love of God coursing within his being that he all but threw his arms about this stranger, a man he had despised so short a time before. No one was more surprised than he himself.

Dramatic, we say. Such a transformation! This same love of God within our hearts is the solution to our daily

lack of power and ineffectiveness, our sinfulness. How we
need to open our lives and let His love come in to drive
away the jealous thought, the envious, the covetous
thought, the doubt, the love of worldly things!

Ephesians 2

OCTOBER 27

New Every Morning

Before the day was over she was tired. Nothing seemed
worth doing. Everything looked the same, the important
and the unimportant. The same things in the same setting.
To add emphasis to the already well-defined feeling, she
muttered, "Musty, dusty, in need of an airing, that's what!"

What is new, the newest thing about? Well, the Smiths'
new baby, next door. In contemplation about this little
bundle of joy, she started an entirely new train of thought.

What a mistake to think that all is old, decrepit, boring!
There is new life within me too, so new it will never be old,
for it is eternal. A new song, a new name, a new commandment. His faithfulness is new every morning. "All things
are become new."

She sat at her window and watched the sun set, rosy
blues and gray in shafts of light. A strange peace crept
over her spirit. Consider, oh, my soul, His loving-kindness.
To live in musty, dusty air is not your lot.

Lamentations 3:23

OCTOBER 28

Physical Sight; Spiritual Insight

Margamma Bai had become a leper shortly after completing her teacher-training course. She left her home, her family, all her friends to live in a leper home. When I came to know her in Shantipur, she had already become matron of the women in the home. Her leadership in things spiritual as well as her ability to organize and care for the physical well-being of the women and girls was recognized by us all. She was a brave, spirited, Christian woman.

And so she served for a number of years. We came home on furlough and had a different assignment when we returned to India. The passing of time brought about many changes.

We visited Shantipur on a Sunday morning. I eagerly looked to see familiar faces in the audience. I saw Margamma Bai sitting among the young girls, but she did not see me. She was totally blind. When the pastor called for special music, she rose with the girls and this is a bit of what they sang:

> Jesus, Thou art the Star of my eyes.
> Don't forget me; take knowledge of me.
>
> We wander on the road; the load of sin is heavy.
> Saviour, we beg you, point out the way.
> Jesus, Thou art the Star of my eyes.
> Don't forget me; remember me.
>
> Until I reach Thy golden castle, Thy great dwelling,
> O Saviour, stay by my side; remember me.

307

Satan gives great grief; he strikes at me.
Save me, Thou who art full of all virtue; save your
loving servant.
For Thou, Jesus, art the Star of my eyes.

Certainly one may be forgiven for weeping at such a time, though why one should weep would be difficult to explain. Of a truth, Jesus is the Light of the world to everyone that believeth.

John 1:4; 8:12

✳

OCTOBER 29

Sabitri by Faith

Sabitri had found refuge in the Shantipur Leper Home, the City of Peace. She had been a worshiper of idols, living in fear of evil spirits. When she heard the Gospel message, she responded to the love of Jesus and accepted Him as her Saviour.

Old, diseased, weak, and illiterate, it was no wonder that she could not memorize the Articles of Faith, the Beatitudes, the Ten Commandments, as could the younger women. However, the flame of faith, fanned by her simple love of Jesus, burned brightly within her. She "took" the name of Jesus. Instead of repeating the name of Ram over and over again, she treasured Jesus' sweet name in her heart.

It was communion Sunday in the church. The strong, both old and young, as well as those who could barely hobble or leaned on others for help, were there. They were all there, save those few too sick to leave their beds. The pastor and a few helpers and friends ministered to these following the church service.

They came to Sabitri's room. So little, so shrunken, so seemingly lifeless she lay in her cradlelike rope bed, completely covered with the coarse shepherd's blanket. She had risen and lain down for the last time, for her emancipation was near.

We called her name, lifting the blanket from her face. She blinked, then comprehending who had come, she tried to raise herself but was unable to do so.

The pastor recalled for her the meaning of Christ's death for us. Too sick to answer his questions she haltingly murmured, *"Mor liyc-maris"* (For me-died). Before the sunset that day she had gone to be with Jesus.

Not by our intelligence, abilities, or education, our refinement, and genteel ways, not by our good works will any of us be saved. We are saved, as is Sabitri, by simple faith in Jesus Christ.

Romans 10:9; Ephesians 2:8, 9

OCTOBER 30

Great Is the Company

It took five years to make a rough draft of the Gospels in the Ostuncalco speech of Guatemala. By that time it was found that there were twenty-two different dialects in the region and the one used for first-draft writing would serve a very limited number of the 330,000 Mam Indians. There was more work. By the end of eleven years "missionaries and shaggy-haired Indian men in colorful home-dyed jackets, working and praying humbly for God's wisdom in this task," produced a translation of the New Testament with a basic language that harmonized and brought together the Mam dialects. A country without the Word became possessors.

This is quite in contrast to many of our homes. Perhaps as long as we can remember each member of our family has had his own particular copy of the Bible, the new one as well as the older laid-aside one; there are Bibles enough to supply each room of the house, besides special Bibles in different languages, different versions in any of several languages, to say nothing of commentaries with running use of Bible texts.

Does such a situation raise thanksgiving within my heart, any consciousness of responsibility, any problem?

Take away my complacency, dear Father. Let me meditate on this: Am I truly thankful for the light of Thy Word? Is there within me a desire to share Thy written Word? How can I do it? Help me somehow to be of that great company, who published the Good Tidings. Amen.

Psalm 68:11

OCTOBER 31

The Thing Called Beauty

Modern women have put so much stress on beauty culture that it has been responsible for the development of a great and lucrative business. The cosmetic counters, beauty parlors, magazine advertisements, the women on the streets themselves are examples of the emphasis.

Certainly there is no evil in softening hair, using lotion

on dishwater-roughened hands. To be careless of one's personal appearance is not a meritorious act. It is sad neglect of duty. A Christian woman at the supermarket with unkempt hair, sagging skirt, twisted stockings, brings no special beauty to her witness. On the other hand, women and girls need often to remind themselves that true beauty does not need the ministrations of high-priced specialists. True beauty lies not in the power of cosmetics and expensive clothing but in temperance and purity, modesty and humility, good temper and calmness of spirit.

There are few of us who have what may be called perfect form and features, a peaches-and-cream complexion. We can recall that within our acquaintance there is that occasional one so noticeably irregular of features that except for beauty of soul she would be counted only homely. We think little of it. Proper care of the body—grace and beauty of the soul, let these be in good proportion.

Jeremiah 4:30; I Samuel 16:7; I Peter 3:4

311

MY CUP RUNNETH OVER

Esther Eby Glass

NOVEMBER 1

My Cup Runneth Over

Early November days are sometimes deceptively fair. Indian summer lingers, loath to depart. The soft, hazy atmosphere gives no hint of the nearness of winter.

Then suddenly, one night, we awake to hear a vixen wind banging the shutters and tearing about the yard in a very rage, shaking the tenacious leaves from the trees, knocking down sticks, and pelting the earth with rain or sleet.

We run to close the windows and fasten the shutters and turn up the thermostat. We find extra blankets and tuck them about the children and Grandma and at last about ourselves.

In the safety and warmth of our comfortable beds we listen to the fury of November and are thankful for houses to keep out the cold, for blankets and thermostats and fuel. Never do we feel this gratitude so keenly as on that first stormy night of November. On no other night are we so conscious that our cups of blessing are full and running over.

Psalm 23:5

Bittersweet

Cups full of material blessings are bittersweet!

We lie in our snug beds, and the very warmth and comfort that should lull us disturbs our sleep. Who are we to be warm when so many shiver in the cold? Who are we to be fed when half of the world goes to bed hungry every night?

The pinched faces of hungry children rise before us, shutting out sleep. The thin, tired mothers of the hungry children reach out hands that tear away our comfortable thoughts and dreams. We can shut our eyes tight, but we can't shut out the beseeching faces or the outstretched hands.

Our cups have been filled by God only that we might empty them for others.

We remember the miserly old woman up the street who lived alone hoarding her possessions. One day she died, and her heirs had a sale of her belongings. How the bidders laughed as the auctioneer opened chest after chest and sold the outmoded clothing and fancywork she had put away year after year. Her cup had been full, full of a musty, dusty, stagnant brew. It never overflowed.

If we try to hold and keep the contents of our cups, we will have nothing in the end but bitter dregs. Cups overflowing to bless others retain their sweetness.

Proverbs 11:24, 25

313

21

On Buying Gifts

Even in early November we are conscious of the approach of Christmas. Catalogs of gifts arrive in the mail, their covers gay with bells and holly. Displays of gifts appear in the local store windows side by side with the Thanksgiving decorations.

If we have packed Christmas bundles for overseas relief giving, or sent packages to missionary friends, we have done this before November. Our cups have run over to reach others in far corners of the earth.

It is so easy to buy gifts if we have money. Even if our budgets are slim, we probably never find it necessary to miss a meal in order to give gifts. We give of our abundance, of that which runs over from our cups.

Sometimes we need to dip out of our cups to others. To empty our cups to others. To give not only what we will not miss, but what we will miss sorely.

We each face the searching thought: When have I hungered that another might be fed? Or felt the biting cold that another might be warmed? Or suffered that another's pain be relieved?

Mark 12:43, 44

Gold-edged Gifts

Whether we have money or not, we have at least two things—time and trouble.

Perhaps no one is asked to divide her time so generously

with others as the minister's wife. And no other person is expected to add so many other people's troubles to her own.

The most precious gifts cannot be wrapped in paper. The hour the minister's wife (or any other Christian woman) gives to pray with you about your problem is a gold-edged gift. You go away blessed, and she postpones cleaning her silver or her hall closet another week.

She dips into her cup to help you in your spiritual life. It is not just the overflow of her time.

Perhaps after your hour of prayer the solution to your problem is not yet clear. But you have found strength to go on, and you say in parting, "Pray for me." You leave her with a share of your trouble. And she gladly takes it. She divides her time, and adds to her prayer burden.

How about you? Do you divide a little of your time in return, offer to do some practical work, mending, baby-sitting, cleaning? Do you promise to pray for her, with her heavy responsibilities?

The most precious gifts are not displayed in store windows. They are ours to give—time and intercessory prayer.

Those who give them give not only the overflow; they dip deep into their cups.

Galatians 6:2

NOVEMBER 5

Sorrow in the Cup

Is there a cup of blessing and a cup of suffering? Or are they one cup?

I have been blessed by the lives of those who have suffered deeply, and have learned through their suffering how to comfort others. And I have seen that the experience that embitters one woman, strengthens and sweetens another. What is the secret?

I have learned something of the secret from Mary. Mary is a widow, whose husband died suddenly on a mission field, leaving her far from her home with a family of young children. God put His hand heavily on Mary's life that day, taking away her husband and changing her life's work as well.

I will not say that Mary's faith never wavered at all, that she did not have long dark hours of sorrow and loneliness. I am sure she had these to endure.

But she believed God was faithful. The secret is as simple as this. And the sorrow dropped into her cup only seems to make the blessings overflow to others. I never sit with her for an hour without coming away a better woman.

I ponder this verse, which she once quoted to me as a favorite. She said it was given her in a dark hour.

"For thy Maker is thine husband; the Lord of hosts is his name; and thy Redeemer the Holy One of Israel; The God of the whole earth shall he be called" (Isaiah 54:5).

NOVEMBER 6

Hidden Sorrow

Not all suffering comes from joys taken away. Sometimes suffering is caused by joys withheld.

We speak words of sympathy to the parents who lose their child through death. But what can we say to the couple who are denied children? Or to the woman who goes through the bitter experience of losing her babies before the required nine months?

One woman, childless for many years, says: "I was particularly bitter when a friend of mine became the mother of twins. She had two babies, and I so much wanted just one! I sat at my organ and played softly the hymn, 'O Love That Will Not Let Me Go.' I could not sing; I could not even speak the words. I knew how Hannah felt when she prayed in bitterness of soul without forming words.

"But when I had made the words of the hymn my own, the Lord gave me strength and peace, though the ache was still there. I carried the ache, and prayed God that from it might come not bitterness, but blessing."

We little know what sorrows are hidden in the hearts of women whose sympathy and kindness overflow so generously to all whom they meet.

"Charity suffereth long, and is kind" (I Corinthians 13:4a).

NOVEMBER 7

Lost: A Son

I wonder how the mother of the prodigal son spent her days while her son was in the far country wasting his substance in riotous living. I wonder if some of her friends blamed his sins on her leniency, while others said she had driven him away by her strictness. Or did they join her in prayer for her wayward son?

"I still believe in the power of prayer," the mother of a modern prodigal said quietly when her son was mentioned. She stands between him and God, holding on in prayer, believing the answer will come in God's time.

Today, O Lord, we pray for wayward sons and daughters. We join our prayers to the prayers of sorrowing parents, who know their children will be lost forever if they do not repent and return to God. May we never add to their heavy burden by our undue criticism. Keep us humble and loving, O Lord. We thank Thee for the prodigals who have returned. May we ever be ready to welcome them and to forgive, as Thou art ready to forgive. We remember that we have all been prodigals. For Jesus' sake. Amen.

Psalm 86:5-7

NOVEMBER 8

Backsliding

Wayward children cause heartache. But, oh, the agony of a wife watching her husband backslide from God. Added to this heartache she bears the double burden of bringing the children to a vital relationship with God which their father no longer enjoys.

I have seen women lifting this double burden. I have seen their children find Christ and join their mothers in prayer for their fathers.

But I have not seen the hours of prayer that I know undergirded this victory. I have not known the wakeful hours, the sorrow of heart, the temptation to despair that has tested this victorious faith.

"I was almost at the point of giving up," one of these women confided to me. "It seemed that the children would

318

follow their father away from the church, and I would be alone. Then our boys accepted Christ, and now the children join me in prayer for their father."

In her darkest hour God honored her prayer for her children. She cannot tell why her prayer for her backslidden husband remains unanswered, but she is still praying in faith.

Dear Lord, today we would kneel side by side in the Spirit with every Christian wife of an unbelieving or backslidden husband. Give these wives the love that beareth all things, believeth all things, hopeth all things, endureth all things. May the love of Christ, shining through them, bring their husbands to repentance and faith. For Jesus' sake.

I Peter 3:1

NOVEMBER 9

When Children Are Different

One day I received a letter from a friend many miles away. Not long afterwards a nearby friend spoke to me over the telephone. These two women do not know each other, but the letter and the phone call carried the same message.

Each of these women is the mother of a number of lively, intelligent children. Each has one child with a mind that is not fully developed. And each felt that her cup of blessing was full and running over when it was possible for her child to attend a special school near home rather than one far away.

I sat and thought of the courage and patience with

319

which these women meet daily a situation I have never faced. Who shall say why this trial should come to some parents and not to others? And who can but feel humble at the sight of the gratitude these parents feel for the help given their children? Each of these mothers spoke deep appreciation for the patience shown her child by her teacher.

As Christian women who are concerned for all of God's children, we must be concerned for these different children also. We can help to establish schools such as the ones my friends find so helpful. And we can pray.

How shall we pray for these children? We can pray, I think, that they may always receive kindness from those they meet. For kindness is the language without words that all children understand.

And this prayer must be more than a pious phrasing of words. We can help our families to remember that God holds us responsible for helping to answer our own prayers!

Romans 15:1

NOVEMBER 10

Sick and Discouraged

How thoughtlessly we sometimes sing beautiful sentiments like the lines: "I thank Thee more that all our joy is touched with pain."

What we really mean is that we are glad that our joys are sometimes touched with pain. But some women's days are all touched with pain, even filled with pain.

Ruby lay on a bed day after day, while her growing family was cared for by their father and other helpers, sometimes competent helpers, sometimes incompetent. "I would give anything," she told me, "to have a hard day's work to do, and to be able to do it." But God took her work away from her temporarily.

Discouragement haunts the bedside of a sick mother. It dogs the steps of an ailing mother who can hardly manage to do her work.

I have no answer for this, but Job has! He had sickness and trouble, and he did not understand the reason at all. But Job is pointed out by James as the outstanding example of patient suffering. And God loved Job very much, all the time He was permitting this testing.

God loves His children while He chastens them. If we can but remember to say in our dark days: "He loves me today. He permits this burden! He loves me! Sometime I will see the fruit of this suffering."

James says that God is very pitiful, and of tender mercy.

James 5:11; Hebrews 12:11

NOVEMBER 11

Nerves

"Nerves are all imagination!" she said in disgust. But she had never had to battle a nervous disorder.

Someone has said that there are just two kinds of people: those who have nerves and those who haven't. And they never will understand each other.

Of course only a doctor can diagnose and prescribe for nervous disorders. But those of us who seem naturally to have nervous dispositions can do some constructive thinking on the subject. And we can follow the thinking with action.

We are usually the people who take on our shoulders more work than we can accomplish without overwork. We finish our work on nervous energy. Our tempers wear thin. Our tongues lose their guard. We are shocked to hear the edge on our own voices! Humiliated, we pray for forgiveness.

We need to lay each day's work out before the Lord, and let Him order our going. The Lord enlists busy people to work in His kingdom. But He wants us to take time to be quiet before Him, too. Nothing wears our nerves thinner than too much work and too little worship.

We need also to learn that we cannot always finish everything we plan. It is good not to put off till tomorrow what we should do today. But it is sometimes better to postpone planned work for more important tasks the Lord sends. It is easier to commit grave decisions about our life's work to the Lord than the details of our daily routine. When we have learned to do this, we have made a second step toward more stable nerves.

Isaiah gives us two prescriptions for quietness.

Isaiah 30:15; 32:17

NOVEMBER 12

Polio and Braces

He walked up the steps to the pulpit on his crutches. He leaned the crutches against the railing and began to preach the Thanksgiving sermon. His text, as I remember it, was: "Giving thanks always for all things unto God and the Father in the name of our Lord Jesus Christ" (Ephesians 5:20).

322

The face that beamed down on us over the open Bible was radiant. One line from the sermon lingers with me: "One day I learned to thank God for polio!"

Oh, no! Not for that! But the radiant face agreed with the words. He had taken his crutches and made of them a ladder to reach nearer to God!

What had he learned in his hours of affliction that many people who have not suffered do not know? He had learned to take into his life some words we often speak, but do not really absorb. Words like these:

"Giving thanks always for all things" (Ephesians 5:20).

"I have learned, in whatsoever state I am, therewith to be content" (Philippians 4:11).

"Most gladly therefore will I rather glory in my infirmities" (II Corinthians 12:9).

NOVEMBER 13

Old and on the Shelf

"Or ever the silver cord be loosed, or the golden bowl be broken" (Ecclesiastes 12:6).

When the golden cup of life is nearly full, almost ready to be broken, the days pass slowly.

"What day is it?" Grandma asks from her armchair. "Every day is so much alike."

Her long life has been like a rose jar, filled with sweet-scented petals. There were sharp thorns pressed among the petals, but thorns have no fragrance. The memories that rise from the jar of her life, overflowing to her friends, are sweet memories as fragrant as roses.

Time hangs heavily on the hands of the aged if no new

activity replaces the tasks that must be laid aside one by one.

We need never relinquish the task of intercessory prayer, and the prayer list grows longer with each new grandchild. Grandma's feet may not be able to move out of the house, but her prayer concern can encircle the earth, and her prayers of intercession wing up to the very throne of God.

Grandma may be old, but she need never be "on the shelf." We can confine the body, never the spirit.

Is every day the same? Every day brings the same opportunity to pray to our Father and to bless those about us.

Psalm 145:2

NOVEMBER 14

Monotony of Every Day

Not only Grandma sometimes thinks every day is alike.

Housewives sometimes rebel at the carbon copy duties, sweeping the same floors, dusting the same furniture, making the same beds. Washing, ironing, dishwashing are repeated over and over.

Housework like prayer is never-ceasing. And housework and prayer go hand in hand. We pray daily for our bread, and then prepare the daily food. We ask God's blessing on our food each time we are ready to eat. And after the meal we wash the dishes. We wash the children, and lay back the covers of the smooth beds we have made, and listen to their evening prayers.

We would not really want to lose the blessed sameness of the daily work and the daily prayer. They are twin gifts from a loving Father to housewives the world over.

Blessed is the woman whose hands keep her house clean and comfortable, and whose prayers keep her family close to God.

Proverbs 31:27

NOVEMBER 15

Housewife Versus Career Girl

On the days when the housework routine seems especially tiresome, I am occasionally tempted to think with just a touch of longing of my friends with careers.

Perhaps in that very day's mail will be a letter describing the interesting travels of Edna the roving reporter, or Elizabeth the editor, or Ann the artist.

I travel from the laundry to the yard to take down the clean, sun-dried clothes. I report a bit of cheery news to Grandma as I put away her sheets and towels. I hear that unique blend of shouting and laughter and motor noises and applied brakes that announces the arrival of the school bus. I prepare to listen to a detailed edition of the day's happenings, complete with humor and features. While I listen I fashion a salad and dessert for supper, my one artistic attempt for the day. The careers of my friends seem a little lonely at this point.

A new thought comes to me. Does the grass on my side of the fence sometimes look greener to the career girls?

I wonder if I sometimes forget to appreciate the satisfying portion in my cup, because I compare it with the colorful brew that glistens in the cups of my friends, a brew I have not even tasted!

It is as though I had asked of the Lord as Peter asked: "Lord, and what shall this man do?"

I think He would answer me as He answered Peter: "What is that to thee? follow thou me" (John 21:21, 22).

NOVEMBER 16
Something Creative

Mary measures yard goods over a counter. Patsy takes dictation and types carefully detailed business letters. Julia's skillful hands turn out dozens of beautifully sewn garments from her complicated sewing machine.

These women are workers. Their work follows one pattern day after day far more closely than a housewife's work does.

Sometimes Mary or Patsy or Julia rebels. "Let me do something creative," she says, as she slams down the last bolt of goods, or shuts with a bang the typewriter or sewing machine.

How do we determine what is creative work? We think at once of sculpture, painting, poetry, literature. These, we say, are creative arts.

Even the sculptor or the artist is only a copyist in the larger sense. He can interpret what he sees through the medium of his art. The more skillful he has become through learning from the masters, the better his interpretation. But in the last analysis, only God can create.

We can be creative too, while we measure cloth, type letters, sew dresses, keep a home clean and a family happy. We can interpret faith and love and hope through the medium of our work. And the more skilled we become through learning at the feet of our Master, the better our interpretation will be.

Only in Christianity is all labor so sanctified.

326

Help me, O Lord, to make each day a masterpiece, a true interpretation of Thy great love and the peace it has brought to my life. Through Jesus Christ. Amen.

I Corinthians 4:6, 7

NOVEMBER 17

About Cleaning

A scrub woman cleaned the floors of an art museum. She never saw the beauty of the pictures that hung on the walls above her. She kept her eyes on the floor which she scrubbed and waxed to a brilliant sheen.

"What a lovely floor!" she said with relief, when she had finished scrubbing. And she went home to sleep.

Sometimes I am like the scrub woman. I clean my house and wash my windows. I do not look through the windows to see the pond lying like a clear-cut jewel on the bosom of the meadow. I only look to see if I have missed a speck of dust somewhere.

I clean my floor and call to the children, "Wipe your feet." I am concerned only for my clean floor, not for the grand idea that prompted that quick rush of muddy feet across the room.

A clean floor is a lovely thing. A shining window lets in more light than a dirty one. A clean floor is a pathway for those we love to walk across. A clean windowpane brings into my house God's sunlight and the beauty of the outside world. Aside from this they cease to be lovely. As an end in themselves they rob me of better things.

Luke 10:41, 42

327

The Joneses

My neighbor is a good manager. Her house is always clean. Her closets never erupt coats and boxes when she opens them. Her wash floats first upon the breeze on Monday mornings. Her garden is green when others are not yet spaded.

God gives some people a beautiful gift of timing. Their work seems always to be done more quickly and with less effort than that of their neighbors.

God allows other people to prosper financially. Their homes may not be showy, but we feel the depth of their carpets and the comfort of their chairs.

God gives to some people impeccable taste. Their homes may be simple to the extreme, but we feel instinctively that every piece of furniture and furnishing is in harmony.

You may say that this is a matter of hard work, inherited money, cultivated taste. I grant this is true in part. But God still is the giver of all good gifts, and permits good as well as evil circumstances.

Did you ever stop to think just which Mrs. Jones you are trying to keep up with? The good-managing Mrs. Jones? The wealthy Mrs. Jones? The artistic Mrs. Jones? Probably we have each tried in a small way to keep up with all three.

I had a beautiful thought one day. I am sure it was a thought from God. It was this: I will try to think of my friends to appreciate them for what they are, what they have, what they mean to me. I will not try to keep up with them! I am much happier when I remember to follow this way.

If I want to keep up with something, it will be with God's will for me. I am afraid I am often far from being the woman He wants me to become. God holds me accountable for the use of the gifts He has given me, whether these gifts be children, talents, or things. He has a plan for me, and He takes care of the Joneses as well.

God Himself fills the cups.

James 1:17

NOVEMBER 19
The Stranger Within the Gates

We have attended large Christian assemblies where we sat among hundreds of other Christians, all of them strangers. We sat together, worshiped together, prayed together. How could we remain strangers?

And yet, it sometimes happens that strangers enter our churches, and when they leave, they are still strangers. If Christ Himself walked into the Sunday morning service in some churches, no one would ask His name.

A church is not a social club. It is a communion of saints! Saints are gathered in common union to worship and commune with God Himself through the Lord Jesus Christ. The very act of common worship should mean that fellow Christians meeting for the first time are not strangers but brethren.

I am ashamed that sometimes I have not greeted visitors in our church. I hid behind shyness. God would have called this shyness by its true name—selfishness!

Hospitality is mentioned often in the New Testament in connection with women. God has given this beautiful gift

329

to women in particular. This gift grows more lovely with use. It can be used at church as well as at home. It is a gift that can be handed down to the children and grandchildren.

Husbands need the gift of hospitality too, but they find it a little hard to use successfully without the help of their wives.

Christian hospitality is an overflowing cup. The more we pour out its contents to others, the more we have!

Hebrews 13:2; Matthew 25:35

NOVEMBER 20

Other Mothers

"Are these your girls?" someone asked the little woman with the three tall girls towering beside her. And she replied confidently, "Yes, they are my girls."

And so they were! Another woman had borne them, but this little mother had brought them up from early childhood. The girls loved her and respected her, although they carried in their hearts a sweet memory of their first mother also. One of them once wrote a fine tribute to her second mother on Mother's Day.

There are so many "other mothers." We call them by names that carry a certain stigma: stepmothers; mothers-in law; foster mothers. I know one woman who has had all of these in her lifetime, and loved them all. She just called them all "Mamma."

A second mother, if she is true to her task, is a type of God! She takes someone else's child and makes him her child. A type is never true in every detail. But the gen-

330

eral thought is there. She loves this child as though he had always belonged to her. He is *called* her child.

Doesn't that remind you of I John 3:1? "Behold, what manner of love the Father hath bestowed upon us, that we should be *called* the sons of God."

Not all of us are stepmothers or foster mothers. If we are mothers, we will probably someday be mothers-in-law. Every mother-in-law can beautify this relationship with love, too, so that her new children will want to be called her children.

Proverbs 14:1

NOVEMBER 21

When I Have Time

"It isn't that I don't want to entertain strangers. Or visit the sick. Or sew for the poor. I just haven't time. My family takes all of my time just now."

I am not sure that anyone has time. In spite of all our laborsaving devices, it seems that women's work is still never done.

When I read the list of virtues that belonged to women of the early church, I see that they describe good women of today too. Paul tells Timothy that the good woman shall be "well reported of for [her] good works;

"If she have brought up children,

"If she have lodged strangers,

"If she have washed the saints' feet,

"If she have relieved the afflicted,

"If she have diligently followed every good work" (I Timothy 5:10).

331

Diligently following every good work could not mean that we should neglect our children or our families to run here and there to help in every good cause. Bringing up children is mentioned first. Yet these other things are mentioned as belonging with the bringing up of children.

Maybe we can't wait until we have time to do these things in a large way. We may have to share our simple meal with strangers instead of cooking a company dinner. We may have to put off making curtains for the living room to sew garments for a family in need. Perhaps once in a while Dad can keep the children while Mother visits a sick or discouraged friend. Sometimes relieving the afflicted will mean missing a sermon to stay with a sick child or a feeble parent. Living a sermon must sometimes be more urgent than hearing one.

Lord, help me to redeem the time today. Let me rejoice and be glad in this day. May this joy be shared with my family and multiplied to meet the needs of others. Through Christ our Lord. Amen.

Psalm 118:24; Ephesians 5:16

NOVEMBER 22

Let Georgia Do It

The expression, "Let Georgia do it," may be slang, but it is expressive slang.

We decide that Georgia has more time than we have. Georgia's children are older and can help her with the work; Georgia's children are younger and do not have so many social demands. Georgia has a bigger house with more room; Georgia has a smaller house and less work. So we decide to let Georgia do it.

332

Let's face the truth. Most of the time Georgia just does the extra task in spite of her other work. She does it not because she has more time than other women have, but because she has learned to make the best use of her time.

Every family has a Georgia who carries the heavy end of preparing for family gatherings or caring for elderly parents. Every church has its Georgias, who teach Sunday-school classes, entertain visitors, serve conference dinners, besides looking well to the ways of their households.

There are Georgias with big houses, and Georgias with small ones. The Georgias have families of varying sizes and children of different ages. They are Georgias only because they do what others do not find time, or take time, to do.

When I read the parable of the talents I think of the Georgias. Their cups of work and responsibility are full, but somehow they seem able to add another task or lift another load. Instead of losing anything by the extra work, they gain new insights and increase their usefulness.

I look at the Georgias, and understand anew the meaning of the verse: "Unto every one that hath shall be given, and he shall have abundance: but from him that hath not shall be taken away even that which he hath."

Matthew 25:15-29

✳

NOVEMBER 23

On Growing

One of the reasons some women try to avoid responsibility is because they have not grown up! They may have had enough birthdays, but they are not mature.

333

There are women who plead ill health or whose head-aches or backaches occur only when unpleasant duties (or the need to make decisions) arise. Their families become slaves to the whims of a mother who has never grown up.

When I am tempted to smile at grown-up women who behave so childishly, I stop and think about myself. I cannot compare myself with this poor woman, or any other woman. The Bible gives me the standard of maturity. I hide my face in shame as I read in Ephesians that God wants me to grow up in all things into Christ.

The writer of Hebrews tells us that many people who ought to be teachers are little more than babies. He says we shall know those who are of full age because "by reason of use [they] have their senses exercised to discern both good and evil."

That verse can be applied to my work in my home and in my church. I must learn to exercise my faculties to know what is good and what is evil in the use of my time, in the training of my children, in the many demands that come from the community and the church. One of the marks of maturity is the ability to discern good from evil, and to choose accordingly.

I need to grow up to be a woman, to be the helpmate to my husband that God created a woman to be. Maturity means not only the ability to choose well, but includes also acting upon decisions. A helpmate helps, lifts her share without complaint.

God wants me to grow up. He not only wants me to do this; He is able to accomplish it in me as I let Him have His way. Perhaps I have not listened carefully enough to the beautiful benediction from Jude that our minister so often pronounces over us as a parting blessing.

Jude 24, 25

Benediction

Peter says in his benediction that after you have suffered a while, God will make you perfect, establish you, strengthen you, settle you. This pictures a mature person, strong and settled. It calls to mind a woman who knows what she believes, and whom she believes. But Peter tells us plainly that this place of maturity is reached only by the path of suffering.

Children never become educated who refuse to learn hard lessons. People who move from community to community to escape problems never solve the deepest problem—the one within themselves.

In like manner I have watched women go from church to church in search of blessing who had not taken the first step in the search—the step of losing self to Jesus Christ. This blessing they were seeking was a place of undisturbed peace, singing, and joy. They eagerly held out their empty cups to be filled with blessing for themselves. But they did not want to lose themselves to have the cup filled.

"Lose oneself?" we ask. "How can that be done?"

We hold out our empty cups to the Father to be filled, willing to take whatever He gives. He puts in first our calling in Christ Jesus. And the cup fills with joy. And then, in infinite love, He puts in suffering.

If we have lost our lives in the love of Christ, we accept the suffering. We do not run away to another place to try to find a new kind of blessing. We take the suffering in our cup for the love of Christ, and it burns and it hurts, but in time it gives strength and stability and peace.

The place of Christian maturity, this place of blessing, can be reached by no other path. We cannot by-pass sorrow or responsibility or work. We must meet them, face them, conquer them through Christ.

And God has promised through Peter that: "The God of all grace, who hath called us unto his eternal glory by Christ Jesus, after that ye have suffered a while, [will] make you perfect, stablish, strengthen, settle you" (I Peter 5:10).

NOVEMBER 25

Calm and Storm

Sometimes near the end of November there comes a soft, warm day. It seems as if an Indian summer day has been slipped into November by mistake. On such a day the children throw down their coats and run out to play. And sometimes, if they wander far from the house, they are caught in a blizzard before they return. Without coats. Without overshoes.

I can see myself in the children. Sometimes I have a season of fair weather too. People speak well of me. Friends nod approval. My skies are all blue, and I do not keep my soul girded for the storms that may come. I pray, but I forget my complete dependence on the Lord. My devotions become hurried and my prayers ramble.

Then, suddenly, without warning, the storm falls and I am not ready!

God loves me infinitely more than earthly parents love their children. I fly to Him, as the wet, disheveled children run home through the storm, and He forgives me.

But I would remember on fair days to thank my Father for the calm and rest they bring. And I would keep close to Him in my joys, not only on stormy days.

He leads beside still waters, and through stormy waves.

"He leadeth me beside the still waters" (Psalm 23:2b).

"When thou passest through the waters, I will be with thee" (Isaiah 43:2a).

NOVEMBER 26

Beauty

Beauty is a jewel that has many settings. We travel many miles to see the sunrise or the sunset over some widely advertised lake or mountain peak. But God has put some beauty in every place. At the most unexpected moment, in the most commonplace corners of earth, He fills our cup with breath-taking beauty.

She had gotten up early in the morning, while weariness still wrapped her like a blanket. If only she could throw off the weariness, as she threw aside the bedcovers. Extreme tiredness is as hard to bear as pain. But her husband had been sick for months, and there were many chores to be done in the barn.

The world outside lay quiet and cold beneath a star-studded heaven. A thin, little moon lingered among the stars. The beauty of the quiet moment enfolded her, lifted her tired spirits, touched her weary body.

The Lord put special loveliness in the earth for early risers, she thought. She remembered rosy dawns in the fall. She remembered summer mornings when the meadows lay bathed in mist, every tree a phantom peering through a veil. She counted a dozen varieties of lovely sunrises as she worked in the dimly lighted barn. Remembered beauty filled her cup.

Ecclesiastes 3:11; Jeremiah 31:25

NOVEMBER 27

Courage for Conquerors

A storm of snow and sleet came upon us unexpectedly, coating the sidewalks and streets with a slippery film. The wind drove the sleet needles into the faces of the few pedestrians courageous enough to venture out.

We were concerned for our guest, a young woman whose home was across the town. I can see her yet, fastening the buckles of her boots, and wrapping her scarf around her face.

"I wouldn't miss walking in this beautiful storm! Let me battle the elements." Out she went, and sometime later called to say she had arrived safely home.

This is the courage for me! Even a storm is a beautiful adventure to the strong of heart. This is the courage our Lord would give us. He would not still all the storms of life, but He would give us strength to walk triumphantly through them and come out safely at home.

We are conquerors through Christ, not after these things, but in them!

Romans 8:37

We Still Give Thanks

November is the month of Thanksgiving. The very word "November" flashes through our minds a series of pictures featuring bounteous harvests, heavily laden tables, joyful family gatherings, and church services of praise to God for all these blessings.

I can remember years when the harvest was not bounteous. The potato crop on which we depended was a stark failure. There was enough to eat, but there was no turkey. All of our relatives lived too far away to join us in a family gathering. But we still had our Thanksgiving service of praise to God.

When I read about drought in other places, I know that each year there are some people whose crops have failed. Or whose business ventures have been unsuccessful. Or who have lost their jobs. There are many folks who cannot attend a happy family gathering.

I pause for a bit to remember these people in prayer. I do not know who they are, but God knows. I feel one with them, for I have been in their circumstances.

And I add a new line to my Thanksgiving prayer. I thank God for the hard places I have traveled, that help me to understand the burdens of others.

In my scrapbook I have an old clipping that tells about the testimony given on Thanksgiving Day by a farmer after eight years of crop failures. It reads in part:

"He was no longer young. He had worked long on the prairie, and his face was weather-beaten and tanned. He was clad in overalls and a coat—all that remained of his Sunday best. But as he spoke all this was forgotten.

"He said: 'Although the fig tree shall not blossom, neither shall fruit be in the vines; the labour of the olive shall fail, and the fields shall yield no meat; the flock shall be cut off from the fold, and there shall be no herd in the stalls; yet I will rejoice in the Lord, I will joy in the God of my salvation'" (Habakkuk 3:17, 18).

‿

NOVEMBER 29

Summons from the King

We sat in the church and listened spellbound while a minister lately returned from Palestine described the conditions in the Near East and kept us busy hunting Scripture references to fit the situations. We felt the return of the Lord was near, at the very door.

Then we came home and the next day we went about our ordinary tasks.

The radio blared exciting news; the newspaper headlines were two inches high.

And still we washed dishes and made beds and swept floors. We read our Bible and prayed with the children and wrote Christmas letters to missionaries. We went to see a friend who was offended at something we had done and asked forgiveness and made peace.

There seems so little that women can do while the world is in an upheaval. Yet I remember that women will be doing their work on the very day the Lord comes. He expects us to keep on working while all about us nations rise and fall. Jesus says that two women will be grinding at the mill, preparing their family's dinner.

Women will be working, caring for their families. But the women who love the Lord will not be afraid while

340

they work. They will be comforting others as well as working.

How wonderful to be awaiting a summons to join the
Lord in the clouds, even while we prepare food for our
families!

Matthew 24:41; I Thessalonians 4:17, 18

NOVEMBER 30

My Cup Runneth Over!

When I think of cups, I remember Christ in Gethsemane praying: "Father, if thou be willing, remove this cup
from me: nevertheless not my will, but thine, be done"
(Luke 22:42).

He took that cup of suffering and drained it for us. I
hear Him say to Peter, as He heals the servant's ear: "The
cup which my Father hath given me, shall I not drink it"
(John 18:11)?

I cannot share that terrible cup of agony and suffering.
I receive from it only blessing, the blessing of salvation.
When I stop to think of this, all the affliction ever dropped
into my cup seems very light indeed. All the love and
sacrifice I have offered to the Lord seems very poor.

I think with David: "What shall I render unto the Lord
for all his benefits toward me?"

And the answer comes to me as it came to David: "I will
take the cup of salvation, and call upon the name of the
Lord."

The Lord gives the cups, and He fills them. I would
take my eyes off the cup and its contents to look at the
Giver, and thank Him for being my God. I would use the

words of David once more:

"The Lord is the portion of mine inheritance and of my cup" (Psalm 16:5).

"My cup runneth over" (Psalm 23:5c).

Psalm 116:12, 13

DECEMBER

AND WHAT DO YOU DO

Dorothy Snapp McCammon

DECEMBER 1

And What Do You *Do?*

Many tourists stop briefly at a famous university here in Tokyo. And it is a quiet joke among the faculty wives that when the campus tour is finished and the university foundation explained, two visitors out of three will ask the wife (whose morning has just been consumed), "And what do *you* do?"

The fact is that those wives, like most of us, are "just" wives, "just" housekeepers, "just" hostesses, "just" committee members. And that "just" is about the same size as the one our Julie handles so lightly when she wearies of too much come-and-go at our house and begs, "Just be a mom." Just!

The professional women among us may be relatively few. But the woman who is not called on daily to perform duties in a dozen different roles is still more rare.

A woman's day is actually anything but humdrum; routine can stay fresh. A consciousness of God's hand in and over our daily schedule can and should transform living into Living!

Now let us make this Christmas month a time of recognizing the opportunities and talents God gives to women. Let us remember that the priceless privilege of mothering our Saviour was given to an ordinary woman, a "handmaid of the Lord." Let us think together, as Christian women to whom God has entrusted much.

May God help us to realize anew that whatever we do to His glory, we must do in His strength. God give us humility to admit that only as we receive from Him can we give to others what is required from us daily.

Let us discover honestly and constructively some of the many answers to our question for this month—"and what do *you* do?"

Remember:

Jesus cautions, ". . . apart from me you can do nothing" (John 15:5b, RSV). But let us say with Paul, "I can do all things in him who strengthens me" (Philippians 4:13, RSV).

*

DECEMBER 2

We Trek

Count for a moment—how many homes have you lived in since you were born? And who can say how many more before this life is done? Yes, we trek. We journey toward a city whose builder and maker is God.

What vivid and exciting memories we all have of "settling into" a new home! Father measuring, sawing, hammering away at odd jobs, workmen making other improvements. Mother sewing, arranging and rearranging, trying to make the new place comfortable, trying to make it home.

Then out of the nest we go—to a dormitory room or a job away from home. And we ourselves labor for that homey effect.

344

And now many of *us* are the mothers, trying to make *our* homes seem snug and secure for *our* families. How grateful we are for husbands who can see the importance of hanging some cherished pictures even before the floors are waxed!

Yet, as Christians we know better. This world is not our home at all, and the things of this world don't really make home. Somehow, and soon, we must believe this deep in our hearts, if the sense of values we communicate to our children, our neighbors, our associates, is to ring true.

Here is a hard assignment, but a good one for early December. In a pre-Christmas covenant—surely with God and preferably with our families too—let's put "things" where they belong. In the giving that we plan, and the gifts that we frankly wish for, let's allow the Spirit to reign!

God will give us practical guidance and tact for working out the details. He'll give us joy beyond our own, as we realize that we are helping others to lighten their loads.

And trekking will be more thrilling, for we will find ourselves less cumbered, with a keener sense of direction, and a clearer vision of our final Goal.

Remember:

Jesus warns His followers, ". . . the Son of man has nowhere to lay his head" (Matthew 8:20, RSV), but He promises, "In my Father's house are many rooms" (John 14:2a, RSV).

DECEMBER 3

We Sing

"Hey, let's do that again!" exclaimed our three-year-old, when our tenor and soprano guests turned our morning singing into a respectable quartet recently. Our family

345

singing has its limitations, of course. An untrained bass and alto, two preschool trebles, and a learning-English Japanese don't produce perfect harmony, musically speaking.

But we *do* produce something a lot more important than that—something called *family* harmony. And akin to that, we produce (when we are all in the right frame of mind) praise to God, acceptable in His sight! Surely direction, not quality, determines the beauty of such songs.

Have you yourself or you as a family been skipping over this avenue of praise to God? Begin singing today! Your children aren't critical, and our neighbors may prefer even imperfect music to some other neighborhood noises. Your Bible is full of it—suggestion, persuasion, command—"O come, let us sing unto the Lord!"

Singing is strength. Many Christians share the testimony that participation in singing at a time of crisis has brought calm and peace. Have you tried it?

Singing is giving. This mother will never forget what Marian Anderson gave one cold evening in a concert hall in Japan. Our tiny boy, whom we'd never yet held in our arms, was struggling for life in an incubator, and this heart was full of fear. Miss Anderson, who believes what she sings, melted that fear as she sang, "He holds the whole world in His hands. He holds the little tiny babies in His hands . . . ."

Singing is prayer. Some of our deepest experiences of dedication and consecration have come through song.

Singing is unity. No memory of home comes more frequently or is more precious than that of the five of us, grouped around Mother at the piano, singing through the hymnal while the dishes waited in the kitchen. They still wait when we all get together.

This month let us turn often to the loveliest song of praise ever sung by woman. It expresses humility, faith, obedience, awe, understanding—all with spontaneity and beauty. It is recorded in the first chapter of Luke, and was sung by the mother of our Lord.

Remember:

The poet wrote, "Let those refuse to sing who never knew our God . . . ." Let us say with the psalmist, "I will sing to the Lord as long as I live; I will sing praise to my God while I have being" (Psalm 104:33, RSV).

∗

DECEMBER 4

We Teach

It was Mike's first visit to a "real" church. (Church is usually just upstairs in our house.) After we silently explored the cathedral, we sat quietly in a pew and thanked God for His presence, the beauty of the building, the people who worship there. And Mike's response was as natural as the prayer had been—it was a three-year-old's reverent, hushed "Hey!"

✿   ✿   ✿

We stopped one morning (between paragraphs of an urgent letter) and unearthed the amazing fact that there are 40,000 muscles in an elephant's trunk. He smells all the way up it, too, but his sight is very poor.

From there the discussion turned naturally and impressively to the wonders of creation, the justice of compensation, and then to the Creator.

✿   ✿   ✿

Mike was starting with unpleasant symptoms of impend-

347

ing illness again. After Julie fanned him to sleep, we prayed together that when he awoke he'd feel better. A couple of hours later he called, and after one look at his grinning face, Julie reported in a delighted voice, "We sure prayed the right prayer that time!"

* * *

". . . What I can I give Him, give my heart." So sang Julie from Rossetti's lovely Christmas poem. But then she stopped and looked troubled. "If I gave my heart, I'd have nothing to pump my blood around with!"

A perfect opportunity to talk, and of course we did.

* * *

We can't exactly make these openings, but we can develop an ear for recognizing them. To reserve such discussion for "worship time" is to eliminate 95 per cent of our God-given chances to teach, to guide, to shape. And to declare ourselves too busy or too poorly informed to pursue the discussion is to sacrifice the remaining 5 per cent.

* * *

Remember:

A teacher rightly called the little lives entrusted to her, "Heaven in My Hand." Then let us pray with the psalmist, "Lead me in thy truth, and teach me . . ." (Psalm 25:5a, RSV).

DECEMBER 5

We Speak

"The love of Him is shutting my mouth," said a German friend about her unspeakable joy in the Lord. But more of us share Peter and John's testimony—"We cannot but speak . . . ."

"But I never gave a speech in my life!" you may protest. Nevertheless you do public speaking; what you say is heard by many and it matters tremendously.

Remember, we speak in many ways. Our silences, our actions, our facial expressions, *and* our voices. It is all too true sometimes that "we cannot but speak." How often have we wished desperately that we could call back the cold silence, the disgusted shrug, the superior look. In fact, when the nonvocal voices speak so clearly and unmistakably, the voiced message is simply wasted.

Too, there are those times when our actions stay in line but our tongues are uncontrolled. The poet longs for a thousand tongues, but most of us have enough trouble managing one!

David recognized the problem of consistent voices when he prayed, "Let the words of my mouth and the meditation of my heart be acceptable in thy sight . . . ." And James probes the sore spot when he observes that "From the same mouth come blessing and cursing. . . . This ought not to be so."

The answer, again, is found in Christ. "If any man be in Christ, he is a new creature . . . ." We all have marveled at this miracle of change in lives newly joined to Christ. Do others observe evidence of newness of life in us?

Pray today for opportunities to speak. Then see to it that your whole life verifies that which you have said.

Remember:

Jesus taught, "Out of the abundance of the heart . . . [the] mouth speaks" (Luke 6:45b, RSV), and James concluded, "If any one thinks he is religious, and does not bridle his tongue but deceives his heart, this man's religion is vain" (James 1:26, RSV).

349

We Write

"Let's read *my* book," says Julie with pride, bringing out some typed, stapled sheets. It is something any mother could compile in a few hours; it's a very special tie between us. You don't need to be a "writer" to write for those who love you. And God is such a One.

It is frustrating to have an idea lurking around the periphery of your conscious thought. It is satisfying to capture it with pen and ink, to analyze it, work it over, make it say what you want it to say. Perhaps we polish it and share it; more often we enjoy the therapeutic value of the "capturing" experience, then consign the product to a drawer or wastebasket.

But too often, we don't even pick up our pens. We think we are too busy; we plan to do it later; we say we surely *wish* we knew how to write.

Has it ever occurred to you that this business of making excuses is a way of cheating ourselves and God too? Surely if He gives us the experiences which evoke the response, He will enable us to express our praise in a way that pleases Him!

Any month is a good writing month, but December almost demands it of us. Did you ever try writing your Christmas notes instead of hunting for just the right card? It's a perfect time for expressing appreciation for God-given friends—faithful pastors, Christian teachers, dedicated doctors, dependable helpers.

Did you ever send someone a carefully written prayer, instead of just saying, "I pray for you"? Paul did. Or how about the family Christmas program? The script can be extremely simple, yet if you do it yourself it will be exactly what you want.

350

There are plenty of writing assignments waiting for you this month—and few excuses!

Remember:

Jude (no journalist) was ". . . very eager to write . . . of our common salvation . . ." (Jude 3a, RSV), and John, an old man, explains, "We are writing . . . that our joy may be complete" (I John 1:4, RSV).

DECEMBER 7

We Share

Insight, understanding, encouragement, sympathy, good ideas—she had them all. She seemed at first like a perfect counselor, one with whom a person could really share. And then the disappointing truth dawned—it was always a one-way sharing. And with that came the second truth—one-way sharing isn't really sharing at all!

True sharing is always reciprocal. If we feel condescending in giving, or apologetic in receiving, we haven't really shared. With that in mind, let us think a moment about what sharing experiences we may participate in this very day.

Joys, dozens of little ones and a few big ones, will surely cross our path today. They're shared back and forth with our children and others nearest us until we scarce can remember whether they're coming or going.

Sorrows, griefs, disappointments, hurts, and troubles will come, with sure results in our lives, whether they begin as ours or others!

Sharing of self, as we feed, clothe, clean, and care for various needs of our families. Outgoing? Yes. Satisfying? Warmly!

351

Sharing of friends, over a cup of tea, a garden gate, or maybe via a note of introduction. Giving? Yes. Rewarding? Richly!

Sharing of goods, with those in need. Who gains the greater blessing—the recipient or the giver? Whichever you are today, act in the name of Christ and accept the blessing meant for you.

Sharing of beauty—a flower, a gem of verse, a beautiful recording, a walk in the woods, a talk under the stars. Invite! Accept! Receive! Give! Beauty always multiplies when truly shared.

Share spiritual strength, the Great Good News of Jesus Christ. Receive humbly from those who would break spiritual bread with you today. Share your faith with someone. It will surely strengthen; it may mean eternal life.

Remember:

A poet wrote: "Art thou lonely, O, my brother?
Share thy little with thy brother.
Stretch a hand to one unfriended,
And thy loneliness is ended."

And Paul exhorted Christians to "Rejoice with those who rejoice, weep with those who weep" (Romans 12:15, RSV).

✳

DECEMBER 8

We Learn

"You should've had me do it," says Julie, five, worriedly mopping the blood from Mother's cut finger. "Then I'd be hurt 'stead of you."

"That's your very nicest one," we parents suggested selfishly. "Are you sure you want to give *it* away?"

352

They both were sure, and there were no regrets later. Only satisfaction that some "children" who hadn't expected a Christmas gift would be pleasantly surprised.

✿ ✿ ✿

"Now the Bible verse you learned that begins with H?"
"Honor your mommy and daddy so they won't spank you."
"And K? Remember? Keep—"
"Oh, I know. 'Keep dirty stuff out of your mouth!'"

✿ ✿ ✿

"Please, just dry things that won't break. Leave the cups for Mother. Yes, I know you want to help, but really you would help the most by just watching."

The cup that broke that morning slipped from Mother's hand. . . .

✿ ✿ ✿

"Why are you crying, Mother? Are you afraid Mike will die? God can tell the doctors what to do—you don't need to worry. Don't you remember, 'I will trust and not be afraid'?"

✿ ✿ ✿

The mothers took turns helping the school cafeteria, and each little girl was eager for the day when her mother was on display. Ruthie was no exception.

"There's my mom," she told Susan, pointing proudly toward the serving counter. "Oh!" gasped Susan with all the frankness of youth, "she's not even pretty!" "No," agreed Ruthie, without a flicker of resentment, "but she's sure awful nice."

✿ ✿ ✿

"Create in *me* a clean heart, O God, and put a new and right spirit within *me*."

✿ ✿ ✿

Remember:

Jesus says, of children, ". . . to such belongs the kingdom of God" (Mark 10:14b, RSV), and James promises, for mothers too, "God . . . gives grace to the humble" (James 4:6b, RSV).

DECEMBER 9

We Choose

"A whole month of daily verbs," you exclaim, "just from the everyday lives of women? *Are* there that many?" Friends, a whole *year* of verbs wouldn't complete a description of our combined busyness. We're surrounded by them, floundering in them, almost strangled by them, these verbs. There are many, many of them; there are too many!

A wise mother writes this advice to her daughter, concerning this month of meditations and also concerning life: "Let me suggest that you work in reverse for a while, discovering what verbs you can eliminate to make life more worth while for yourself, your family, and your world. It usually takes years of living to reach this wonderful discarding stage, but one *could* start at any time."

Let's start today! Let us think of verbs we can profitably eliminate from our lives, making more room and time for the things that count. An excellent practice would be to write beside each verb we discard, the Biblical basis for doing so. Here is a beginning; now turn it into *your* list.

Begrudge	Hate
Boast	Indulge
Covet	Lie
Deceive	Pout

Dispute	Rebel
Doubt	Resent
Exaggerate	Worry
Fear	

Remember:

these teachings of Jesus: ". . . lay up for yourselves treasures in heaven . . . . For where your treasure is, there will your heart be also" (Matthew 6:20a, 21, RSV). ". . . Martha, you are anxious and troubled about many things; one thing is needful. Mary has chosen the good portion . . ." (Luke 10:41, 42a, RSV).

DECEMBER 10

We Cook

"It was observed," writes his intimate friend about Brother Lawrence, "that in the greatest hurry of business in the kitchen he still preserved his recollection and heavenly-mindedness." We will leave it open to conjecture just why this quotation had to be written about a *man*—the point here is, kitchens and heavenly-mindedness need not be mutually exclusive.

In fact, when we consider what proportion of our days and years is spent in kitchens, it becomes imperative to a Christian woman's spiritual welfare that she find things about her kitchen activities which turn her thoughts heavenward!

Do good appetites seem synonymous with activated bottomless pits, at your house? Just visit a friend with a sickly husband or child, and you will come home thanking God for a healthy, hungry family.

When you are tempted to refer to yourself as the family drudge, remember the wives who watch with longing hearts from beds or wheel chairs, as others care for their families.

If Christmas cookies and candies and boxes seem more burden than fun, stop and pray for those who *can't* send food to hungry loved ones behind iron curtains.

When you are tired of trying to estimate quantities for the family feast, remember the refugee woman who came here yesterday. Hollow-cheeked and big-eyed, she said quite frankly that if it weren't for her child she would long ago have ended her life. Her part-time job in an Italian bar paid only food. There wasn't much there for her four-year-old's breakfast. Now even that job is gone.

Let's start a list of tangible kitchen equipment for keeping kitchen thoughts turned heavenward:

1. A bulletin board with Scriptures you want to memorize, pictures worth meditating on, hymns to learn.

2. A note pad, for jotting down names of folks who would be cheered by a pot of jam, a box of cookies, a hot casserole.

3. A prayer list, with pencil attached.

4. A savings bank, which will expect a share for someone needy each time you decide to serve the family some luxury item.

5. A Bible with a flour-resistant binding and a good concordance. Now you add to the list; then use it.

Remember:

In Proverbs we read this about a good wife and mother: "She looks well to the ways of her household . . . . Her children rise up and call her blessed; her husband also . . ." (Proverbs 31:27a, 28a, RSV). And a thoughtful saint reminded herself, each time she saw someone less fortunate, "There, but for the grace of God, go I."

We Reflect

We were gathered in the chapel of Michi Kawai's beloved Keisen School, attending a service commemorating the anniversary of her death. Probably no one else even caught a glimpse of what, to this visitor, was the most impressive sight of the day.

To the right of the platform hung a huge, framed photograph of Miss Kawai, but just then her likeness was barely discernible. Instead, the light fell so that fifteen wholesome, purposeful student faces were clearly reflected from the glass.

The layout of that picture was correct. Miss Kawai's life had been filled with Christian girls, and their lives had been touched and changed by hers. Now her earthly days and work were closed. Theirs were just opening, full of hope and promise. One felt sure that she would have been pleased with her place in the background.

Influence is a tremendous power on our lives—almost fearsome! No matter how young or old we are, our lives are constantly being influenced. We cannot alter the fact. Our reading, our associates, our entertainment, our friends, our loves, our enemies—in a real sense, all of these leave an indelible mark on our lives. They become a part of us; we reflect them.

Paul writes, "You are an open letter about Christ" (II Corinthians 3:2, Phillips). If you are a Christian, he is talking to you. But what that letter says about Christ is for you to decide.

Consider, too, the fact that *we* are reflected in whatever lives ours touch. What do others see of us in our children, our husbands, our students, our closest friends? Influence from our lives is a sacred and inescapable responsibility.

Some apparently lovely objects can appear very warped in reflection. But clear reflections of the very ordinary are often extremely beautiful.

Remember:

The poet vows, "I would be true, for there are those who trust me." And Paul reminds us, ". . . We, though many, are one body in Christ, and individually members one of another" (Romans 12:5, RSV).

*

DECEMBER 12

We Listen

"Then you understand me, what I talk about!" she cried in obvious relief. "You are the first one in Tokyo—oh, God is good." The tears welled up and ran freely down her cheeks. She was a strange mixture—Russian, had always lived in China, speaking broken English, stranded in Tokyo. But she was a woman who needed to talk, and she had found someone with enough parallel experiences to understand her story. She had found a sympathetic listener, and to her it was a reminder that God is good.

❄ ❄ ❄

"And Mikie, listen, then we all got off the bus and the teacher took us to the park, and listen, you know what we did then—do you? Mother, Mikie won't listen to me! Mother, aren't you listening either? Mikie, come on, I'm gonna go find Daddy. . . ."

❄ ❄ ❄

She was in her 90's when we knew her, and it took some faith to hand tiny Julie over into her shaky arms. But she always reached for her, and she never dropped her. Then

358

she always talked of her own baby, some seventy years old at that time! She didn't ask for two-way conversation; she was starving for someone to listen. She invariably asked God's blessing on her visitors as they left her room, and they invariably received it.

❃ ❃ ❃

"Oh, the comfort, the inexpressible comfort of feeling safe with a person—having neither to weigh thoughts nor measure words, but pouring them all right out just as they are, chaff and grain together; certain that a faithful hand will take and sift them, keep what is worth keeping, and with the breath of comfort blow the rest away."

❃ ❃ ❃

Remember:

James advises, "Let every man be quick to hear, slow to speak . . . " (James 1:19b, RSV), and Paul reminds us, "If I . . . have not love, I am nothing. . . . Love is patient and kind . . ." (I Corinthians 13:2b, 4a, RSV).

DECEMBER 13

We Mingle

Our Japanese friends have taught us two ways in which to make mingling more enjoyable and refreshing. We hasten to fill the "awkward pauses" in conversation; they find the silence comfortable and restful. We seldom forget the watch on our wrist; they rarely remember it. Do you take time to mingle? Mingling takes time!

Is it natural to mingle? Follow our Mike down the street. The policeman salutes him; the bus driver honks at him; the shopkeeper calls him by name; the delivery boy sets him on his bicycle and rides off with him. A child not yet affected by the "laws" of society is an outgoing, mingling little being.

Is it easy to mingle? Not always. Some of us lack a sense of need. We are too satisfied with our present clique; we have no desire to make new friends. Some of us are too shy or modest; we forget that we have something worth while to contribute to others. Both of these types need to meditate on the term "redemptive friendship." It implies opportunity, challenge, responsibility.

Is it dangerous to mingle? It could be. Mingle, mix, blend, merge, disappear—so runs the possible course for losing one's identity. Strength of character, of faith, of values, of purpose—these are prerequisites for "safe" mingling. And they are a guarantee to your associates that what rubs off, from your life to theirs, is worth keeping. Remember that mingling is a two-way process.

Is it Christian to mingle? Follow Christ for a few days. "The whole city was gathered . . . many were gathered together . . . all the crowd gathered about him . . . many were sitting with Jesus . . . a great multitude followed . . . the crowd came together again . . . a very large crowd gathered about him . . . ." He was seldom alone!

Is it necessary to mingle? Absolutely, if you belong to Christ. "Go . . . teach . . . learn . . . heal . . . witness . . . forgive . . . receive . . . ask . . . give . . . seek . . . find . . . rejoice . . . weep . . . love . . . pray"—these are some of the basic commands of Christ to His disciples.

Remember:

your social responsibility according to Jesus Christ: "Let your light so shine before men, that they may . . . give glory to your Father . . ." (Matthew 5:16, RSV). And remember the only spirit, in which this can be done: "He

[Christ] . . . told this . . . to some who trusted in themselves that they were righteous and despised others: '. . . every one who exalts himself will be humbled . . .'" (Luke 18:9, 14, RSV).

DECEMBER 14

We Thank

"I guess it was all right," said a Christian girl of a public prayer she heard, "but it sounded awfully queer." The prayer *was* unusual; it was only thanksgiving. It was so different from the ordinary "give me and forgive me" variety, that even Christians found it strange. But to God's ear it was surely sweet music, a kind He must long to hear more often.

Thanks for gifts and blessings which are exactly what we've been wanting—that kind of thanks comes easy. Health, food, clothing, work to do, home, children, and the spiritual blessings which change darkness to light—for these we cannot thank God too often. These mercies which are new every morning dare not become commonplace in our thinking. Let us keep fresh our wonder at God's daily goodness!

But some days come when it seems that we need to search deep and bend low before we can be sincerely thankful. Can you give thanks to God for being proved wrong? For humiliating correction from a child? For His withholding something you desperately want?

How about the thanks you receive? How faithful are you at keeping your left hand uninformed about your right hand's generosity? How willing are you to do a favor which you know will never be repaid? Are you hurt when someone forgets to thank you, or gives credit to the wrong person?

In some families, "taking it for granted" has become a bad substitute for expressed thanks. Carefully shined shoes, a helping hand with the dishes, a yard mowed before it is mentioned, a telephone call to save worry—such daily evidences of thoughtfulness and love deserve a spoken "thank you."

A child who is courteously thanked at the proper times will soon begin to voice his appreciation without prompting. And if he has always heard God included in the natural "thank you's," he will early establish a grateful heart toward the Giver of all truly good gifts.

❋   ❋   ❋

> Thou that hast given so much to me,
> Give one more thing—a grateful heart.
> Not thankful when it pleases me,
> As if Thy blessings had spare days,
> But such a heart whose pulse may be Thy praise.
>
> —*G. Herbert.*

❋   ❋   ❋

Remember:
the psalmist's refrain: "O give thanks to the Lord, for he is good; his steadfast love endures for ever" (Psalm 118:1, RSV), and Paul's admonition to Christians: ". . . give thanks in all circumstances; for this is the will of God in Christ Jesus for you" (I Thessalonians 5:18, RSV).

✳

We Wait

"Perhaps tomorrow"—that is all it says, as it hangs by the desk of a busy executive. But that brief motto helps us understand the dedicated spirit in which he lives. It explains the efficient urgency with which he works. He is waiting for a great day, and for him, waiting time is preparation time. Christ is coming! When? Perhaps tomorrow.

Now some people are quite the opposite—they put off everything until tomorrow. They don't have time today to speak a word for Christ—later. They don't take time to read a good book—some other time. They don't have time to visit a sick friend this week—sorry. They can't stop and do things with their children or grandchildren—maybe tomorrow. But those people are waiting for a day that will never come; the tomorrow *they* talk about is *now*, and when they realize it, it will be yesterday, and it will be gone.

Some who read this today are suffering; they know from experience what it means to watch for the morning. They wait confidently for help, believing God's promise that He will not ask His children to bear more than they can endure. Let us learn from them of waiting in faith. May God find us available today to serve as channels of courage and relief.

Some who read these lines could teach us much about waiting. Their threescore years and ten have been fully lived, and they are done with the hustle and bustle of "everyday waiting." Now they wait for that great tomorrow when they will see Him face to face. Let them hear from us today that their useful days are not finished, that as they wait with patient grace and assurance for tomorrow, they contribute much to our today.

But the majority of women who read this together today are neither old in years nor suffering in body or spirit. Yet we, too, will wait today. We will wait our turn at the supermarket; we may wait in line for the bus. We will wait for the family to come when we call them to meals; we may wait for the repairman who promised to call. We will wait for a dawdling child whose play is, to him, more important than our time; we may wait for a letter that is overdue. We will wait for a spark of interest from a spiritually cold acquaintance; we may wait for an answer to our prayers.

No matter who we are, nor what our age, health, or station in life, today we will wait. It behooves us to prepare spiritually for the waiting this day holds, that we may possess our souls in patience. Let our first waiting be before the Lord!

Remember:

Milton's comforting words, "They also serve, who only stand and wait," and the beautiful promise from Isaiah, ". . . They who wait for the Lord shall renew their strength, they shall mount up with wings like eagles, they shall run and not be weary, they shall walk and not faint" (Isaiah 40:31, RSV).

✳

DECEMBER 16

We Read

"That's what God made schoolteachers for," shrugs the bored American wife. "Wait until you're six and they'll teach you to read." So she sits here in Tokyo month after month, with two servants to open the commissary supplies at mealtime, and refuses to read to her lonely little boy. That, it would seem, is a record reading-low for a parent!

And almost as low on the ladder of reading decency are the parents who read only trash. Three guesses what their children will read. Good taste in reading is by no means innate; such taste is more often "caught" than taught.

Few of us are willing to join either of these two categories; our temptation may begin a little higher up, say on the "easy reading" rung. "Oh, all right," we yield to the coaxing child, "I'll read just one book. But choose an easy one, and short." The chances are that we choose our own books by the same standards. If it doesn't make us think, or squirm, or change, or grow—we like it!

Now that last sentence describes exactly what the world's best Book *does* do. And to a degree what all worthwhile literature will do. There are many rungs along the way, but this is the top of the ladder. And it is the spot toward which Christian women must be striving. Blessed are those who hunger and thirst for righteousness, for they shall be satisfied.

"Grace before reading," suggests a lover of good books, "is every bit as important as grace before meat." Indeed, why not?

Obviously, however, not even God Himself could bless some reading diets to the strengthening of the reader. We would do better to go back one more step and pray earnestly and openly for guidance as we *select* our diet.

Then the grace before reading can be sincere thanksgiving; then the expected miracle of transformation—from paper page to enriched life—will surely be wrought.
Remember:

Paul admonishes Christians to "Let the word of Christ dwell in you richly" (Colossians 3:16a, RSV), and he reminds Christians that ". . . God's temple is holy, and that temple you are" (I Corinthians 3:17b, RSV).

We Intercede

Chinese friends told us of a frail foreign missionary interned in Chungking during the war. Each morning his work required that he come across the river and climb the many steps to the city. Each evening he toiled wearily home again, heavy pack on his back, up the hundreds of steps on the other side. Finally his friends tried to voice their pity and concern, but his radiant face stopped them short. "It's truly the nicest time of my day," he assured them, "and the steps are always too few. You see, that is the time each day when I pray for my friends."

❋   ❋   ❋

"I like to feel in all the work
    Thou hast to do,
That I by lifting hands of prayer
    May help Thee too . . . ."

❋   ❋   ❋

God's Prayer Reminder

I cannot tell why there should come to me
    A thought of someone miles and years away,
In swift insistence on the memory,
    Unless there be a need that I should pray.

We are too busy even to spare a thought
    For days together of some friends away;
Perhaps God does it for us; and we ought
    To read His signal as a sign to pray.

366

Perhaps just then my friend has fiercer fight,
   A more appalling weakness—a decay
Of courage, darkness, some lost sense of light.
   And so in case he needs my prayer, I pray.

Dear, do the same for me! If I intrude
   Unasked upon you, on some crowded day;
Give me a moment's prayer, as interlude,
   Be very sure I need it; therefore pray.

—*Marianna Farmingham.*

❋   ❋   ❋

Remember:

James encourages Christians to ". . . pray for one another [because] "The prayer of a righteous man has great power in its effects" (James 5:16, RSV), and Paul says, "Have no anxiety about anything, but in everything by prayer and supplication with thanksgiving let your requests be made known to God" (Philippians 4:6, RSV).

DECEMBER 18

We Judge

"I isn't, isn't I, Mother? She didn't, didn't she, Mother? They shouldn't, shouldn't they, Mother?" So come the appeals, tens of times daily, from our Michael-of-many-negatives.

Women lawyers are scarce, and women judges in the courts are almost unheard-of. But when it comes to the total number of decisions handed down in a day's time, we women are surely the world's judging majority.

It sobers us when we realize that little folks can form their idea of justice only from what they see, hear, and experience. And how alert they are to signs of judgment in the air! "Who, Mother, who are you talking about?" "Why did you make me do that?" "Why doesn't Chikochan want me to play at her home?" "I don't want to play with the little kids; I want to listen to you big people talk."

There are awful dangers in setting ourselves up as judges, but we are judges, and judge we do! It takes some discipline to restrain ourselves in situations where we are obviously not qualified to judge. It takes more to keep our fingers off the cases where we feel ever so qualified, but are not invited!

It is humiliating to review a day of household judgments. How many were colored by momentary partiality, reached too quickly in impatience, passed needlessly in foolish anger, or meted out before all the facts were known?

Sobering, dangerous, humiliating—judging is all of these and more. The only reason we dare undertake such a role is because we have free access to God's wisdom. Another saving feature (which the bench judges don't enjoy) is the fact that when we err we can (and should) frankly admit the error and correct it.

Go slowly in your judging today. Make sure, first of all, that the situation requires a judgment; then that the task is really yours. Recognize again the fact that silences speak judgment too. Undertake the job only after you have sought God's help.

And remember this—a wrong judgment, openly corrected in Christian humility, may well be a stronger witness for God than a hundred correct decisions from which He receives no glory.

Remember:

Jesus reminds us, ". . . with the judgment you pronounce you will be judged . . ." (Matthew 7:2a, RSV).

Then pray with Solomon, "Give thy servant . . . an understanding mind . . . that I may discern between good and evil" (I Kings 3:9a, RSV).

DECEMBER 19

We Write—from Full Hearts

This prayer came from a full heart, at Christmas time, when music seemed to fill the air. "Thou Giver of all perfect gifts, I thank Thee today for the good gifts that are mine. I thank Thee that because Thou art my Father and my Creator, Thou dost perfectly understand me. I thank Thee that in Thy perfect knowledge Thou art able to speak to me in many ways—not only by Thy Word and with the silent voice of Thy Spirit, not only through Thy children, but Thou dost also speak to my heart by the sheer beauties of Thy creating hand.

"O Lord, I want to acknowledge today Thy marvelous gift of music. I thank Thee that Thou hast moved in men's hearts to capture and record the heavenly harmonies they have felt and heard. I thank Thee for the lives of great men who have suffered scorn, felt physical deprivation, given all they had to pursue music. Dear God, how wonderfully gracious Thou art to give them, as the fruit of this temporal self-denial, something eternal, indestructible, and soul-nourishing!

"I thank Thee, Father, that no one is excluded from sharing music. That even when I do not grasp the technicalities of musical structure, I can feel, in the soul Thou hast given me, a deep response to such beauty. I thank Thee that I can worship Thee in song, and that beautiful chords from the pens of men always strike a vibrant response from my soul, turning my thoughts to Thee.

"Lord, my prayer is that today, the world over, Thy children may discover anew and share freely this joy of knowing Thy presence more fully and richly through music.

"And when they and I have drunk deep of the joy and peace of close communion with Thee, send us forth, O Lord, to be instruments of Thine in a discordant world. May we be so closely in tune with Thee that Thou canst put Thy hand upon us and bring forth chords of peace and harmony. May the music of our lives always resound to Thine own honor and glory, we pray for Jesus' sake. Amen."

Remember:

The poet prayed,
>"Lord, speak to me that I may speak,
> In living echoes of Thy tone . . . ,"

and the psalmist reminds us, "It is good to give thanks to the Lord . . ." (Psalm 92:1a, RSV).

DECEMBER 20

We Serve

None of us knew his real name; we called him "Mr. George." He was a shabby, hungry-looking Indian gentleman attending graduate school in New York. But his heart, even then, was in a children's home in South India. Many

370

individuals and church groups tried to give a helping hand to this friendly fellow, and he always accepted cheerfully —offerings, overcoats, anything! After a few weeks' interval, the donor would invariably receive a letter of thanks from the institution Mr. George served in India. It was impossible to give anything *to* him; we could only give *through* him. Serving, after all, is just that—it is being a channel, from a source to a need.

Serving can be plain hard work. There is usually nothing very glamorous in the daily schedule of a nurse, a clerk, a teacher, a housewife, an attendant in an old people's home, a telephone operator. Their services are fleetingly appreciated by lives they touch, but for them it may be the dull route to a pay check; dutiful drudgery; inescapable routine.

Helmut Gollwitzer, in his prison camp diary, *Unwilling Journey,* gives a key to a new outlook as he discusses forced labor and Christians. He and his fellow Christians determined to obey the Scriptural passages which told them they must conceive of their work as done "to the Lord." They discovered that "every thrust of a spade could be transformed from a task undertaken with reluctance into a service done to the Lord. . . . It [the command] was not an exhortation from the outside imposed from above, but was a possibility promised as a gift—and thereby a door was opened indeed; forced labor need not remain forced, it could be transformed from a meaningless drudgery into a service full of meaning . . . into a service offered to the Lord."

Does your daily "service" more nearly resemble forced labor? Then share the revelation these prisoners received in their hour of need!

Inspect the terms that describe your serving. Away with

371

words like grudging, hesitant, minimum, choicy, false humility.

Now to the work of today, with a newly chosen set of adjectives: prayerful, joyful, selfless, honest, loving, tender, sacrificial, proud (in the right sense), faithful, united!

Offer these and yourself to God; He can make vital use of such a combination.

Be a channel today, from a Source to a need.

Remember:

Paul's admonition: ". . . whatever you do, do all to the glory of God" (I Corinthians 10:31, RSV), and the words of Jesus about service: ". . . as you did it to one of the least of these my brethren, you did it to me" (Matthew 25:40, RSV).

DECEMBER 21

We Covenant

We smiled at each other right there in Union Church. "Let your first waking thought be of God," the pastor advised. "Repeat it again and again." Our smile came in remembering that the first waking sound of our household those days was repeated again and again, all right, but it was an insistent little voice saying, "Wanta big bottle muk!"

He was right, that pastor. A definite turning to God before the activity of the day begins makes His presence more real all day. A very practical idea is to *record* certain important points regarding our relationship with God. Get them crystallized, then make sure each morning that they are still true.

Here is a sample. It was found in a borrowed book in

West China, spent some time in the States, and now lives under a desk glass in Tokyo.

The Morning Act of Faith . . .

I believe on the Son of God; therefore I am in Him,
  having redemption through His blood and life by His
  Spirit.
He is in me, and all fullness is in Him.
To Him I belong by creation, purchase, conquest,
  and self-surrender.
To me He belongs for all my hourly need.
There is no cloud between my Lord and me.
There is no difficulty inward or outward which
  He is not ready to meet in me today.
I believe I have received not the spirit of fear-
  fulness, but of power and of love and of a sound
  mind.
The Lord is my keeper.
Amen.

—H. C. G. Moule.

Remember:

David's words, "O Lord, in the morning thou dost hear my voice . . ." (Psalm 5:3a, RSV), and he prayed, "Search me, O God, and know my heart! Try me and know my thoughts . . ." (Psalm 139:23, RSV).

DECEMBER 22

We Believe

"There is now no one and nothing for me to depend on except the Lord Jesus and His Word," writes a friend. Then she adds in simple victory, "but more we don't need."

There, in a breath, is the difference faith makes.

* * *

Betty is at home in the country near Tokyo. She's going to die soon, and she knows it. She knows that before she dies she will have to endure intense suffering, because she knows her disease and also that her body can't take sedatives in any form.

She knows all this, but at the same time she knows a contagious brand of assurance and comfort and peace. Because she knows Christ, and she believes His promises.

And that makes all the difference.

* * *

Word had just come of Bill's tragic death. Almost automatically Ruth placed a phone call, then wondered what comfort she could speak. But her dear friend, Bill's widow, spoke first: "Oh, Ruth, the Lord's grace really is sufficient!" Her testimony never wavered, nor will it. Her faith makes all the difference; he had it too.

* * *

Faith makes the difference in December. At your house, does the word "Christmas" start discussions about Santa Claus, or a Babe in a manger?

Which Christmas stories do your children love best? The ones you love, probably. Which do they believe? The one you taught them to believe, of course.

And what difference will this make to their lives? Most likely the same difference it makes to yours. Pray God it be an eternal promise.

* * *

Remember:

David had these two things to say about belief: "The fool says in his heart, 'There is no God'" (Psalm 14:1a, RSV); "The fear of the Lord is the beginning of wisdom" (Psalm 111:10a).

374

DECEMBER 23

We Write—from Concerned Hearts

A concerned heart in a far country found release in writing this, one December.

"Christmas is coming! Where you live, everybody celebrates Christmas as a holiday, a day when the whole family comes home, when the factory gives you a bonus and you have the day off with pay. Tragically, in the so-called Christian land of America, Christmas doesn't mean much more than that to many people.

"To them, Christmas is a time of happiness, when even the cynics forget themselves and join in a vague spirit of good fellowship.

"Christmas is a time of hope, when modern stargazers see new stars, and optimistically—usually only briefly—claim them for their leading lights and hitch their wagons to them.

"Christmas is a time of peace, when even the disillusioned and the men of ill will catch an echo of the angels' song, and close their eyes for a few moments to the ugly reality about them.

"Christmas is a time of giving, when even the Scroogiest of men fall into the commercial traps set for them, and spend more money on others than they have for a whole year.

"How empty, how shallow, how futile, how unsatisfying and pitiable are these feeble graspings after joy!

"What is it that makes Christmas more than this? Christmas must mean Christ! Christ born! God with us! God in man! The Lord's Son, our Saviour come to earth! Prophecy fulfilled, faith rewarded, life abundant now, eternal life entered into!

"A time of happiness? Of course, in the knowledge of Him. Of hope? Yes, abiding hope in Christ. Of true peace? Ah, deep peace through our Lord Jesus Christ. Of giving? Yes, unstinted giving to others through Him, and consecrated giving of very self to Him.

"Here lies the open secret of real joy at Christmas; Christmas must mean Christ in our hearts. This season is a good time for soul-searching. Why do you rejoice as it comes near?"

Remember:

Mary said, ". . . my spirit rejoices in God my Saviour . . ." (Luke 1:47, RSV), and Paul writes, "Rejoice in the Lord always" (Philippians 4:4a, RSV).

DECEMBER 24

We Find

Here is a lovely old Christmas tale, preserved because it contains much truth.

"The three Wise Men came to Bethlehem, full of hope and excitement. And when they saw that the star had led them to a baby in a woman's arms, all three were almost overwhelmed with chagrin and dismay. As they sat and pondered this strange happening, they heard Mary singing to her new baby, as mothers are wont to do. They listened.

" 'My soul doth magnify the Lord!' she sang. 'The Lord!' exclaimed the first wise man. 'Then I have found my Sovereign, my Monarch, my King, my Lord!' And he offered his gold, while Mary sang on.

" 'And my spirit hath rejoiced in God . . . ,' she continued. 'In God!' cried the second, his face alight. "Then I have found Him—the God for whom my spirit has hungered!' And he presented his incense to the babe. Still the mother sang.

" 'My soul doth magnify the Lord and my spirit hath rejoiced in God my Saviour!' 'My Saviour!' echoed the third, 'My Saviour!' And he offered his vase of myrrh."

And so one found in Jesus the King of his desire. Another found in Jesus the God he had so passionately sought. And the third found in Jesus the Saviour for whom his very soul was aching.

And here is truth. For surely from that day until this, every person who truly seeks in faith finds in Jesus exactly what he most needs. This is the essence of the Christmas story; it is the essence of the Gospel of Jesus Christ.
Remember:

God says through Jeremiah: "When you seek me with all your heart, I will be found by you . . ." (Jeremiah 29:13b, 14a, RSV), and the poet sings,
"I came to Jesus as I was, weary and worn and sad;
I found in Him a resting place, and He has made me glad."

DECEMBER 25

We Kneel in Wonder and Adore!

Who can add to Christmas?
The perfect motive—God so loved the world.
The perfect gift—He gave His Son.
The only requirement—Whoever believes on Him . . .
The reward of faith—Shall have eternal life!
The natural response—

"Oh, come to my heart, Lord Jesus,
    There is room in my heart for Thee!"
Remember:

The prophet foretold: ". . . his name will be called 'Wonderful Counselor, Mighty God, Everlasting Father, Prince of Peace.' . . . Immanuel [God is with us]" (Isaiah 9:6b; 7:14b, RSV), and the angel announced: ". . . You shall call his name Jesus, for he will save his people from their sins" (Matthew 1:21b, RSV).

✳

DECEMBER 26

We Love

How do we love? Eternally, fleetingly? Selflessly, selfishly? Spontaneously, dutifully? Steadily, sporadically? Enrichingly, greedily? Purely, lustfully? Deeply, superficially?

Evelyn Underhill wrote wisely in this regard: ". . . it is all right to love people all you can, so long as you live with and in God." Here is a safe guiding principle—let our loving be done with and in God. Then self has no demands or desires; then "God is at work in you, both to will and to work for *his* good pleasure" (Philippians 2:13, RSV).

Here is a tremendous check list by which we must "grade" our love. It is just four verses and a bit more, but it could change the whole world. Read it slowly, line by line, with an honest mind and an open heart.

"Love is patient and kind;
    love is not jealous or boastful;
    it is not arrogant or rude.

Love does not insist on its own way;
it is not irritable or resentful;
it does not rejoice at wrong,
but rejoices in the right.
Love bears all things,
believes all things,
hopes all things,
endures all things.
Love never ends."

God gave the list, through Paul. He gave the love, through Christ. He gives it still, through you.

Remember:

John observed that ". . . he who abides in love abides in God, and God abides in him" (I John 4:16b, RSV), and Paul summarized the fruits of the Spirit: ". . . love, joy, peace, patience, kindness, goodness, faithfulness, gentleness, self-control . . ." (Galatians 5:22, 23a, RSV).

DECEMBER 27

We Write—from Needy Hearts

Here is another reason why we write, or should.

A brilliant Christian girl, studying in a Tokyo university, lost her radiance. Her face was clouded and troubled, and she found it impossible to express her trouble in spoken words, either to us or to God. Worse, she almost convinced herself that she shouldn't really need to bother God with her troubles.

Finally she agreed to try a written discipline of faith.

379

She wrote, honestly and completely, the things that were making the shadows. Then she wrote a statement of her faith in God's ability and willingness to share, to bear, her burdens. On the basis of the second paper, she committed the first to Him.

She came back from this experience her happy self. When old troubles recur, she renews her commitment. When new ones come, she adds them to the list, then lays it at His feet again.

If you could see her face, you would know that it works. Another way to prove it? Try it yourself.

Remember:

the psalmist's exhortation. "Cast your burden on the Lord, and he will sustain you . . ." (Psalm 55:22, RSV), and Jesus' invitation, "Come to me . . . and I will give you rest" (Matthew 11:28, RSV).

DECEMBER 28

We Overlook

We hasty American women with our large-scale ambitions and bigger and better aspirations miss a lot of life's loveliness; we just plain overlook it. Our oriental friends observe [correctly!] that we are not really so busy; we just *seem* busy! Somehow, with no freezers, driers, or disposal units to simplify their work, they find more time to enjoy the beauty of an earthenware cup, the grace of a lovely branch, the wonder of a single bud.

Children take time to wonder. We made two new friends this week. One was a wealthy widow, on a luxury tour around the world. The other was four-year-old Andy, with three frogs in a wastebasket. For an exciting, educational time, we'll travel with Andy any day.

How many readers have given five minutes' contemplation to the internal structure of a fig recently? Or lain on the floor to visit face to face with a canary? Or dropped off to sleep watching clouds scud across the moon? It does appear at our house that when one is three or five years old, such experiences are wonderful. And that abused word by the way, means "adapted to excite wonder."

A friend tells how her dormant sense of wonder was suddenly quickened when a cocoon, which she was explaining to her children, came to life in her hand! It was a profitable shock. Until then, she had just been a dutiful guide for her small explorers. Now she is one of them!

Yes, we adults overlook a great deal. To explore successfully *with* a child is to explore *as* a child. Nor is the process complete until we share, in our own terms, the child's open wonder and exultation at what we discover.

We hope the phrase, "with eyes of wonder," describes any child. Surely it should fit a child of God, living in His amazing creation. Try it on yourself—does it?

Remember:

Job's tardy discovery: "I had heard of thee by the hearing of the ear, but now my eye sees thee" (Job 42:5, RSV), and the psalmist's song of praise, after reviewing God's creation: "O Lord, our Lord, how majestic is thy name in all the earth" (Psalm 8:9, RSV)!

DECEMBER 29

We Rest

Gladys was a tiny, sponsor-less saint of God, active

among and deeply devoted to Chinese youth. In fact, she had given up her British passport and become a Chinese citizen. She had an absolute minimum of possessions and a rare maximum of devotion to God. The combination was not a coincidence.

But even Gladys had her limitations. She had a mind and body that got tired. And God, in His goodness, always provided a quiet home, nourishing food, and loving friends when that need for rest came. Willing hands took Gladys in, and ministered to her until she was rested again.

We all need rest, and often it is when we need it most that we fail to recognize the need. When our bodies get weary, we usually force ourselves to drag along in a dull, low-efficiency rut. We say we must! When our minds are tired, we frequently act as though the solution is simply to screw the tension tighter. And when spirits wane, spiritual vision dims. Then it is that we need someone to remind us that we cannot continue to give out, unless we stop and take in.

Resting and vegetating are not synonymous, even in the dictionary. They *must* not be so in a Christian's vocabulary! Not that most of us could find the time, place, or money to vegetate, even if it were desirable. No, most of us must recognize our limits, muster our resources, and deal with the problem right where we are. Let's think of some helps:

Tackle one job at a time. What we haven't done can make us more tired than what we are doing!

Sometimes the rest we need is simply a change, say from waxing to mending.

Clear-cut decisions are restful! Indecision contributes to and springs from weariness. Which will it be—fresh cookies after school or a clean attic? Decide and then abide.

A quick bath or a short nap can do wonders toward making the rest of the day attractive to you, and you attractive to your family.

A good brisk walk or game can re-create order in a foggy brain.

Time spent with the Word of Life and the Lord of Life always results in renewed perspective and strength.

Now remember the Golden Rule. What Gladys do you know? What would God have you do for her today? An invitation to lunch, a guaranteed quiet afternoon in bed, an offer to baby-sit, an extra child or two from school for the night, a lent concert ticket—the possibilities are exciting, even if you are tied down at home or flat broke!

And the results promise to be exciting too, if it is the love of God which prompts your kindness. In fact, there may well be rejoicing in heaven before the day is over.

Remember:

This steadying Goal: "Consider him . . . so that you may not grow weary or faint-hearted" (Hebrews 12:3, RSV), and this comforting Refuge:

> "Jesus, I am resting, resting,
> In the joy of what Thou art. . . ."

DECEMBER 30
We Write—from Satisfied Hearts

A year-end inventory (good spiritual exercise!) prompted this.

Sufficiency

"Rich memories are not, I think, proportionate to years.
This life is short in years, and yet my memory store is
packed

With fragments—moments, snatches, words unspoken,
　　friendships brief.
　　Were I to know this day would be my last—I have not
　　lacked.

"Each morning, dawning fresh, brings with it gifts in sol-
　　emn trust;
　　Heights still unscaled and vistas new, hard work de-
　　manding skill.
The past is gone. Today is mine! That challenge satisfies.
　　Were there *no* memories in my heart, I could be happy
　　still.

"Who knows the lot tomorrow holds? We are not meant to
　　know.
The Great Creator knows our feeble frame, our frail stuff,
And so He teaches us not how to know, but how to trust.
Had I no past, no present, only faith—it were enough!"

We take lots of time these days for figuring taxes and
analyzing budgets. Why not take time today for some
quiet reflection on the intangibles this year has brought
you? (Prose will do just as well; form doesn't matter.)

Don't decide before you start what kind of year you have
had. Be fair with yourself and God. If you proceed with
an open mind, you are certain to come out praising Him
for His goodness.

If the results surprise you, when you get them into black
and white, that is sure evidence that the inventory was
needed and the time well invested.

Remember:

The poet encourages us to "Count your blessings, name
them one by one . . . ," and Paul speaks of God as "Him

384

who . . . is able to do far more abundantly than all that we ask or think . . ." (Ephesians 3:20b, RSV).

DECEMBER 31

We Anticipate

It's still your decision today. For a few hours yet you *can* ignore tomorrow. You can stand with your back to it and not see it at all. Some things about the old year you hate to leave; some possibilities in the new year you dread to face. How about it, honestly? Think for a few minutes right now. Do you wish you could stop the clock of life?

Do you secretly wish you could keep your family just as it is now?

Do you really think the world might be a safer place if scientific research would just stop?

Are you pretty comfortably situated, economically— enough so that you'd gladly live like this the rest of your life?

And about world conditions. It isn't exactly peace, of course, but would you settle for this, lest cold war turn hot, or partial war turn global?

Would you frankly be glad if you knew you never need- ed to change homes again—that "this is it" for the rest of your days on earth? Of course you're not perfect, but do you privately think maybe you are good enough, and that you have grown about as much spiritually as you are going to?

Well, for another few hours you can waste your time thinking like that. It's shameful Christian behavior, but no one will know unless you tell it.

But then you must go, whether you like it or not; over the threshold and into a new, unknown year!

Why not, then, spend the time getting ready, instead of dreaming of a deepfreeze existence? Face things realistically, but face them with Christ! When your hand is securely in His and things go right between you, tomorrow will hold challenge instead of fear. Life will promise growth, and anticipation will be high spiritual adventure, Then you can say with Kipling:

> "We are standing
> at the opening verse
> of the opening page
> of the chapter
> of endless possibilities."

Remember:

God's word to Joshua—and to you: "Be strong and of good courage; be not frightened, neither be dismayed; for the Lord your God is with you wherever you go" (Joshua 1:9, RSV). Take this too. It is from Jesus to His followers. "Be of good cheer; I have overcome the world" (John 16:33b).

BIOGRAPHICAL DATA

Alderfer, Helen Wade (Mrs. Edwin), now of Scottdale, Pennsylvania, grew up in Illinois and was graduated from Goshen College, where she met her minister husband. They served in the MCC program in the Philippines, where Mrs. Alderfer was unit matron and conducted a nursery school and community library. They have also lived in Culp, Arkansas, and Blooming Glen, Pennsylvania. Mrs. Alderfer is the mother of four children, has been editor of the *Prayer Guide* of the Mennonite Women's Missionary and Service Auxiliary, and was recently appointed Home Life Editor of *Christian Living* magazine.

Brenneman, Helen Good (Mrs. Virgil), was born at Harrisonburg, Virginia, and grew up near Hyattsville, Maryland, a suburb of Washington, D.C. She attended Eastern Mennonite and Goshen colleges. The Brennemans served with the MCC in Europe and are now at the Iowa City Mennonite Church, where he is pastor. Mrs. Brenneman is the mother of four children and the author of *Meditations for the New Mother* and *But Not Forsaken.*

Clemens, Lois Gunden (Mrs. Ernest), grew up near Flanagan, Illinois. She received her B.A. from Goshen College, her M.A. from George Peabody, and her Ph.D. from Indiana University. Until her recent marriage she was Associate Professor of French and Spanish at Goshen College. She has served with MCC in France and

Puerto Rico. She was interned in Germany during World War II and has worked in various voluntary service projects in the United States. She is now at home in Lansdale, Pennsylvania.

Glass, Esther Eby (Mrs. Forrest J.), is a native of Denbigh, Virginia, in the Tidewater country, but has lived since her marriage in 1922 on a 60-acre farm near Lancaster, Pennsylvania. Two teen-age children and a shut-in mother are also a part of the Glass family. Mrs. Glass has taught Sunday-school classes for many years, speaks frequently to women's groups, and has written a great deal for Mennonite publications. She is the author of *The Seven Gales* and *When You Date*.

Graber, Minnie Swartzendruber (Mrs. J. D.), was born at Eagle Grove, Iowa, spent her girlhood years in Versailles, Missouri, and was graduated from Hesston Academy and Goshen College. In 1925 she was married to Joseph D. Graber and in November of the same year they sailed as missionaries to India. Since their return in 1942 she has been active in the women's organization of her church, first as president of the Indiana-Michigan district and for the last seven years as president of the national Mennonite WMSA. The Grabers have two children.

Lind, Miriam Sieber (Mrs. Millard), was born at Filer, Idaho, and grew up in Idaho, Illinois, and Indiana. She received her B.A. from Goshen College and studied a year at the Goshen Seminary. Mrs. Lind says she belongs to a family of bookworms made up of her minister-editor-writer husband, five sons, and a daughter. Her interest in writing has ranged from children's poetry and stories through devotional poetry and articles to an occasional bit of adult fiction. She is the author of *Such Thoughts of Thee*. The Linds live near Scottdale, Pennsylvania.

McCammon, Dorothy Snapp (Mrs. Don), was born at Walworth, Wisconsin, but grew up at Bristol, Indiana. She received her B.A. from Goshen College and remained there for two years to teach commerce. After her marriage to Don McCammon in 1945, they attended graduate school at Cornell University (N.Y). and the University of Oklahoma. Mrs. McCammon has put their four years of missionary experience in China into a volume, *We Tried to Stay*. Until her recent furlough Mrs. McCammon served as pastor's wife at the Tokyo Mennonite Center and as treasurer for the Mennonite Board of Missions and Charities in Japan. The McCammons have a daughter, Julia. Their son Michael died early in 1958.

Metzler, Ethel Yake (Mrs. Edgar), grew up at Scottdale, Pennsylvania. She received her B.A. from Goshen College and then returned to Scottdale where she was assistant editor of the *Youth's Christian Companion* for several years. She now serves as pastor's wife at Kitchener, Ontario. Mrs. Metzler has been active in youth work at Laurelville Camp and in Mennonite Youth Fellowship. She is editor of *Youth Program Ideas*, Volumes I and II. The Metzlers have three children.

Rich, Elaine Sommers (Mrs. Ronald), was born at Plevna, Indiana, in 1926. She received her B.A. from Goshen College and her M.A. from Michigan State University. She has taught English and speech at Goshen and Bethel colleges and has written for Mennonite publications. She now lives with her husband, two sons, and a daughter at North Newton, Kansas, where her husband is Associate Professor of chemistry.

Smucker, Barbara Claassen (Mrs. Don E.), is married to a seminary professor and lives in Lombard, Illinois. Before her marriage she attended Bethel College for one year and then transferred to the school of journalism at Kansas State College where she was graduated. She taught high school at Harper, Kansas, and also was a news reporter at Newton, Kansas. The Smuckers have served Mennonite pastorates at Wadsworth, Ohio; Lancaster, Pennsylvania; and Freeman, South Dakota. They have three children. Mrs. Smucker is the author of *Henry's Red Sea* and *Cherokee Run*.

Waltner, Winifred Schlosser (Mrs. Erland), was born at Kihsien, Honan, China, where she grew up, the daughter of Free Methodist missionaries. She attended the American School at Kikungshan, China, received her B.A. from Greenville College and her M.R.E. from Biblical Seminary in New York. The Waltners have had pastorates at Philadelphia, Pennsylvania, and Mountain Lake, Minnesota, and spent eight years on the Bethel College campus. They now live with their four daughters at Elkhart, Indiana, where he is president of Mennonite Biblical Seminary.

Wenger, Grace, was born in 1919 near Lancaster, Pennsylvania. She was graduated from Elizabethtown College and received her M.A. from the University of Pennsylvania. For three years she was an elementary teacher in the public schools of Pennsylvania. For thirteen years she taught English in the high school at Eastern Mennonite College, and she now teaches at Lancaster Mennonite School, Lancaster, Pennsylvania.